Children
with Learning Disabilities
A Five Year Follow-up Study

Children with Learning Disabilities

A Five Year Follow-up Study

Elizabeth Munsterberg Koppitz, Ph.D.

Board of Cooperative Educational Services
Yorktown Heights N.Y.

GRUNE & STRATTON

New York and London

© 1971 by Grune & Stratton, Inc.
All rights reserved. No part of this publication
may be reproduced or transmitted in any form or
by any means, electronic or mechanical, including
photocopy, recording, or any information storage
and retrieval system, without permission in
writing from the publisher.

Grune & Stratton, Inc.
111 Fifth Avenue
New York, New York 10003

Library of Congress Catalog Card Number 70-167977

International Standard Book Number 0-8089-0726-3

Printed in the United States of America

To Werner

To Werner

Table of Contents

1. **Introduction**   1

     DESCRIPTION OF THE LD PROGRAM INVOLVED IN THE FIVE YEAR FOLLOW-UP STUDY 4
     LD PUPILS INVOLVED IN THE FOLLOW-UP STUDY 8

2. **Characteristics of the LD Pupils at Entry into the LD Program**   10

     REFERRING SCHOOL DISTRICTS 12
     SEX OF LD PUPILS 13
     AGE OF LD PUPILS 14
     IQ SCORES OF LD PUPILS 15
     VISUAL-MOTOR PERCEPTION OF LD PUPILS 15
     ACHIEVEMENT OF THE LD PUPILS 19
     BEHAVIOR OF THE LD PUPILS 20
     DEVELOPMENTAL AND MEDICAL HISTORIES OF LD PUPILS 22
     SOCIAL BACKGROUND OF LD PUPILS 25
     CHARACTERISTICS OF LD PUPILS AT TIME OF ENTRY INTO SPECIAL CLASSES: SUMMARY 26

3. Admission Data and Pupils' Status Five Years after Coming to the LD Program · 34

    REFERRING SCHOOL DISTRICTS · 38
    SEX OF LD PUPILS · 41
    AGE OF LD PUPILS · 41
    IQ SCORES OF LD PUPILS · 42
    VISUAL-MOTOR PERCEPTION OF LD PUPILS · 44
    ACHIEVEMENT OF LD PUPILS · 45
    BEHAVIOR OF LD PUPILS · 47
    DEVELOPMENTAL AND MEDICAL HISTORIES OF LD PUPILS · 49
    SOCIAL BACKGROUND OF LD PUPILS · 51
    ADMISSION DATA AND PUPILS' STATUS FIVE YEARS AFTER COMING TO THE LD PROGRAM: SUMMARY · 52

4. The Actual Progress of the LD Pupils · 58

    PROGRESS OF THE FORTY-TWO LD PUPILS WHO RETURNED TO REGULAR CLASSES · 58
        Length of stay in LD program before pupils' return to regular classes · 59
        Relationship between time spent in the LD program and pupils' actual progress · 61
    ADJUSTMENTS OF FORMER LD PUPILS TO REGULAR CLASSES · 65
        Former LD pupils who made a good adjustment to regular classes · 67
            Successful return to regular classes after one year in the LD program · 68
            Successful return to regular classes after two years in the LD program · 74
            Successful return to regular classes after three years in the LD program · 77
            Successful return to regular classes after four or five years in the LD program · 81
        Former LD pupils who made a fair adjustment to regular classes · 84
        Former LD pupils who made a poor adjustment to regular classes · 87

5. Progress of Long-term LD Pupils   95

    GROUP A: DULL CHILDREN   98
    GROUP B: CHILDREN WITH POOR REASONING AND GOOD MEMORY   110
    GROUP C: CHILDREN WITH SPECIFIC LEARNING DISABILITIES   115
    GROUP D: CHILDREN WITH EMOTIONAL AND BEHAVIOR PROBLEMS   126

6. Pupils Who Were Referred for Hospitalization   137

    GROUP A: AUTISTIC CHILDREN   139
    GROUP B: UNCONTROLLABLE AND VIOLENT CHILDREN   145
    GROUP C: CHILDREN WITH SYMBIOTIC ILLNESSES   150
    GROUP D: SEVERELY DISTURBED PARENT-CHILD RELATIONSHIPS   157
    GROUP E: ASOCIAL AND DELINQUENT CHILDREN   163

7. Pupils Who Were Withdrawn and Those Who Returned   166

    PUPILS WHO WERE WITHDRAWN FROM THE LD PROGRAM   166
    PUPILS WHO LEFT AND THEN RETURNED TO THE LD PROGRAM   176

8. Summary and Implications of Five Year Follow-up Study of LD Pupils   180

    PURPOSE OF LD CLASSES AND SELECTION OF PUPILS FOR THESE CLASSES   180
    AGE AND IQ SCORES OF LD PUPILS   183
    VISUAL-MOTOR PERCEPTION AND LD PUPILS   186
    ACHIEVEMENT OF LD PUPILS   187
    BEHAVIOR OF LD PUPILS   192
    DEVELOPMENTAL AND MEDICAL HISTORIES OF

LD PUPILS   194
SOCIAL BACKGROUND OF LD PUPILS   195
CONCLUSIONS   197
RECOMMENDATIONS FOR A COMPREHENSIVE SPECIAL
EDUCATION PROGRAM   199

References   **208**

Index   **211**

List of Tables

1. Distribution of age, sex, and IQ scores for 177 pupils enrolled in LD program. 14
2. Level of Bender Gestalt Test scores related to LD pupils' CA and MA. 18
3. Achievement levels of LD pupils. 19
4. Developmental and medical histories of LD pupils. 24
5. Social background factors of LD pupils. 26
6. Pupils' status five years after coming to LD program. 35
7. Referring school districts and pupils' status five years after coming to LD program. 39
8. Admission age and pupils' status five years after coming to LD program. 41
9. IQ scores and pupils' status five years after coming to LD program. 43
10. Bender Gestalt and Wepman Test scores and pupils' status five years after coming to LD program. 45
11. Achievement and pupils' status five years after coming to LD program. 46
12. Behavior and pupils' status five years after coming to LD program. 48

13.	Comparison of behavior and social background factors in three groups of LD pupils.	49
14.	Developmental, medical and social background factors of LD pupils.	50
15.	Comparison of pupils who returned to regular classes after 1 to 2, or 3 to 5 years in the LD program.	60
16.	Progress of 42 pupils in LD program prior to return to regular classes.	61
17.	Average annual reading gain of 42 LD pupils.	63
18.	Adjustment of 41 former LD pupils to regular classes.	66
19.	Terry's progress during three years in the LD program.	78
20.	Progress of 71 long-term LD pupils.	96
21.	Progress of four groups of long-term LD pupils.	98
22.	Adam's progress in the LD program.	108
23.	Darlene's progress in the LD program.	113
24.	Russell's progress in the LD program.	119
25.	Bruce's progress in the LD program.	129
26.	LD pupils who were referred for hospitalization.	140
27.	Pupils who were withdrawn from LD program.	167
28.	Pupils who left and then returned to LD program.	176
29.	Mental age of kindergarten pupils with different IQ levels.	184

Preface

After working for several years as a psychologist in clinical settings, I became convinced that a more effective and efficient way of helping youngsters who suffered from emotional and learning problems would be to work in the public schools. Since children enter school at an early age, it is in the schools where pupils with potential behavior and learning difficulties can be identified and worked with before their problems become unmanageable and disabling. Ten years ago I decided, therefore, to join the staff of a newly organized public school program for children with learning disabilities. Special classes were set up for pupils of supposedly normal mental potential who had emotional and learning difficulties. It was the stated purpose of these classes to provide special education so that the children could overcome their problems and could return successfully to regular classes within a year or two.

It soon became apparent that the special classes were able to help some youngsters as planned, but not others. It was further found that most children progressed slowly and required many years of special education before they could return to regular classes; that some youngsters benefitted a great deal from the program even though they could never return to regular classes; and finally, that there were some who were unable to adjust to or profit from the special classes altogether. A question therefore presented itself: Which children can benefit from special classes, and why? A survey of the literature on special classes for children with learning disabilities failed to provide a satisfactory answer to this question. So I decided to find out for myself what special classes actually could and could not do for various youngsters with different types and degrees of emotional and learning disorders.

I began to keep detailed notes on each child I worked with and reevaluated the pupils at frequent intervals to assess their yearly progress. These informal notes soon developed into a systematic five year follow-up study of the first 177 pupils, age 6 to 12, who were enrolled in the special classes for children with learning disabilities. The results of this follow-up study proved to be most valuable for my own work as psychologist. They helped me to gain a better understanding of the youngsters' problems and assisted me in making more meaningful recommendations and prescriptions for the pupils' education. I believe that the findings of this study will also be helpful to others working with children with learning disabilities. This book presents the results of the five year follow-up study and the conclusions drawn from them.

The follow-up study was carried out with the approval of the director of special education, and I also received much help and encouragement from colleagues and friends, for which I am grateful. But the study was conceived and executed mainly by myself and on my own time. It was neither sponsored nor financially supported by any agency or grant. The ideas, conclusions, and recommendations presented in the book are my own and do not necessarily agree with those of the administration of the special education program.

This book was written for psychologists, teachers, administrators, school social workers, and all others concerned with the education of children with learning disabilities. The book does not deal with learning problems *per se,* but rather with the *children* who have learning and behavior disorders. An attempt is made to define the various factors that contribute to the youngsters' problems and that affect their progress or lack of it in the special classes. It is shown what public school special classes can and cannot do to help children with learning disabilities. Furthermore, recommendations are made for a preventive approach to special education so as to avoid or minimize learning and behavior disorders, rather than trying to correct them after they have developed and grown out of all proportion. It is also hoped that this book will stimulate further research in the important area of learning disabilities and special education.

E. M. K.

Acknowledgments

Thanks and appreciation are due to the many people who helped to make this study possible. I especially want to thank Paul Irvine, Director, and Don Coe, Assistant Director of Special Education of the Board of Cooperative Educational Services, and my friends and colleagues Helen Murray, Betty Dietz, Esther Chu, Mary Wilson, Becky Troika, Helene Elitcher, and the many special class and regular class teachers and counselors who contributed generously of their time. I am also indebted to the special class pupils who participated in the follow-up study and from whom I learned a great deal. But, above all, I want to express my gratitude to my husband, Werner J. Koppitz, to whom this book is dedicated. Without his continued help and support this book would never have been completed.

Elizabeth M. Koppitz

Chapter 1

Introduction

This is a book about children. It is a book about children with learning disabilities. There is an extensive literature on learning disabilities and on specific programs designed to remedy learning problems in children. Most of the published studies focus on learning disorders as such or on teaching methods or techniques, rather than on the children who have the disorders (Cruickshank and Johnson, 1958; Early, 1969; Ebersole et al., 1968; Haring and Phillips, 1962; Hellmuth, 1966a, 1966b; Johnson and Myklebust, 1967; Kirk, 1962; Mallison, 1968; Strauss and Lehtinen, 1947). For the purposes of this study, a child is said to have a learning disability if his school achievement is more than one year below his mental age, and if he cannot get along or profit from attendance in a regular public school class despite normal intellectual potential (i.e., an absence of mental retardation) and a lack of gross motor impairment. The child's learning disability might result from any one or several of the following: immaturity or developmental lags, neurological impairment, severe early deprivation, brain injury, genetically determined cerebral dysfunction, serious emotional disturbance, minimal brain malfunction, or other reasons. The term *learning disability,* as used here, does not indicate any specific underlying cause or etiology for the problem.

Special public school classes or programs for children with learning disabilities (LD hereafter) are a relatively new phenomenon. Most of them were organized within the last decade and their number is increasing every year (Mackie, 1965; NEA, 1967; Richards and Clark, 1968). Some local school districts try to meet the needs of LD pupils in self-contained special classes while other districts set up "resource rooms" or hire itinerant teachers who assist the LD pupils for a part of each day (Lazure and Roberts, 1969). Some districts join other local districts and develop cooperative special education classes or programs. No one seems to dispute that LD pupils need extra help over and beyond what most regular classes can offer them, but there is no agreement among educators regarding the merits and negative effects of placing LD pupils into special classes (Christoplos and Renz, 1969; Harvey, 1969; Miller and Schoenfelder, 1969; Towne and Joiner, 1969). There is a consensus, however, that more evaluation of special class programs and more longitudinal studies of children with learning disabilities are needed.

Only two studies along this line have come to my attention. Rawson (1968) followed a group of bright, dyslexic private school pupils into adulthood, while Kotting and Brozovich (1969) conducted a follow-up study of public school pupils who had attended special classes for the emotionally disturbed for only a year or two. No study was found on the actual progress of LD pupils while in special classes for a longer period of time. Most public school special classes have the stated goal of providing intensive and individualized training and help for LD pupils for just one or two years, after which time they are expected to return to regular classes. It is apparently assumed that learning problems can be successfully corrected in a limited period of time.

The vast majority of LD programs are located in elementary schools only and do not make provision for older children with learning problems, or for long-term special education. Yet, anyone working with LD classes soon discovers that most pupils still have learning disabilities even after one or two years in special classes. How effective are LD classes? How adequately do they meet the children's needs? What is the actual progress made by the pupils who are enrolled in public school LD classes?

The purpose of this book is to explore the characteristics of children with learning disabilities who are referred to special public school classes and to discover what happens to these youngsters once they are placed into the special classes. Presented here are the findings and implications of a five year follow-up study of 177 pupils with learning

Introduction

disorders who were enrolled in special public school classes for educationally handicapped children. This is not a report on a carefully designed and executed research project; rather it is an analysis of actual school records, test protocols, and teachers' reports that were collected and used in the process of conducting the special class programs. By necessity some of the research methods employed are not as precise nor are the data used as complete as might be wished or as would be expected from a laboratory experiment.

The data collected come from the first 177 pupils, age 6 to 12, who were enrolled in a newly created public school LD program. The children entered the program over a span of four years. When possible, each youngster was studied for five years following his admission to the special classes. Thus a total of eight years elapsed from the time the first LD pupils entered the special classes until five years after the last group of pupils was admitted. During this eight-year period, the LD program under discussion underwent numerous changes in administration, teaching staff, ancillary services, the location of the classrooms, and the teaching methods and instructional materials used. Such changes (hopefully all for the better) are not only unavoidable, but even desirable in a still-new and developing educational program. Most public school classes for children with learning disabilities are still subject to much experimentation and improvement. This was also the case in the LD program in which the present study was conducted. For this reason, no attempt will be made here to evaluate the program itself; instead, the discussions will be limited to the pupils who were enrolled in the program. The LD program involved was at least equal to, if not better than, many other special classes programs in public schools throughout the country.

Public school classes for children with learning problems are given different names in different localities. In some states, the classes are referred to as classes for youngsters with minimal brain dysfunction (MBD); some classes are designated as classes for the educationally handicapped (EH) or as classes for children with learning disabilities (LD); others are called classes for emotionally disturbed and/or brain-injured children (ED/BI); or they are considered to be classes for children with perceptual problems, etc. Regardless of the label attached to the classes, the pupils in them resemble each other in the types of learning problems and behavior disorders they display.

After a visit from a county consultant for educationally handicapped children in a Western state, a letter containing the following statement was received: ". . . your LD children and our EH children are the same, which is comforting and means that we *are* communicating about the same subject. . . ." Private schools for learning-disabled youngsters, on the other hand, tend to serve somewhat different populations from public school LD classes. Private schools can afford to be more selective in their admission policy. It is therefore important not to assume that the findings or results from studies of private school pupils with learning problems (Rawson, 1968) would necessarily be comparable to those of public school LD classes (Kotting and Brozovich, 1969).

DESCRIPTION OF THE LD PROGRAM
INVOLVED IN THE FIVE YEAR FOLLOW-UP STUDY

The LD classes in which the five year follow-up study was conducted were part of a large cooperative special education program which served thirteen smaller school districts. The thirteen school districts are located in a Northeastern state in rural, semirural, suburban, and small town communities with a total school population of approximately 50,000 children. The LD classes were housed wherever room was available: they were situated in regular schools, in old abandoned school buildings, in church buildings, and in converted residences. The LD pupils were transported by bus to the most appropriate special class closest to their home.

During the time of the five year follow-up study, the number of pupils in the cooperative LD program increased from 40 pupils in five classes to more than ten times that number of children and classes. The average number of pupils in each class was eight; although some classes had as few as five or six children, others—especially those with older children—had as many as ten youngsters. The children were grouped in the LD classes on the basis of age, social and emotional maturity, the specific type of learning problem presented, behavior, and geography. Mentally retarded pupils were not included in this study. They were enrolled in special classes for educable and trainable children. In the LD classes no distinction was made between children who were diagnosed as suffering from learning disabilities primarily because of emotional problems and those who were said to have learning disorders primarily because of neurological malfunction. A child's functioning rather than his diagnostic label determined his class placement. One of the advantages of the rather extensive cooperative LD program was the large number of pupils available, so that good class groupings could be achieved. An attempt was made to keep the distance each

Introduction

child had to travel to class to a minimum, but the child's educational needs were given primary consideration. When a child's problems could not be met within an LD class located in his home district, he would be transported to a class peculiarly suited to his needs, even if the class was situated in a different school district.

The LD program was initially designed to serve children age 6 through 16. By the time the follow-up study was completed, the cooperative program encompassed classes ranging from kindergarten through high school with an age range from $4^1/_2$ to 21 years. The children referred to the program were highly atypical. Even after the LD classes had greatly expanded in number they never enrolled more than one to one-and-one-half percent of the total school population. The school districts served by the cooperative LD program were regarded as quite good; most had well-trained teachers as well as reading and language specialists, social workers, and psychologists and counselors. The schools and the teachers were able to cope successfully with a vast array of problems presented by the pupils. A child's difficulties had to be truly major or very persistent before referral to a special class was even considered. It should be emphasized that the pupils were referred to the LD program only after the local schools had tried to the best of their ability to help the children within the regular school program.

Children were enrolled in the LD classes after going through an elaborate referral and screening procedure. The referral for special class placement was usually initiated by the child's homeroom teacher with the approval of the principal. In a few cases parents requested, very wisely, that their child be considered for placement in the LD classes. Prior to an official application for admission to the LD program, each child was evaluated by the local school psychologist and by a consulting psychiatrist, while the school social worker (if available) obtained the child's developmental and social history, and discussed with the parents the plan for the transfer of the youngster to a special class. Parental cooperation is, of course, essential for successful placement of a pupil in an LD program. A complete set of the educational, psychological, psychiatric, and social work reports accompanied each official application for the admission of a child to the special education classes.

The referral data for each child were thereafter carefully examined by the screening committee for the LD classes. This committee consisted of the administrators, the psychologists, the social workers, and the teachers, as needed. In cases of doubt, a child and his parents were asked to come in for an interview, or some members of the screening committee went to observe the child in his home school. If possible, the children were screened in the spring for admission to the LD program in September, the beginning of the new school year. However, if a youngster moved into the area or if a critical situation developed, children were also enrolled in the special classes during the school year. Admission to the LD classes after the spring vacations rarely proved successful and was discouraged.

The criteria for acceptance into the LD program were the presence of learning disabilities and the belief that the pupils would profit from special class placement and could function better in a small group setting. The LD pupils included both boys and girls, black and white. They came from a wide variety of backgrounds including affluent upper middle-class families as well as isolated backwoods enclaves and urban and rural slums. There were as many children from solid, upward-striving middle-class homes as there were from marginal homes and from welfare families living in poverty areas.

The staff of the LD program included administrators; classroom teachers; psychiatric social workers; school psychologists; consulting child psychiatrists or neurologists; language therapists; reading consultants; teachers for gym, music, and art; and teacher aides and volunteers. The teachers were either trained and certified in special education or (especially in the early days of the LD program) they were regular classroom teachers with special interest and experience in working with learning disabilities. All teachers were encouraged to take in-service training courses and to attend local, state, and national meetings on special education.

The teaching methods used in the LD program varied considerably from class to class and from one age level to the next. Whereas private schools are usually built around specific educational philosophies and teaching methods, the public school LD program here under discussion followed no set theory or philosophy. This was not necessarily bad as it allowed for much flexibility and experimentation within the classes.

The teaching materials and techniques used were determined largely by the teachers' preferences and philosophies, by the type of problems the children presented, and by the fads and fashions current in a given year. During the years in which the present study was carried out, several new approaches and methods in dealing with learning disabilities were introduced and enthusiastically applied. Most of them were quietly dropped the following year in favor of still different techniques. Older methods were "rediscovered" with just as much fervor. It is good to be aware of new developments and to try out new ideas.

Introduction

One only wishes that more time were allotted to truly evaluate a given method before either adopting or discarding it. In the last analysis it appears, however, that the success or failure of an LD class rests with the personality and skill of the teacher rather than with special teaching techniques or materials.

Educational and clinical evaluations and observation of all LD pupils were conducted at the beginning and end of each school year, and throughout the year as needed. Regular staff meetings were held to discuss problems or questions presented by the LD students. The social workers kept close contact with the children's parents and parent-teacher-social worker conferences were held every semester, or more often when needed. The psychologist and/or administrator joined these meetings if it was considered desirable or necessary. In addition, the mothers were encouraged to attend a voluntary monthly guidance group conducted jointly by the social worker and the psychologist.

Whenever an LD teacher felt that one of his or her pupils was ready to return to a regular class, a full-scale reevaluation of the youngster was conducted. Once again, educational, psychological, and psychiatric findings were presented to the screening committee to see if the child should be referred back to his home school. If a consensus was reached that the youngster could hold his own in a regular class, return proceedings were initiated. Meetings were arranged with the principal and the teachers of the child's home school in order to select a suitable class for the youngster, and to work out a modified class schedule if needed. On occasion a child would be sent back to a regular class on a trial basis before a final decision was made. The easiest and smoothest transfers from the LD class to the regular class occurred when the special class was located in a regular school. In such a case, the LD pupils had a chance to participate in one or more regular classes while they were still enrolled in the LD class. This gradual reintegration into a regular class proved most helpful.

A youngster who was not yet ready or able to return to a regular class could remain in the LD program. A child could receive special education in an LD class as long as he needed it, or up to his 21st birthday, either in an academic track or in a vocational training program. All LD pupils who continued in special education for the remainder of their formal education graduated with a diploma from their local high school and a certificate from the LD program.

Some youngsters proved to be too disturbed to benefit from the special public school classes and had to be referred to a residential treatment center or to a mental hospital for psychiatric care. The LD program was first and foremost an educational program, albeit a therapeutic one. It was able to help children with learning and emotional problems *if* they could function in a public school class, but if a child needed primarily psychiatric treatment and could not be managed in a public school class, he was excluded from the LD program. Other children were withdrawn from the program by their parents or by the local school districts. Still others moved away. In a few instances, boys and girls were transferred from the LD classes to different types of special classes that were better suited to their specific needs. As is true in most large special education programs, there was a steady increase in the number of pupils and a constant shift or change in the LD pupil population.

LD PUPILS INVOLVED IN THE FOLLOW-UP STUDY

As the first and, for several years, the only psychologist with the LD program under discussion, I had the opportunity to know and to work with all the pupils who were admitted to the LD classes in the early years of the program. The present study includes the first 177 boys and girls, age 5 years 9 months to 12 years 11 months, who entered the LD program. Children who were 13 years old or older at the time of admission to the special classes were not included in this study. The 177 children involved in the follow-up study represent the total population of the younger pupils admitted to the LD program during the first four years of its existence. All of these youngsters were seen and evaluated upon entry into and at regular intervals during their participation in the LD program. At the end of the five year study, the pupils ranged in age from eleven years to 18 years. All the children were originally believed to have normal or near-normal mental potential even though some of them had below average IQ scores.

The initial evaluation of each child included an analysis of his referral data; that is, his clinical folder was examined for his educational, psychological, developmental, and medical reports; for descriptions of the child's behavior at home and in school; and for his family background. Shortly after his admission to the special classes, each child was given the Bender Gestalt Test (Koppitz, 1964) and the Wide Range Achievement Test (Jastak, Bijou, and Jastak, 1946, 1965). The same two tests were again administered at the end of each school year.

Introduction

At the end of the study, each pupil's whereabouts were established, if possible, and his total functioning was reevaluated.

The five year follow-up study is divided into four parts:

1. Evaluation of the characteristics of the LD pupils at the time of their admission to the special classes.
2. Relationship between the admission data and the pupils' status five years after coming to the LD program.
3. Evaluation of the pupils' progress and functioning while in the LD program and at the end of the five year follow-up study.
4. Summary and implications of the findings.

Chapter 2

Characteristics of the LD Pupils at Entry into the LD Program

No single variable or characteristic can describe the LD pupils or the reason for their referral to the special classes. I maintain that one cannot really understand a child unless one knows something about six major areas regarding his functioning and background. These areas are:

THE CHILD'S ABILITY TO CONTROL HIMSELF:

How well developed are his inner controls? How long is he able to concentrate? How restless and distractible is he? How impulsive is he? Is he hypoactive or lethargic? How well can he tolerate frustrations? Does he have temper tantrums?

THE CHILD'S INTEGRATIVE FUNCTIONING:

How well developed is his visual-motor and auditory perception? How well can he translate what he perceives into motor activity? Can he repeat or copy what he hears or sees in the correct sequence or form? Can he coordinate visual and kinesthetic perceptions? Can he retain and recall what he learns? Can he integrate time and space perception?

Characteristics of Pupils at Entry into LD Program

THE CHILD'S REASONING ABILITY:

Has the child common sense? Can he understand and deal with everyday situations? Can he comprehend abstract concepts? Can he apply them? Does he understand what he reads? Can he learn from experience? Can he transfer what he has learned previously to new situations?

THE CHILD'S EMOTIONAL ADJUSTMENT:

How does the child feel about himself? How does he perceive his position in his family and in his neighborhood? How does he meet challenges and problems? Does he have self-confidence or does he withdraw? Does he derive satisfaction from actual experiences or does he escape into fantasy for gratification?

THE CHILD'S SOCIAL ADJUSTMENT:

Is the child able to relate to others? What is his attitude toward his parents and siblings? Does he have friends? Is he liked by his peers? How does he get along with teachers and authority figures? How does he react to frustration and criticism by others? How considerate is he of others?

THE CHILD'S BACKGROUND:

What socioeconomic group does the child come from? What is his cultural, religious and national background? What kind of development and medical history did he have? With whom does he live? Has he experienced any prolonged separation from his family or any other trauma?

All of the areas outlined above interact and affect each other; however, they are also distinct from one another. That is, a child may be outstanding in only one of these areas, or he may have difficulty in only one area and not in the others. For instance, a youngster may be extremely hyperactive and distractible, yet he may be bright and well integrated, and may have fairly good social and emotional adjustment. Another child may have serious malfunctioning in visual-motor perception, yet he may have normal intelligence, good control and satisfactory emotional and social adjustment. Some well-controlled, well-functioning children are grossly deficient in abstract reasoning, whereas other children who are bright, well controlled, and integrated may show poor emotional adjustment. Some very bright youngsters do well in all areas with the exception of social adjustment. A child's control, integration, and conceptualization depend largely on his level of maturity and on the functioning of his central nervous system; his emotional and social adjustment, on the other hand, depends mainly on the child's interaction with his environment and on his experiences with others.

One can find in almost any classroom children who have problems in *one* of the areas mentioned above. I have come to the conclusion that pupils who have problems in only *one* of the six areas are most often able to hold their own in regular classes and do not come to the attention of the school psychologist. They are usually not the ones who are referred to the special classes. The LD pupils on the other hand tend to have difficulties in two, three, or even more, areas. It is not uncommon to find youngsters who have problems in the area of control *and* in integration *and* in emotional and social adjustment.

Each LD pupil was evaluated, at the time of admission to the LD program, on nine different characteristics or factors which reflected on the six areas mentioned earlier. Information on the nine characteristics was derived from the youngsters referral records and from the tests administered to the LD pupils. The nine characteristics investigated were as follows:

The child's — school district
— sex
— age
— IQ scores
— visual-motor perception
— academic achievement
— behavior
— developmental and medical history
— social background

It was hoped that these nine characteristics, taken together, would give a well-rounded picture of the LD pupils as they were at the time of entry into the special classes. Each of the nine characteristics will be discussed separately for the 177 LD pupils and then in relationship to each other, in order to show patterns of functioning that might be regarded as typical for special class pupils.

Referring School Districts

The 177 pupils involved in the five year follow-up study displayed a considerable variety of learning and behavior problems. They also varied greatly in age and in mental ability. The children came from thirteen school districts that served communities with disparate socio-economic levels. The teachers and the administrators in the various school districts also differed markedly in their attitude toward the special classes. Some of the districts helped to establish the LD program and enthusiastically supported it—others viewed the LD classes initially with suspicion or even rejection. One district declared with all sincerity that it did not have any children with learning disabilities. Needless to say, this school district soon discovered that it too had children with learning disabilities and has been referring pupils to the LD program for many years.

The numbers and the types of children referred to the LD classes depended to a large extent on the attitude of the local school districts toward the LD program. Some school districts expected the special classes to help the LD pupils to "catch up" so they could return successfully to regular classes. Other districts regarded the classes as a "last resort" for children who could not be managed in the regular classes.

Larger school districts tended to send more pupils to the LD classes than did smaller school districts. However, there was no one-to-one relationship between the size of a school district and the number of pupils referred to the special classes. In addition to the size and the attitude of the school districts, the school budgets also determined the number of children who were referred to the LD classes. The amount of progress made by the pupils in the LD program depended, of course, on the types of youngsters who were sent to the classes. The following numbers of pupils were referred to the LD program from each of the districts: District A sent 13 pupils; District B, 12 pupils; C, 6 pupils; D, 15 children; E, 13 pupils; F, 36 youngsters; G, 12 boys and girls; H, 4 pupils; I, 39 pupils; J, 8 children; K, 4 youngsters; L, 13 pupils and District M, 2 pupils.

Sex of LD Pupils

It has been documented repeatedly than many indices of pathology (e.g., infant mortality, birth trauma, emotional disturbances, learning problems, behavior disorders, deliquency, etc.) are consistently higher for boys than for girls. It is to be expected therefore that many more boys than girls would be referred to the LD program. As shown in Table 1, the overall ratio of boys to girls for the 177 LD pupils was 6:1. But this ratio varied at different age levels. Among the six-, nine- and ten-year-old LD pupils there were relatively fewer girls: the ratio of boys to girls was 8:1 and 9:1 respectively. Relatively more girls were admitted to the LD classes at ages seven, eleven, and twelve. The ratio of boys to girls at these age levels were 4:1 and 5:1. These findings might reflect the tendency to protect girls more and for a longer period than boys. Boys were referred to the special classes as early as age six whereas girls were not sent until age seven. The increase of girls at age eleven and twelve may be due to their developmental stage. These youngsters had entered the difficult preadolescent period and often showed an intensification of problems that might have existed all along. At age eight, the ratio of boys to girls among the LD pupils was 6:1.

Table 1.

Distribution of age, sex, and IQ scores for 177 pupils enrolled in LD program.

Age (in years)	All Pupils	Boys	Girls	79 down	80–89	90–99	100–109	110–119	120 up
6*	28	25	3	7	11	1	5	2	0
7	34	28	6	10	9	7	4	4	0
8	35	30	5	4	10	10	6	2	2
9	30	27	3	2	10	10	3	3	1
10	19	17	2	2	2	8	5	1	1
11	17	14	3	2	6	2	4	2	1
12	14	11	3	4	3	1	3	1	2
	177	152	25	31	51	39	30	15	7

IQ Scores†

*Age 6 years includes three pupils age 5 years 11 months.
†The four autistic nontestable children are not included here.
The Age Mean for all LD pupils was 8 years 11 months.
The IQ Mean for all LD pupils was 92.

Age of LD Pupils

Table 1 shows the age levels at which the 177 LD pupils entered the special classes. A total of 127 children, or three-fourths of the LD pupils were between six and nine years of age. Approximately one-fourth of the pupils were ten to twelve years old at the time of admission to the LD program. The mean age for all LD pupils was eight years and eleven months.

IQ Scores of LD Pupils

The clinical records of the LD pupils included IQ scores derived from either the Wechsler Intelligence Scale for Children (WISC) (Wechsler, 1955) or from the Stanford-Binet Intelligence Scale (Terman and Merrill, 1960) which had been administered just prior to the youngsters' referral to the special classes. Only in four cases were the IQ scores missing. The four exceptions were autistic children who proved to be "untestable." The discussion of IQ scores of the LD pupils will deal therefore with only 173 children instead of all 177 LD pupils. Table 1 shows the distribution of IQ scores for the youngsters according to their age level.

A comparison of IQ scores of the pupils at different age levels revealed that most of the youngest and oldest pupils were of dull normal or borderline intelligence, while most of the eight- to ten-year-old children were of average mental ability. It appears that duller children with learning difficulties are referred to special classes earlier than brighter children with learning problems. The duller youngsters tend to be still much too immature at the time of school entry to cope with a regular kindergarten class or with a first grade. LD pupils of average ability are usually able to maintain themselves, after a fashion, in the primary grades and do not become serious behavior problems until age eight or after two years of failure in regular classes. By that time the youngsters are thoroughly frustrated and have developed emotional and behavior problems in addition to their learning difficulties.

Two explanations suggest themselves for the relatively high number of dull eleven- and twelve-year-old LD pupils. First, it must be pointed out that the LD program did not exist when these particular pupils were six or seven years old, and therefore they could not have been referred to the LD classes at a young age. It is also possible that these LD pupils were able to maintain themselves in regular classes in elementary school, but were unable to do so in the large middle school where they were given less support and structure. The IQ mean score for all LD pupils was 92; more than half of the 173 children had IQ scores between 80 and 99. That is, LD pupils fall typically into the lower half of the average range of mental ability.

Visual-Motor Perception of LD Pupils

Visual and auditory perception, intersensory integration, and the ability to translate that which has been perceived into motor responses are all closely related to a child's overall performance and achievement in school. In this study, the Bender Gestalt Test (Bender, 1938), a test of visual-motor perception, was selected as a measure of the children's integrative maturity and functioning. In the course of the follow-up study it became apparent that the youngsters' auditory perception and their ability to recall and sequence sounds and symbols also had a profound effect on their progress and achievement in the LD program. It was observed that some youngsters had difficulty with visual-motor perception *only,* while others had problems *only* in the area of auditory perception and/or recall, but not in the visual-motor area. Many more LD pupils, however, had problems in *both* visual-motor perception and auditory perception and/or in sequencing and recall. Unfortunately no complete data were available for all LD pupils on their maturity or adequacy in auditory perception or on their memory function.

The Bender Gestalt Test was administered to all pupils shortly after they entered the LD program. All of the Bender Test protocols were scored according to the Koppitz Developmental Scoring System (Koppitz, 1964). The Bender Test scores were grouped into four categories: Good (scores more than one SD above the mean), High Average (scores between the mean and plus one SD), Low Average (scores between the mean and minus one SD), and Poor (scores more than one SD below the mean). The Bender records were scored both in relationship to the pupils' chronological age (CA) and compared to their mental age (MA).

It is often incorrectly assumed that poor performance on the Bender Gestalt Test reflects problems in visual-motor perception. This is not always the case. An immature or poor Bender Test protocol in and of itself does not indicate problems in visual-motor perception or integration. A child's performance on the Bender Gestalt Test is related to his age and mental ability, and to his integrative maturity. One would expect very young and very dull children to produce immature Bender Test records even if they do not have specific problems in visual-motor perception.

One can only speak of specific malfunctioning in visual-motor perception and in integration if there is a *marked discrepancy* between a youngster's Bender Test score and his mental age. For instance, if an eight-year-old child with an IQ score of 75 and a mental age of six obtains a Bender Test score that is on the level of six-year-olds, then that child is functioning up to his mental age level and cannot be said to have specific problems in visual-motor perception. His poor performance on the Bender Test merely reflects his general immaturity and

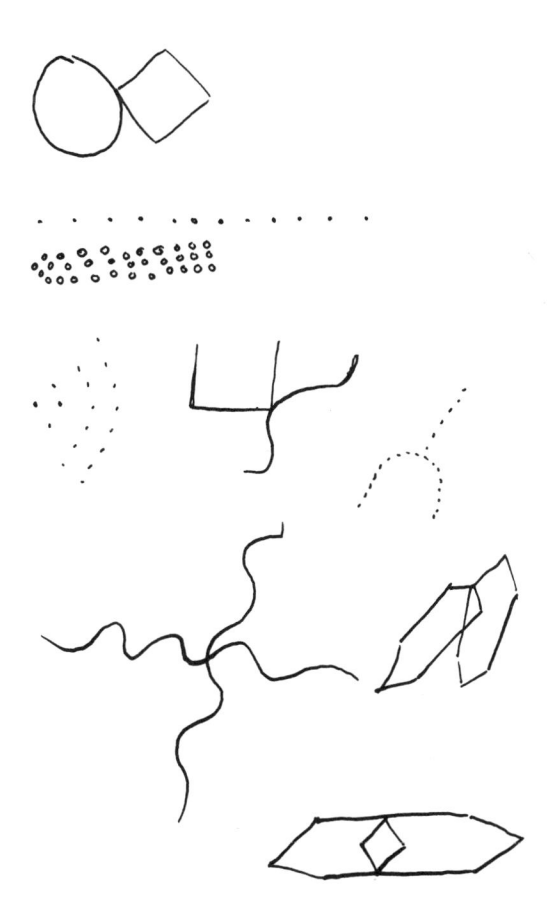

Characteristics of Pupils at Entry into LD Program 17

**Plate 1.
Angelo, CA 10-6.**

All plates in this book have been reduced to 50% of original size, from 8½″ x 11″ sheets.

mental slowness. But if this same youngster should produce a Bender Test protocol that is similar to those of five-year-old children, then one can say that he has malfunctioning in visual-motor perception and in integration, in addition to his mental limitations. The child's Bender Test score would be regarded as below average in relation to his mental age.

The situation differs somewhat for children with a mental age of ten years or above. Plate 1 shows the quite adequate Bender Gestalt Test record of a ten-year-old LD pupil of above-average intelligence who suffered from minimal brain dysfunction. Children with a mental age of nine or ten can usually copy the Bender Test designs without error; the performance on the Bender Test cannot improve beyond the ten-year mental age level. If, therefore, a twelve-year-old child obtains a Bender Test score that is on the level of a ten-year-old, then that Bender Test score should be regarded as good since the Bender Test score cannot get any better. But if a twelve-year-old child obtains a Bender Test score on the level of an eight-year-old youngster, he can be said to have malfunctioning or immaturity in visual-motor perception and integration.

Table 2.

Level of Bender Gestalt Test scores related to LD pupils' CA and MA.

Level of Bender Gestalt Test scores	Bender Test scores related to CA	Bender Test scores related to MA
Good	3	5
High Average	19	35
Low Average	53	65
Poor	102	72
	177	177

Table 2 shows the level of Bender Test scores for all LD pupils, both in comparison to their chronological ages and in comparison to their mental ages. Almost 90 percent of the pupils scored on the Bender Test below the mean compared to other children with the same chronological ages. However, since many of the LD pupils also had below average mental ability one would expect them to produce Bender Test records that were below their CA levels. When the Bender records of the LD pupils were compared with those of children with similar mental ages, it was found that 137 of the LD pupils were still markedly below their mental ages in visual-motor perception. That is, 77 percent of the LD pupils showed specific malfunction in visual-motor perception. It would appear, therefore, that immaturity or malfunction in visual-motor perception is a common characteristic of LD pupils at the time of referral to the special classes.

As was mentioned before, many LD pupils also revealed problems in auditory perception and in memory, but no complete test data were available for these areas. It seems safe to hypothesize that immaturity or malfunction in perception and integration contributed significantly to the LD pupils' learning problems and to their need for special class placement.

Achievement of LD Pupils

All children referred to the LD program have—by definition—learning problems and can be expected to show poor achievement. Shortly after their entry into the LD classes, the Wide Range Achievement Test (Jastak, Bijou, and Jastak, 1946, 1965) was administered to all pupils. This brief diagnostic test assesses only the children's word recognition in reading, spelling, and arithmetic computations. The test was not meant to serve as a full scale achievement test; it was chosen as a convenient measure of the LD pupils' academic performance on which to compare the achievement of the children. Table 3 shows the number and the percentage of LD pupils who were reading, spelling and doing arithmetic at their appropriate grade level, or one, two, or three or more years below the expected grade level.

Table 3.

Achievement levels of LD pupils.

	\multicolumn{6}{c}{Wide Range Achievement Test}
	Reading		Spelling		Arithmetic	
Level of functioning	N	%	N	%	N	%
At grade level	33	19	13	7	20	11
1 year below grade level	47	26	34	19	54	30
2 years below grade level	56	32	68	38	57	32
3 years below grade level	41	23	62	35	46	26
	177	100	177	99	177	99

Most of the six- to nine-year-old pupils were functioning one or two years below their expected achievement level. The ten- to twelve-year-old LD pupils were usually achieving two or more years below their age-grade level. The spelling scores for all LD pupils were consistently lower than either the reading or the arithmetic scores. There was much unevenness in the performance of the individual children; none of them were at grade level in all three areas of achievement. The majority of youngsters obtained achievement scores that were at least two years below their grade level, but it was surprising that so many children were actually functioning in reading at grade level or only one year below it. It is of course recognized that six-year-old pupils cannot function more than one year below their grade level. The data on Table 3 suggest that poor achievement was only one among several factors or characteristics that brought the youngsters to the LD classes. Obviously, many children in regular classes are also functioning one year below grade level and are *not* referred to the LD program. Achievement *alone* is rarely a reason for referring a child to a special class.

Behavior of LD Pupils

Most LD pupils showed not only learning disabilities, but also behavior problems. The admission data for all LD pupils were checked for twelve different types of behavior which are believed to contribute to children's difficulties in getting along in regular classes, and which may have accounted in part for the youngsters' referral to the LD program. The behavior investigated occurred *prior* to the pupils' coming to the special classes. It had been reported by the regular classroom teachers and by the examining clinicians. The actual behavior displayed by the pupils *in* the LD classes often bore little resemblance to the behavior reported in their referral records.

A child's behavior may be a response to internal or external stresses or demands that are present at a given moment, or it may be a reaction to some past experience or conflict which has not yet been resolved. Since it is often difficult to determine from the referral record the causes for a child's disturbed or disturbing behavior, it is not possible to predict what his behavior will be like once he enters the LD classes. It is common for LD pupils to go through a "honeymoon period" after entering the special classes. It sometimes takes days, sometimes weeks before some of the child's behavior problems become evident.

The behavior of some children improved greatly in the LD classes, especially if the youngsters had been under undue pressure in the regular classes. On the other hand, some children behaved worse in the special classes than they were said to have acted in the regular classes. This occurred most often when the child and one or both parents were opposed to the youngster's placement in the LD program.

The present discussion is limited entirely to the behavior of the LD pupils that was reported to have occurred prior to their admission to the special classes. The following is a list of the twelve types of behavior that were investigated:

1. *Restlessness,* hyperactivity, distractability.
2. *Low frustration tolerance,* inability to take failure or criticism, hypersensitivity.
3. *Explosiveness,* poor inner control, impulsivity, temper outbursts.
4. *Anxiety,* tenseness, compulsivity.
5. *Withdrawal,* passivity, lethargy, depression.
6. *Aggressiveness,* destructive behavior, hitting, biting, kicking.
7. *Attention seeking,* demanding, controlling, clinging.
8. *Rebelliousness,* defiance of authority, uncooperativeness.
9. *Somatic complaints,* nervous mannerisms, headaches, stomachaches, tics, thumbsucking, rocking, tapping of fingers and feet, hair twisting or pulling.
10. *Schizoid behavior,* fading in and out, talking to self, disorganized, poor reality contact, bizarre behavior.
11. *Delinquent behavior,* stealing, fire setting, truancy.
12. *Autism,* inability to relate to others, non-conforming to an extreme degree, following of inner drives to the exclusion of the outer world, extreme rigidity, lack of adaptability, failure to learn from experience, lack of affect, inability to communicate verbally.

With the exception of autism, none of the other behavior categories listed are mutually exclusive. If a child was checked for autism, then none of the other behavior categories were checked. Otherwise a child might be said to show one or several types of behavior. For example, a child may be restless and have a very low frustration tolerance. He might be also explosive and aggressive and rebellious. Another child might be hypersensitive and wiggle constantly in his seat but he might be able to cope with failure in a non-acting-out way. He may display tension by rocking in his seat or by pulling his hair out. A schizoid child may keep to himself and may muddle along only to become severely depressed when overwhelmed by demands he cannot handle. Bizarre behavior may change places with somatic complaints. Some children vacillate between aggressive acting-out behavior and withdrawn or passive behavior. No LD pupil was said to have displayed all of the different types of behavior listed, but most of the children were reported to have shown at least one, or more often several, of the behavior problems before coming to the LD classes.

By far the most prevalent behavior problem reported was restlessness and hyperativity. No less than *ninety-one percent* of the LD pupils were thus described by their teachers. Low frustration tolerance (54%), Explosiveness (43%), and Anxiety (42%) were also frequently observed and made the youngsters' adjustment in regular classes difficult. About one third of the children were said to have been aggressive (33%) and/or showed attention-getting behavior (32%). Eighteen percent were thought to be rebellious and ten percent had shown delinquent behavior. More than a third of the LD pupils were reported to be withdrawn (38%), fourteen percent displayed somatic complaints or nervous mannerisms, and no less than thirteen percent showed schizoid behavior. Four youngsters (2%), all boys, were autistic.

No two LD pupils showed exactly the same behavior, and it was not possible to speak of any typical behavior of LD pupils. All that can be said is that each child was reported to have shown *some* kind of behavior problem, but that no child was sent to the LD program *only* because of behavior disorders. It is certain that the children's behavior was just one of several contributing factors that resulted in their referral to the LD program.

Developmental and Medical Histories of LD Pupils

The developmental and medical histories of the LD pupils, as reported in their referral records, were checked for significant factors that might have some bearing on the children's learning difficulties and on their need for special education (Birch and Gussow, 1970). Unfortunately not all of the clinical records of the LD pupils included adequate developmental or medical histories, nor did all the children have neurological examinations or EEG's. Because of this, the data presented here cannot be regarded as complete and must be thought of as merely suggestive.

It was found that the developmental and medical histories of the six- to eight-year-old pupils were usually more comprehensive than those of the nine- to twelve-year-old children. In general, more of the younger children had had complete medical and psychiatric workups. More of them were also diagnosed as "brain-injured" or as suffering from "minimal brain dysfunctioning." More of the older pupils were regarded as "emotionally disturbed." This is not unexpected since many of the so-called "organic signs" or "soft signs" (e.g., speech problems, perceptual malfunction, restlessness, hyperactivity, immaturity, etc.) improve with age. They tend to disappear or to become less noticeable by the time the children are ten or eleven years old. At that age level neurological examinations and EEG's are frequently negative and no longer reveal the positive signs that were evident when the children were younger. A complete developmental and medical history often shows that these "emotionally disturbed" children had the same kinds of developmental patterns and medical histories as the younger LD pupils who are diagnosed as suffering from brain dysfunction. Furthermore, parents sometimes forget to report early traumatic events or developmental delays in the life of the older LD pupils because these appear to be no longer "relevant" to a twelve-year-old's acting-out behavior.

The referral records of the LD pupils were checked for six developmental and medical factors.

PRENATAL AND/OR BIRTH TRAUMA:
Severe bleeding during first three months of mother's pregnancy; toxemia or serious illness during last three months of mother's pregnancy; difficult or abnormal delivery; bruised baby; "blue baby;" RH factor; premature baby or birthweight less than 5 lbs.; placement in incubator after birth; etc.

SLOW DEVELOPMENT:
Walking and/or talking not until after two years of age.

IMMATURE OR UNEVEN DEVELOPMENT:
Marked overall immaturity for child's age level; grossly undersized; extreme unevenness in development; good verbal skills but extremely poor coordination and visual-motor ability; good reasoning but extremely poor language and verbal ability; etc.

SERIOUS ILLNESS AND/OR ACCIDENT:
Jaundiced at birth; extremely high fever with convulsions in infancy; congenital syphilis; meningitis or encephalitis; serious head injury or concussion; prolonged period of unconsciousness; brain tumor or brain operation; etc.

MEDICAL DIAGNOSIS OF BRAIN DYSFUNCTION OR BRAIN INJURY:

Diagnosis by a child neurologist or psychiatrist; grand mal epilepsy, petit mal epilepsy; cerebral palsy.

ABNORMAL EEG

Table 4 shows the number and the percentage of LD pupils who revealed each of these factors in their developmental and medical histories. Once again, it must be emphasized that the results presented in Table 4 are only suggestive and not complete for all LD pupils. Furthermore, the four autistic children were not included on Table 4 since their developmental history was not reported in detail.

Table 4.

Developmental and medical histories of LD pupils.

Developmental and medical factors	N	%
Prenatal and/or birth trauma	47	27
Slow development	36	21
Immature, uneven development	49	28
Illness and/or accident	53	31
Diagnosis of brain dysfunction	78	45
Abnormal EEG	43	25

None of the six factors are mutually exclusive; in fact, they rarely occur alone. An LD pupil might, for instance, have experienced complications at birth and then developed slowly and was later diagnosed as having minimal brain dysfunction. Another child might have developed seizures during an attack of high fever in connection with a serious case of measles and was subsequently found to have an abnormal EEG and was diagnosed as brain-injured. On the other hand many children who are diagnosed as suffering from "minimal brain dysfunction" do not show any positive signs on a neurological examination, nor do they have abnormal EEG's or a traumatic developmental history. The LD pupils varied so much in their developmental and medical histories that it was not possible to derive at any "typical" developmental or medical pattern for children with learning disabilities. According to Table 4, forty-five percent of the LD pupils were diagnosed as having some kind of brain dysfunction. It is probable that the percentage would be higher if complete medical data had been available for all the LD pupils.

Social Background of LD Pupils

A child's learning ability and behavior depends to a large extent on his inborn personality (Thomas, Chess, and Birch, 1970), and his endowments and on the way in which they were molded and developed by the significant people and events in his environment. One cannot study or understand a child and his problems without knowing something about his social background and his family. The LD pupils came from a wide range of socioeconomic backgrounds and many different types of families. It is obvious that children who came from poor families are more likely to have experienced physical deprivation in early childhood than those from middle class families. But emotional neglect or rejection and family instability occur in all walks of life. Regardless of whether they lived in exclusive upper middle class suburbs or came from welfare families in crowded poverty areas, many of the LD pupils were exposed to parental conflict, alcoholism and abuse, illness, separation or death of parents, or to a lack of understanding and to unrealistic demands by the parents.

The referral records of all LD pupils were checked for four factors that were thought to contribute to children's ability to learn and to their adjustment in school (Birch and Gussow, 1970).

SEVERE NEGLECT IN EARLY LIFE:

Severe emotional and/or physical neglect and deprivation during part or all of the child's first three years of life.

CURRENT DEPRIVATION:

Child lives at time of follow-up study in a socially and economically marginal home; family is on welfare, father is unemployed or has no steady employment; overt rejection and neglect of child by parents is experienced.

UNSTABLE HOME:

Child lives in broken home due to death or absence of one parent, serious mental or physical illness of one or both parents, chronic disability of one or both parents (e.g., blindness, deafness, severe crippling by arthritis, etc.), intense parental conflict, abusive or alcoholic parent, etc.

FOSTER HOME:

Child is living at time of follow-up study in a foster home or institution.

Table 5.

Social background factors of LD pupils.

Social background factor	N	%
Severe neglect in early life	40	23
Current deprivation	24	14
Unstable home	64	37
Foster home	17	10

Table 5 shows the frequency of occurrence of the four background factors in the social histories of the LD pupils. The referral records of the children, from which the information was gathered, were often incomplete regarding the youngsters' early lives. The findings presented on Table 5 should therefore be thought of as merely suggestive. The figures given are probably too low. It was found, for instance, that some parents were unable or unwilling to share the details of their homelife with the school social worker. The parents presented the picture of a wholesome and stable family life which, it was then later learned, proved not to be in accord with the facts. In other cases, the family situation had changed and the present home situation had indeed become stable and harmonious following the remarriage of the mother or after the father had found a new job, etc. Intense hardship, conflicts, or periods of parental separation in the child's early life were happily put aside and no longer discussed or reported, even though they might have had a lasting effect on the child.

All that can be deduced from Table 5 is that at least one fourth of the LD pupils suffered from severe emotional and/or physical deprivation in early life and that fourteen percent of them still lived in deprived home situations at the time of the follow-up study, another ten percent had been removed from their homes and were living in foster homes. More than a third of the LD pupils lived in unstable families. Instability in the home in itself is not unusual and most children learn to cope with it after a fashion—but for the LD pupils, who tend to be vulnerable, poorly integrated, and who often have low frustration tolerance, an unstable home can be most upsetting and damaging.

CHARACTERISTICS OF LD PUPILS
AT TIME OF ENTRY INTO SPECIAL CLASSES: SUMMARY

In the preceding sections of this chapter the admission data for the

Characteristics of Pupils at Entry into LD Program

177 LD pupils were analyzed for different characteristics which were discussed separately. At this time the various characteristics will be summarized and related to each other since no child displayed only *one* of the characteristics or only *one* problem. Children with learning disabilities differ markedly from each other. There is of course no such thing as the typical LD pupil. However, certain behavior and learning patterns and social background factors occur often enough among LD pupils to be considered representative for the group as a whole.

In summing up the admission data, one can say that the children who were referred to the LD classes were mostly boys who were between six and nine years old. They were usually poorly integrated, had problems in visual-motor perception, and showed weak inner controls. They tended to be restless, explosive, anxious and had a low frustration tolerance. Frequently they were aggressive and/or withdrawn and their achievement was at least one year, and usually two years, below their grade level. The mental ability of the LD pupils fell most often into the lower range of normal intelligence, that is, between IQ 80 and 100. The youngsters usually had to cope with the double handicap of suffering from minimal brain dysfunction and of living in an unstable home environment. No child was referred to the special classes because of *only* learning problems or *only* behavior problems, instead they all had multiple and complex difficulties that required treatment and help in many different areas.

The case of Carl* is presented here to illustrate the characteristics of LD pupils at the time of their admission to the special classes. Carl had difficulty in school from the time he first entered regular kindergarten. Since he was a well-developed youngster of apparently normal intelligence, the teachers hoped that he would "outgrow" his problems. He was extremely restless and unable to follow directions; he could not participate in group activities, but he was quiet and was not disruptive. He showed no marked improvement in his behavior or in his learning in the first grade. By the end of the second grade Carl had still made only minimal academic gains while his behavior had greatly deteriorated. He was quite disturbed and disturbing in the classroom. He no longer withdrew quietly, instead he began acting out and was aggressive to his peers and negativistic toward school.

At that point, the second grade teacher initiated a referral for Carl to the LD program. According to her report, Carl was hypersensitive

*The names of all the pupils mentioned in this book have been changed to protect the identities of the children.

about his lack of academic skills. He was still only functioning on the pre-primer level in reading and could not write or copy letters and numbers without reversals. He seemed to have little difficulty understanding what he heard, but he could not retain what he learned. Carl never participated in group discussions. When he was required to open a book or to produce written work he became extremely anxious. When forced to do school work he would lose his temper and strike out at his classmates or become defiant to the teacher. Because of his unpredictable and aggressive behavior, Carl was rejected by his peers and was a social isolate. He had no friends in school or in his neighborhood. Carl spent much of his time alone in a world of fantasy.

According to Carl's social history, both of his parents were greatly concerned about their only son, but they disagreed on how to handle him. The overanxious, emotionally labile mother tried to bribe and push Carl into academic achievement. She worked with him every day when he came home from school, offered him rewards and hired a tutor for him on Saturdays. The father, an ambitious professional man, had little understanding of or patience with Carl. He tried to shame him into doing better in school by comparing him unfavorably with his older sister who was an honor student in high school. On occasion the father would threaten Carl that he would "send him away" if he did not "shape up." At no time did the father try to conceal from Carl his disappointment in him and his disapproval of his school failure. Both parents agreed that there was nothing "wrong" with Carl and that, "he could learn if he only tried a little harder." They refused to accept the report of the school psychologist and of the consulting school psychiatrist that Carl had real learning disabilities as well as emotional problems, and that he showed signs of minimal brain dysfunction.

When the home school finally decided to refer Carl to the LD program, his parents were most upset and strenuously opposed such a move. They did, however, agree to get a complete psychiatric and neurological workup for their son. Carl was seen by a child psychiatrist and neurologist who informed the parents that Carl was indeed suffering from "minimal brain dysfunction due to unknown causes." There was nothing in his developmental or medical history to account either for the neurological impairment that was evident or for the abnormal EEG he had revealed. The psychiatrist confirmed that Carl had serious learning and behavior problems and strongly recommended that he be sent to the LD program. The parents went along with these recommendations reluctantly. Carl was eight years eight months old when he entered the LD classes.

Characteristics of Pupils at Entry into LD Program

As was stated earlier (p. 10), one cannot really understand or help a child unless one knows something about his inner controls, his integrative ability, his reasoning, his social and emotional adjustment, and his family background. Carl's referral records and test results revealed the following picture:

Carl's inner controls were weak. He was reported to be restless, could not concentrate for more than a few minutes at a time and had a very low frustration level; his behavior was uneven and unpredictable, fluctuating between withdrawal and impulsive striking out at others, especially against peers.

Carl's integrative ability was extremely immature. His performance on the Bender Gestalt Test (Plate 2) was on the level of a six-and-a-half-year-old child and showed problems in visual-motor perception (Koppitz, 1964). Carl had difficulty reproducing angles and curves (figure A, 6, 7, 8); he had a tendency to perseverate on figure 6; and figures 2 and 3 showed immature rotations of the design. Rotations and reversals were also revealed on Carl's numbers (e.g., $\mathcal{E}, \mathcal{Z}, \mathcal{H}, \mathsf{P}$) and letters (for example, d=g, p=d, b=d, m=n). Difficulty in visual-motor perception was also reflected on Carl's poor performance on the WISC Block Design Subtest.

Furthermore, Carl showed major problems in recall and sequencing of sounds and symbols. His performance on the Digit Span Subtest was defective and he had difficulty recalling even elementary bits of factual information on the WISC Information Subtest. The combination of problems in visual-motor perception *and* in oral recall and sequencing might well account for Carl's lack of progress in reading. For, if he was not sure of the shapes or sequences of letters and if he could not remember the sounds that went with the letters, then he could not learn to read. It was therefore not surprising that Carl's grade level scores on the Wide Range Achievement Test were only 1.3 in reading and 1.2 in spelling.

Carl's reasoning ability was average. There was no doubt that Carl was essentially a youngster of normal intelligence. This was confirmed by the quality of his Human Figure Drawing (Plate 3) and by his WISC IQ scores. The Human Figure Drawing showed normal mental development for an eight-year-old boy (Koppitz, 1968, p. 29). On the WISC Carl obtained a Verbal IQ score of 92, a Performance IQ score of 94, and a Full Scale IQ score of 93. Carl's relatively high scores on the WISC Subtests of Comprehension (Weighted Score 13) and Picture Arrangement (Weighted Score 11) revealed his good commonsense reasoning and his good understanding of social relationships. Carl's

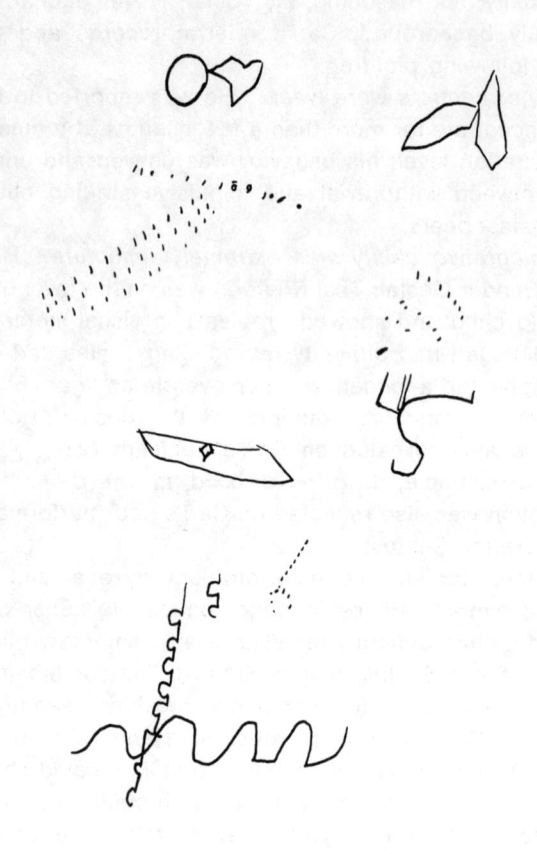

Plate 2.
Carl, CA 8-7.

Characteristics of Pupils at Entry into LD Program 31

Plate 3.

Carl, CA 8-7.

abstract verbal reasoning was also in the average range. His WISC Weighted Scores on Similarities and Vocabulary were both 10. Since Carl could not remember aurally presented numbers long enough to work with them, he did very poorly on the WISC Arithmetic Subtest. His arithmetic score on the Wide Range Achievement Test, which presented the problems in written form, was on the mid second-grade level. Carl was the type of youngster who cannot work independently in arithmetic. Such children have to have their "noses pointed in the right direction" before they can carry out a specific task. They have difficulty in directing themselves since they cannot recall the meaning of signs or where to begin a problem. For instance, Carl was never sure if you begin an addition problem by adding the first or the last digits or whether a given number was a six or a nine. Carl's problems with arithmetic were due not to reasoning, but rather to poor directionality and memory.

Carl's emotional adjustment was quite poor. His extremely low self-concept was shown by his lack of self-confidence and by his fearfulness and frequent withdrawal. It was also reflected on the tiny size of his Bender Gestalt Test designs (Plate 2) and on his Human Figure Drawing (Koppitz, 1968, chap. 5). The drawing (Plate 3) shows Carl's intense anxiety in the heavy shading of his boy's neck and limbs and in the omission of hands and feet. Carl's figure has literally no feet to stand on. He is "up in the air" and has withdrawn into the realm of fantasy. Without hands he cannot reach out toward others and cannot manipulate material or cope with problems. The large head of the boy reveals Carl's intensive feelings of intellectual inadequacy and concern over his lack of academic achievement.

Carl's social adjustment was most unsatisfactory. He was a social isolate who had no friends other than his cat and his turtle. He felt rejected by his father and deeply resented his more adequate sister. His peers avoided him. Carl was threatened by his mother's overanxious concern. He distrusted adults. Carl was a lonely and unhappy youngster who had no one he could turn to.

Carl's developmental and social background explained in part the reasons for his difficulties. He was immature and showed weak inner controls and poor integration, all of which contributed to his learning disabilities. When he failed to measure up to his parents' expectations in school they exerted excessive pressure on him, producing much anxiety and emotional tension in Carl. His lack of success in school contributed in turn to the parents' disagreement in handling him. The parents' conflict over Carl increased the mother's emotional instability

Characteristics of Pupils at Entry into LD Program

and provoked resentment toward the boy in both parents since he created so many problems at home. Carl was a threat to his mother's and father's feeling of adequacy as parents. The parents were neither neglectful nor indifferent toward Carl, but their lack of understanding of him had contributed unwittingly to his difficulties. If Carl had been a bright, well-integrated child like his sister, then he too would have been an honor student and his parents would have been most accepting and loving. They just did not know how to cope with a vulnerable child like Carl who looked so intelligent but could not function normally.

Once Carl was enrolled in the LD program, the teacher tried to help him with the many problems he had. Carl needed guidance to improve his inner control and his social adjustment with peers. He required special training in visual-motor perception and sequencing, in reading and writing, and in memory. In addition, his parents needed to be repeatedly counseled in order to support and give them guidance. An LD class in a public school must be concerned with *all* areas of school functioning, not just with achievement.

Carl's special class teacher and the psychologist worked out jointly a plan to help Carl. Priorities were established. It was decided that Carl had first of all to develop a better self-concept, and that he needed to acquire confidence in his teacher and in the LD program if he was going to benefit from it. Without such confidence all efforts on the part of the LD staff would be in vain. Books and formal academic instructions were not introduced until Carl was ready and able to face them without panic. Specific training in his areas of weakness (visual-motor perception and sequencing) were alternated with social studies and science which were taught on the level of his mental age, that is, on the third grade level, without the benefit of books.

While all this was going on, the social worker of the LD program worked intensively with Carl's parents to bring about a better understanding and acceptance by them of Carl and of the LD program. The success Carl was able to achieve during his stay in the LD classes was due not only to Carl's own ability and to his teacher's efforts, but also to the change of attitude on the part of his parents—and this change resulted in large measure from the efforts of the social worker. The LD staff worked closely together as a team whose main goal was to meet the individual needs of each pupil, so that he could develop and learn in school up to the level of his ability.

Chapter 3

Admission Data and Pupils' Status Five Years After Coming to the LD Program

The purpose of the LD program, as stated initially, was to help the pupils in the special classes to correct or to compensate for their learning problems so that they could return within a year or two to regular classes. However, it was discovered before long that this stated goal for the LD classes was unrealistic and too narrow. Some LD pupils were indeed able to return to regular classes as planned, but many more were unable to do so. Many pupils required long-term special education, while some youngsters were unable to benefit from the LD program and could not be maintained in the special classes.

This chapter explores the status of the LD pupils five years after they first came to the special classes. How many youngsters actually did return to regular classes? How many remained for the entire period of the follow-up study in the LD program? How many children left the special classes, and for what reasons? And finally, could the pupils' success or failure in the LD classes have been predicted from their referral data?

Table 6 shows the status of the 177 LD pupils at the end of the five year follow-up study. Forty-two children (24%) returned from the special classes to regular classes. That means that forty-two pupils were sent back to their home schools and into regular classes, on the recommendations of the LD staff, sometime during the five-year period following

Table 6.

Pupils' status five years after coming to LD program.

Pupils' status	N	%
Returned to regular classes	42	24
Remained in LD classes	71	40
Referred for hospitalization	26	15
Withdrawn by parents	17	10
Moved away	15	8
Transferred to other classes	6	3
	177	100

their entry into the special classes. It does not necessarily mean that the youngsters were actually in regular classes at the end of the five-year period. For as will be shown later (p. 89), some children who were returned to regular classes were not successful and did not remain there. In fact, some pupils even returned to the LD program on their own request.

Seventy-one (40%) of the LD pupils remained in the special classes for five or more years. These children remained continuously in the LD program during the entire five-year period following their admission to the special classes. Included in this group are a few youngsters who were pulled out of the program for only a few weeks or months but who were never absent for more than one semester. Children who were absent from the LD program for a whole year or more were listed under "withdrawn" or "moved" even if they returned to the LD program at a later time.

Twenty-six youngsters (15%) were too disturbed to benefit from the special classes and had to be referred for intensive psychiatric care or hospitalization. These children were given a psychiatric exclusion from the LD program and were referred to residential treatment centers or to mental hospitals. However, in some cases the parents refused to cooperate and did not accept the recommendations of the LD staff. While most of the children did go to residential treatment centers, a few youngsters were placed on home tutoring and received out-patient treatment. The referral for hospitalization occurred sometime during the five years following the youngsters' admission to the special classes. But this did not mean that the children were necessarily still under psychiatric care at the end of the follow-up study. Some youngsters responded well to treatment and were able to return to the LD program, or even to regular classes in a relatively short time; other pupils were not so lucky.

Seventeen (10%) of the LD pupils were withdrawn by the home school or by their parents from the special classes *contrary* to the recommendations of the LD staff. In most instances the youngsters were then sent to private schools or to regular classes.

Fifteen children (8%) moved with their families out of the area served by the LD program. These moves were usually necessitated by a change in the father's employment or by a separation of the parents. In only one case was it known that the family moved deliberately to get the child out of the LD program. Most of the youngsters and their parents were reluctant to leave the special classes. The moves occurred some time during the five years after the children first came to the special classes, but in this age of high mobility a move is rarely permanent. Thus a few of the pupils who are listed as "moved" actually returned to the LD program a year or more later when the family was able to move back into the area served by the program.

Six children (3%) were transferred to a more suitable special class when it was found that the youngsters were misplaced in the LD classes. In each case the child was moved from one type of special class to another. One child was referred to a school for the deaf, others were moved to classes for educable mentally retarded youngsters.

The findings on Table 6 show that approximately one fourth of the LD pupils were returned to regular classes within the five-year period following their enrollment in the special classes. This figure might be considered low by those who believe that learning disabilities can be "cured" or eliminated with the help of special teaching techniques and an increase in motivation for learning on the part of the child; for the LD staff members who actually worked with the youngsters it was a pleasant surprise to learn that as many as one fourth of the pupils *were* actually sent back to regular classes. No matter how the figure is looked at, it has considerable implications for the planning of public school LD classes. It is unrealistic even to suggest that most children with serious learning disabilities can be placed for a year or two into special classes, after which time they will be able to return successfully to regular classes. This just does not happen (Kotting and Brozovich, 1969).

According to Table 6, forty percent of the LD pupils were still in the special classes by the end of the five year follow-up study. What this figure does not show is that an additional 10% of the children were again in the LD program by the time the study was completed. Several of the youngsters came back to the LD program after an unsuccessful try in regular classes; some others returned to the LD classes after a period of residential treatment or hospitalization; again others were reenrolled in the LD program after being withdrawn or having moved away for more than a year. Actually no less than 50% of the 177 LD pupils who were included in the follow-up study were still or again in the special classes five years after they first entered the program. It appears therefore essential that an LD program be designed at the outset to offer the pupils long-term special education on both the elementary school and the high school levels, rather than just setting up one or two classes for short-term help in the elementary school. Or, if only a limited LD program is available, the choice of the pupils has to be highly selective (p. 74).

Even though 26 LD pupils had to be referred for residential treatment or hospitalization, most of the youngsters were (at least initially) appropriately placed in the LD program. Only a few of them should never have been admitted to the LD classes to begin with. In some cases, the need for more intensive psychiatric care for a child was apparent from the outset, but the youngster's parents were not yet able to accept this fact. In such instances, a temporary placement in the LD program served as a helpful intermediate step toward getting the services the child needed. In a few cases, the children's home situation deteriorated drastically during the five years of the follow-up study. This added to the child's problem and finally resulted in a serious emotional breakdown.

Needless to say, not all parents are willing or able to reconcile themselves to the fact that their children have learning disabilities. Some parents agree to special class placement for their son or daughter but have quite unrealistic expectations for the outcome of such placement. They are then disappointed when no miracles occur and when the child's problems have not vanished in a few short weeks or months. According to Table 6, seventeen disappointed or disillusioned parents withdrew their children from the LD program.

Moving is a common occurrence in our highly mobile society. Table 6 shows that 15 youngsters left the LD program when their families moved away. What Table 6 does not show is that several families with children with learning disabilities moved into the area served by the LD program especially in order to get special education for their youngsters. A good LD program will attract families with children who need LD classes.

Six youngsters were transferred from the LD classes to different types of special classes. The younger a child is at the time of referral to the LD classes, the more difficult it is to make an accurate diagnosis of the youngster's mental ability, the extent of his learning disability, and the severity of his emotional problems. It is also very difficult to tell the difference between marked immaturity and specific disabilities in perception in five- or six-year-old children. Because of this, the young pupils with many and confusing problems were placed into so called "observation classes" where they could be studied and observed until a valid diagnosis could be made. It often required many weeks or even months before a clear picture of a given child emerged, and before a suitable placement for the youngster could be determined. It was not uncommon to discover that some young children had serious learning problems as well as emotional problems, but that both of these were only secondary to moderately severe mental retardation. Depending on the child's main needs and his overall functioning, he might be then transferred to a class for educable retarded children or to a class for youngsters with multiple problems. It was found that retarded, brain-injured, and emotionally disturbed children can feel just as outclassed in a group of brighter LD pupils as in a regular class. In several cases, the slow youngsters became so frustrated in the LD classes that they began to show aggressive and acting-out behavior. Their behavior improved again as soon as they were placed into a slower moving, less competitive special class.

The intake data for all 177 LD pupils will now be once more evaluated in order to find out how they relate to the children's status by the end of the five year follow-up study. Once again each of the nine characteristics discussed earlier will be examined, first separately, and then together, to explore whether definite patterns emerge for different groups of children. The findings might prove helpful in predicting the progress of new pupils in the LD program; they might also be of use when planning LD programs in the years to come.

Referring School Districts

The marked diversity in the socioeconomic background of the thirteen school districts served by the cooperative LD program here under discussion was pointed out earlier (p. 6). Table 7 shows how much the youngsters from the various school districts differed in their status five years after coming to the LD program. The percentage of LD pupils who returned from the special classes to regular classes ranged from 46%, 31%, and 30% for Districts L, I, and E, respectively, to zero for Districts H, K, and M. Certainly this difference is not pure chance, nor is it due to the size, the affluence, or the racial or social composition of the

Admission Data and Pupils' Status Five Years After Entry

district. The main determining factor appears to be the selection of pupils for the LD program. The long-range progress shown by the LD pupils seemed to depend even more on what the children themselves brought into the situation, on what they had to work with, than on the educational program they were exposed to. In other words, if a child lacked a certain basic ability or if he was severely disturbed to begin with, his prognosis in the special classes was less favorable than if he was less impaired or less disturbed.

Table 7.

Referring school districts and pupils' status five years after coming to LD program.

						Status						
School Dist.	Total Adm. N	Reg. Class N	%	LD Class N	%	Hospi- talized N	%	With- drawn N	%	Moved N	%	Transferred N	%
A	13	1	8	8	62	2	15	1	8	0	0	1	8
B	12	2	17	6	50	2	17	1	8	0	0	1	8
C	6	1	17	3	50	0	0	1	17	0	0	1	17
D	15	1	7	7	47	2	13	4	27	1	7	0	0
E	13	4	30	5	38	3	23	0	0	1	8	0	0
F	36	10	28	10	28	4	11	5	14	6	17	1	3
G	12	3	25	4	33	3	25	0	0	2	17	0	0
H	4	0	0	2	50	2	50	0	0	0	0	0	0
I	39	12	31	16	41	6	15	1	3	3	8	1	3
J	8	2	25	4	50	1	13	0	0	1	12	0	0
K	4	0	0	2	50	1	25	0	0	0	0	1	25
L	13	6	46	3	23	0	0	3	23	1	8	0	0
M	2	0	0	1	50	0	0	1	50	0	0	0	0
	177	42		71		26		17		15		6	

Table 7 revealed that 62% of the pupils from District A and half of the pupils from Districts B, C, D, H, J, K, and M required long term special education. In Districts L, F, G, and E, only one fourth to one third of the children remained for five or more years in the LD program. The Districts differed even more on the percentage of youngsters who were referred for hospitalization. District H had only four children in the LD program, two of whom were so disturbed that they had to be given a psychiatric exclusion and were referred to a mental hospital. The other two youngsters were of borderline intelligence and required long-term special education. In most of the other districts, the number of children who were referred for hospitalization was between 13 and 25 percent. None of the pupils from Districts C, L, and M had to be excluded for psychiatric reasons.

The selection of the pupils for referral to the LD program depends mostly on the classroom teachers, the administrators, and the psychologist and consulting psychiatrist in the local schools. Parental approval and cooperation is solicited before the child is referred to the special classes. The length of time the LD pupils remain in the LD classes depends on the special education staff and on the parents of the youngsters. Some parents never fully accept special class placement for their son or daughter. Other parents are at first agreeable to such a placement but become later discouraged when they see no radical change or rapid progress in their child's achievement. Sooner or later the parents ask that their youngster be returned to regular classes. If the LD staff is convinced that the child is not yet ready for a return to regular classes and recommends that the youngster remain in the LD program, then the parents have two options open to them: They can either accept the judgment of the LD staff and leave their child in the LD program, or they can withdraw him from the special classes against the recommendations of the LD staff. It is here where the socioeconomic differences between the school districts are most apparent.

Table 7 reveals that the two school districts in the most affluent communities had the highest percentage of pupils who were withdrawn from the LD program. In Districts L and D, approximately one fourth of the LD pupils were withdrawn by their parents and were sent to private schools. It is probable that some of the parents in Districts E, G, H, J, and K would also have liked to send their children to private schools, but they could not afford to do so. The implications are clear: The LD pupils from upper middle class communities rarely remained in the public school special classes for five years or more. If the children were not able to return to regular classes within a period of two or three years, the parents tended to withdraw them and sent them to private schools instead. This trend had a marked effect on the composition of the LD population. The younger LD pupils represented a much wider range of ability and social background than the older children in the program.

In District M, one child was withdrawn from the LD classes by his local school district against both the child's and the parents' wishes. In this case, budgetary considerations and transportation problems prevailed over the LD staff's recommendations and the parents' requests.

As might be expected, there was no clearly defined relationship

between the referring school districts and the perc
who moved away or who had to be transferred to diff
special classes. In both instances the number of pupils
small.

Sex of LD Pupils

The overall ratio of boys to girls among the LD pupils was
the time of admission to the special classes (p. 13). The same sex r
existed for the group of LD pupils who returned to the regular class
For those children who remained in the LD program for five or mor
years the ratio of boys to girls was 5:1. The proportion of girls in the LD classes who were in need of long term special education was apparently somewhat higher than that of boys. Twenty-four boys were referred for hospitalization compared to only two girls. The boy girl ratio for the children who were given psychiatric exclusion from the LD program was therefore 12:1.

Table 8.

Admission age and pupils' status five years after coming to LD program.

Admission Age	*Status* *Regular class*	*Still in LD class*	*Hospitalized*
6 years	4	14	5
7 years	4	19	3
8 years	9	17	2
9 years	12	8	2
10 years	6	7	3
11 years	5	3	6
12 years	2	3	5
	42	71	26
Age Mean	9-0	8-0	9-9

Age of LD Pupils

Table 8 reveals that a child's age at the time of his referral to the LD program had a significant relationship to his status during the next five years. If a youngster was six or seven years old when he first came to the special classes, then there was a good chance that he would remain in the LD program for five or more years. The children who were referred to the LD classes prior to or at the end of kindergarten or the first grade tended to be more impaired and more disturbed than those youngsters who were maintained in regular classes through the primary grades. Children who were eight to ten years old at the time of admission to the LD program had a much better chance of returning to regular classes within a five-year period. The pupils who were referred for hospitalization included children of all ages, but most often they were ten to twelve years of age.

Chi squares were computed comparing the number of younger (age 6 to 8) and older (age 9 to 12) pupils who remained in the LD classes for five or more years, who returned to regular classes, and who were referred for residential psychiatric care. The results showed that the long-term LD pupils were significantly younger when coming to the special classes than either the children who returned to regular classes ($X^2 = 8.61$, P. 01) or the group who were given a psychiatric exclusion ($X^2 = 6.99$, P.01). [Typographical limitations prevent the use of a chi. Therefore, Y has been used in its place throughout this book.] There were no statistically significant differences in the ages of the latter two groups of pupils.

IQ Scores of LD Pupils

Table 8 indicated that the younger LD pupils most often required long-term special education. It was shown on Table 1 that most of the younger LD pupils were of dull normal or borderline intelligence. It could be expected therefore that the IQ scores of the LD pupils would also be related to their status five years after coming to the special classes. Table 9 shows that this was indeed the case.

All but four of the LD pupils who returned to regular classes had an IQ score of at least 85 or better. The four exceptions, boys with IQ scores of 84 or less, did not do well in the regular classes. Thus it appears that an IQ score of 85, at the time of admission to the LD program, is a required minimum if an LD pupil is to return to a regular class within a five-year period. The IQ mean score for the youngsters who returned to regular classes was 98, or average, compared to an IQ mean score of 87, or dull normal, for the long-term LD pupils.

It seems that modest mental ability, as measured on the Wechsler Intelligence Scale for Children or the Stanford-Binet Intelligence Scale, is one of the factors which accounts for the need of some LD pupils for long-term special education. This factor had been also stressed by Ames (1968). Almost two thirds of the long-term LD pupils obtained IQ scores in the dull normal or borderline range. The fact that one

Table 9.

IQ scores and pupils' status five years after coming to LD program.

IQ scores	Regular class	Status Still in LD class	Hospitalized*
120 up	2	0	2
110–119	4	5	3
100–109	11	7	4
90–99	15	14	3
85–89	6	7	4
80–84	3	22	3
70–79	1	15	2
69 down	0	1	1
	42	71	22*
IQ mean score	98	87	94

*The four nontestable autistic children are not included.

third of the long-term LD pupils had IQ scores in the average or high average range suggests, however, that limited mental ability was not the only reason for the youngsters' need for the LD program.

In contrast to the group of LD pupils who returned to regular classes and those who remained in the LD classes, the children who were referred for residential psychiatric care showed an almost even distribution of IQ scores. They ranged all the way from the superior to the mentally defective. The mean IQ score for these youngsters was 94, or average. Table 9 indicates that lack of mental ability was not a prime cause for the LD pupils' inability to benefit from the special classes and for their need for residential treatment.

Chi squares were computed comparing the number of children with IQ scores both above and below 85 who returned to regular classes, those who were long-term LD pupils, and those who were referred for hospitalization. It was found that the long-term LD pupils were significantly duller than the youngsters who returned to the regular classes ($X^2 = 20.05$, P .001). The long-term LD pupils were also found to have significantly lower IQ scores than the children who were excluded ($X^2 = 3.33$, P .05). There was no statistically significant difference between the IQ scores of the pupils who returned to regular classes and those who were referred for residential psychiatric care.

The implications seem to be that average intelligence in and of itself is no assurance that an LD pupil will be able to return to a regular class within a five-year period. The child might have to remain in the LD program for five or more years, or he might even require more intensive psychiatric care and have to be referred to a hospital. Without adequate intellectual potential, however—that is, without an IQ of at least 85 or better—an LD pupil has little chance of returning successfully to regular classes. It is imperative therefore that an LD program set realistic goals for its pupils. Dull children need long-term special education and should not be expected to return to regular classes. If a quick return to regular classes is required for all pupils, then the enrollment in the LD classes should be restricted to children of at least average ability.

Visual-Motor Perception of LD Pupils

It was shown on Table 2 that the majority of LD pupils display, at the time of entry into the LD program, immaturity and/or specific malfunction in visual-motor perception. Specific problems in visual-motor perception were defined as a marked discrepancy between a child's functioning level on the Bender Gestalt Test and his mental age. In this study the Bender Gestalt Test served in a dual capacity as a test of visual-motor perception and as a measure of a youngster's integrative ability (p. 10).

At this time the relationship between the LD pupils' Bender Test scores and their status five years after coming to the special classes will be explored. Chi squares were computed comparing the Bender Test scores (Poor compared with Low Average or better) of the LD pupils who returned to regular classes, who were long-term LD pupils, and who were referred for hospitalization. No significant differences were found between the Bender Test scores of the LD pupils who returned to regular classes and the long-term LD pupils. However, the children who were in need of residential psychiatric care showed a significantly higher frequency of very poor performance on the Bender Test than the youngsters who returned to regular classes ($X^2 = 8.63$, P .01) and the long-term LD pupils ($X^2 = 5.28$, P .05).

Table 10 shows that about two thirds of the pupils who were referred for hospitalization had very poor Bender Test scores, compared to only one third of those who remained in the LD program for five or more years and only one fourth of those who returned to regular classes.

Not all LD pupils were given the Wepman Auditory Discrimination Test (Wepman, 1958); therefore, the data shown on Table 10 are incomplete. They nevertheless are suggestive. It appears that poor auditory

Table 10.

Bender Gestalt and Wepman Test scores and pupils' status five years after coming to LD program.

Level of Bender scores	Regular class	Status Still in LD class	Hospitalized
Good	2	1	1
High Average	9	15	4
Low Average	20	29	4
Poor	11	26	17
	42	71	26
Wepman scores			
Poor	3	19	2

perception has considerable influence on a child's progress in the LD program. With a few exceptions, all those youngsters who revealed poor auditory perception as measured on the Wepman Test required long-term special education. The three youngsters with poor auditory perception who returned to regular classes did not do well in these classes. It was further noted that most of the long-term LD pupils who did poorly on the Wepman Test also performed poorly on the Bender Gestalt Test. It appears therefore that children who have difficulties in both auditory perception *and* visual-motor perception are likely candidates for long-term special education.

Achievement of LD Pupils

The achievement of the LD pupils was measured with the Wide Range Achievement Test (p. 19). Table 11 gives the levels of academic achievement of the three groups of LD pupils at the time of their entry into the special classes. Chi squares were computed comparing the number of children whose achievement was less than two years below grade level with those whose achievement was two or more years below grade level. As might be expected, the LD pupils who returned to regular classes were from the outset better readers than the long-term LD pupils ($X^2 = 13.51$, P .001) and the youngsters who were referred for hospitalization ($X^2 = 4.54$, P .05). There were no statistically significant differences in the reading scores of the children who were referred for hospitalization and those of the long-term LD pupils.

Table 11.

Achievement and pupils' status five years after coming to LD program.

Achievement level	Regular class Read.	Regular class Arith.	Still in LD class Read.	Still in LD class Arith.	Hospitalized Read.	Hospitalized Arith.
At grade level	13	6	9	8	6	4
1 yr. below grade level	17	15	15	25	5	2
2 yrs. below grade level	7	15	30	22	8	5
3 yrs. below grade level	5	6	17	16	7	15
	42	42	71	71	26	26

A different picture emerges when the arithmetic achievement of the LD pupils was compared. Significantly more children who were in need of residential psychiatric care showed poor arithmetic achievement than did the youngsters who returned to regular classes ($X^2 = 3.80$, P .05) and the long-term LD pupils ($X^2 = 3.42$, P .05). There were no statistically significant differences in the arithmetic scores of the two last-mentioned groups.

The relationship of low arithmetic scores and the need for hospitalization may seem puzzling until it is recalled that the children who were in need of psychiatric care also revealed exceptionally poor integration on the Bender Gestalt Test. Research has shown (Brenner et al., 1967; Koppitz, 1970; Kotting and Brozovich, 1969; Swift and Spivack, 1968) that a close correlation exists between performance on the Bender Gestalt Test and achievement in arithmetic, and that both are related to children's integrative ability and their overall behavior.

A child's reading and arithmetic levels at the time of entry into the special classes cannot predict, by themselves, the youngster's status five years later. In general, it seems that a child who can read at grade level or not more than one year below grade level, has a better chance of returning to regular classes than one who reads two or more years below his grade level. If the youngster functions three or more years below grade level in reading, his chances of returning to regular classes within a five-year period are very slim indeed. A pupil whose arithmetic achievement is three or more years below grade level is most likely vulnerable and poorly integrated, and he may require a period of residential treatment if other conditions are unfavorable.

Behavior of LD Pupils

As was pointed out earlier (p. 22), all LD pupils had shown one or more types of behavior problems in school prior to their coming to the LD program. Disturbed or disturbing behavior in the classroom was one of the major factors that contributed to children's need for the special classes. It was also emphasized that the LD pupils differed widely from each other in the kinds of behavior they had displayed.

Table 12 shows the frequency of occurrence of the twelve types of behavior under discussion and their relationship to the pupils' status five years after coming to the LD program. With the exception of autism, all the other types of behavior listed occurred to some extent in all three groups of pupils studied. The four autistic children were unable to function in groups of children and required so much individual attention and constant personal supervision that they could not be maintained in the program. All four of these youngsters had to be excluded from the LD classes and were referred to hospitals or to special schools for autistic children.

Chi squares were computed comparing the number of LD pupils with and without a given behavior problem who returned to regular classes to those who were long-term LD pupils and to those who were referred for hospitalization. Six of the twelve behavior categories listed on Table 12 failed to differentiate significantly between the three groups of pupils. These were restlessness, low frustration tolerance, attention seeking, rebelliousness, somatic complaints, and schizoid behavior. These particular types of behavior had been accentuated in the youngsters by the pressures and frustrations they had experienced in the regular classrooms. Once the children were transferred to the smaller, more relaxed, and protective special classes, these types of behavior tended to improve. Young children with minimal brain dysfunction are very sensitive and often overreact in large, overstimulating regular classrooms. Because these youngsters are so poorly integrated and immature, their behavior deteriorates or regresses rapidly when they cannot cope with a situation; at such times they may appear to be quite bizarre. Happily, much of this extreme behavior responds to change in the child's class placement and to the subsequent lessening of frustrations and of the pressures on him. Time and maturation are

Table 12.

Behavior and pupils' status five years after coming to LD program.

			Status					
	Total Admission (N = 177)		Regular class (N = 42)		Still in LD class (N = 71)		Hospitalized (N = 26)	
Reported behavior	N	%	N	%	N	%	N	%
Restlessness	158*	91	37	88	68	96	21*	95
Low frustration tolerance	94*	54	23	55	34	48	14*	64
Explosive	74*	43	17	40	26	37	16*	73
Anxiety	72*	42	22	50	26	37	19*	86
Withdrawn	65*	38	23	52	23	32	10*	45
Aggressive	57*	33	10	23	21	30	12*	55
Attention-seeking	56*	32	7	16	25	35	7*	32
Rebellious	32*	18	9	20	9	13	7*	32
Somatic complaints	25*	14	8	19	8	11	4*	18
Schizoid	23*	13	5	11	9	13	4*	18
Delinquent	18*	10	4	9	3	4	8*	36
Autistic	4	2	0	0	0	0	4	15

*The four autistic children are not included.

also factors that bring about a reduction in the restlessness and vulnerability of LD pupils. In addition, many LD pupils benefit from special education, from counseling, and from medication, all of which can increase their ability to cope with frustrations and enables them to concentrate better.

It is interesting to note that the LD pupils who returned to regular classes were initially more withdrawn than were the long-term LD pupils ($X^2 = 4.59$, P .05). This was the only type of behavior in which these two groups of youngsters differed significantly. It is therefore hazardous to make predictions as to which LD pupils will remain in the special classes and which will return to regular classes within a five year period, purely on the basis of the behavior that the children exhibited prior to their entry into the LD program.

Very different results were obtained when the initial behavior of the LD pupils who were referred for hospitalization was compared with that of the other two groups of pupils. The findings are shown in Table 13.

The youngsters who had to be excluded from the LD program were more often explosive, anxious, aggressive, delinquent and, as was men-

Table 13.

Comparison of behavior and social background factors in three groups of LD pupils.

Behavior	Regular class vs. hospitalization X^2	P	Still in LD class vs. hospitalization X^2	P
Explosive*	4.79	.05	9.38	.01
Anxious*	5.84	.05	14.73	.001
Aggressive*	4.76	.05	3.56	.05
Delinquent*	5.18	.05	13.72	.001
Autistic	4.36	.05	7.87	.01
Background				
Early neglect*	3.89	.05	13.09	.001
Current deprivation*	6.65	.05	3.52	.05
Unstable home*	8.88	.01	7.49	.01
Foster home*	3.60	.05	8.69	.01

*The four autistic children are not included.

tioned above, autistic. All of these differences in frequency of occurrence were statistically significant at the .05 level or higher. Thus it seems that acting-out children who are referred to special classes have a much poorer prognosis in an LD program than non-acting-out children. It was also observed that the youngsters who were referred for residential care all had a larger number of different behavior problems than did the children in the other two groups of LD pupils. For instance, it was not uncommon to find that a child who was in need of hospitalization was not only extremely restless, anxious, and easily frustrated, but that he also was explosive, aggressive, *and* delinquent.

Developmental and Medical Histories of LD Pupils

It was mentioned earlier that many of the developmental and medical records of the LD pupils were not complete, so that the data presented here are just suggestive. Nevertheless, Table 4 showed that more than one fourth of the children had experienced prenatal and/or birth trauma, had suffered severe illnesses in early life or serious accidents, had shown uneven or slow development, and/or were immature and had obtained abnormal EEG records. Almost one half of the LD pupils were medically diagnosed as suffering from brain dysfunction.

At this time the relationship between the developmental and medical histories of the LD pupils and their status five years after their admission to the LD program will be examined. Table 14 shows the frequency of occurrence of the various developmental and medical factors among

Table 14.

Developmental, medical, and social background factors of LD pupils.

	Pupils' status 5 years after coming to LD program					
	Regular class (N = 42)		Still in LD class (N = 71)		Hospitalization (N = 22)*	
Developmental and Medical factors	N	%	N	%	N	%
Prenatal/birth trauma	7	17	19	27	6	27
Slow development	7	17	11	15	3	14
Immature	17	40	21	30	4	18
Illness/accident	9	20	26	37	7	32
Brain injury diagnosed	21	52	38	54	7	32
Abnormal EEG	13	29	21	30	6	27
Social background						
Early neglect	11	25	10	14	12	55
Current deprivation	2	5	10	14	7	32
Unstable home	11	25	23	32	15	68
Foster home	4	9	4	6	7	32

*The four autistic children are not included.

the three groups of pupils studied. It can be seen that the youngsters who returned to regular classes had had a somewhat higher rate of immaturity and had a somewhat lower rate of birth trauma, serious illness, and accidents than the other two groups of children. The youngsters who were referred for hospitalization were less often diagnosed as immature or brain-injured. However, when chi squares were computed comparing the number of pupils whose histories showed the key medical and developmental factors and their status five years after coming to the LD program with those whose histories did not exhibit these factors, no statistically significant differences were found for the three groups of pupils on any of the items investigated.

On the basis of these limited data, it appears that a child's developmental history or medical diagnosis by itself cannot predict the youngster's status five years after admission to an LD program. The findings also offer support for the conviction that it is impractical and meaningless to group children in special classes on the basis of diagnostic labels. Similar findings have been reported by other investigators (Bortner and Birch, 1969; Dubnoff, 1966; Fenichel, 1966; Kotting and Brozovich, 1969).

Social Background of LD Pupils

Certain social background factors that were reported in the referral records of the LD pupils were shown on Table 5. It was found that more than one third of the children came from unstable homes and almost one fourth of them had suffered from serious emotional and physical neglect in early life. Fourteen percent of the youngsters were still living in deprived homes at the time of their admission to the LD program; ten percent lived in foster homes. Table 14 shows the relationship between these background factors and the children's status five rence were statistically significant at the .05 level or higher. Thus it years after their entry into the special classes. It is immediately apparent that the frequency of occurrence of the four social background factors differs markedly between the three groups of LD pupils. Chi squares revealed that these differences were statistically highly significant for the children who were referred for hospitalization (Table 13). The youngsters who were in need of residential treatment had more frequently experienced serious emotional and physical neglect in their early lives than either the children who returned to regular classes or the long-term LD pupils. Furthermore, the hospitalized group was living significantly more often in deprived and unstable homes at the time of entry into the special classes than the other two groups of pupils; and proportionately more of them were living in foster homes.

These findings indicate that a child's social background is more closely related to his status five years after entry into the LD program than his diagnostic label or his developmental history. They also point up the importance of taking a youngster's home environment into consideration when planning his class placement and education. It is not enough just to concentrate on a youngster's academic problems in a special class. Work with the pupils' parents is an essential part of any LD program if the child is to benefit from special education.

Any child, but especially a child with learning problems, must be treated and worked with as a social being who lives in and responds to a given environment. LD pupils tend to be vulnerable children who react even more strongly to their home situation than do most other children. Whereas most well-integrated children can and do survive in an unstable home without too much serious damage, the LD pupils cannot cope as easily with instability and deprivation. The LD pupil's long-range academic progress will depend as much on changes in his home situation as on changes in his school situation. Any meaningful prediction regarding an LD pupil's status five years after entry into special classes must be based in part on knowledge of the child's social background.

ADMISSION DATA AND PUPILS' STATUS FIVE YEARS AFTER COMING TO THE LD PROGRAM: SUMMARY

In the preceding sections of this chapter, data concerning nine characteristics of LD pupils were discussed both separately and in relation to the children's status five years after their admission to the special classes. The purpose of this investigation was to discover whether any of these characteristics could predict the pupils' progress in the LD program. If such predictions can be made successfully, they might have considerable value for the parents, the teachers, and the administrators in helping the LD pupils.

When a child is referred to an LD program, the parents almost invariably ask: "How long will my child be in the special class? When will he return to the regular classes?" Such questions are understandable and valid. The answers the parents usually receive tend to be either vague or unwarrantedly optimistic. If meaningful long-range predictions regarding an LD pupil's progress could be made on the basis of his referral data, then the parents could be provided with more realistic answers to their questions.

Teachers are trained to teach and want to see results from their efforts. When a child does not learn as fast or as well as a teacher expects, the teacher often blames herself for having failed or gets impatient or angry with the child. If a child's long-term rate of learning and growth in the LD classes can be realistically predicted at the time of the youngster's admission to the LD program, then the teacher could assess her success or failure with the pupil on a more objective basis and would not get discouraged if marked progress were not immediately evident.

Valid predictions concerning the progress of LD pupils would also help administrators in planning special class programs. On the basis of the admission data, the administrators could then anticipate each year the number of pupils who would require long-term special education, vocational training, an academic type of special class, and the number who would remain in the LD program for only a limited time.

The present study revealed that, with the exception of autism, none of the characteristics investigated had a one-to-one relationship with the pupils' status five years after their admission to the LD program. It can be stated with certainty that autistic children, as defined here (p. 21), cannot benefit from a public school LD class. These youngsters need more intensive and specialized educational and treatment facilities. It is not safe to make any long-range predictions regarding an LD pupil's status five years hence solely on the basis of any other *single* characteristic or factor in his admission record. Most of the characteristics studied occurred significantly more often in some groups of LD pupils than in others, but none of these relationships were strong enough to have predictive value by themselves.

No human variable or factor exists in isolation. It is therefore logical that predictions about an LD pupil's progress cannot be based on separate bits of information or single characteristics, rather they must be based on all aspects of the child's admission data. When the individual characteristics of LD pupils are combined into clusters or patterns, a very different picture emerges. Such composite pictures or patterns of intake data are, of course, only generalizations and do not necessarily apply to every single child in a group of pupils. Nevertheless, such patterns can be used as general guidelines for meaningful long-term predictions for children who are referred to the LD program.

TYPICAL ADMISSION DATA OF LD PUPILS WHO WERE ABLE TO RETURN TO REGULAR CLASSES WITHIN A FIVE-YEAR PERIOD AFTER COMING TO SPECIAL CLASSES:

These youngsters tended to be between eight and ten years old when they entered the special classes; that is, they had been able to be maintained in regular classes during the primary grades. They were of at least average intelligence (minimum IQ 85), but usually showed immaturity or malfunction in visual-motor perception and control. They were often anxious, restless, hyperactive, and very easily frustrated. Even though they were, at times, disruptive in the classroom, they were not extremely hostile nor were they acting-out youngsters. Their achievement level was seldom more than one, at most two years below their appropriate grade level. The children revealed no serious problems in the area of language development, auditory perception, and in memory and sequencing.

Some of these youngsters were diagnosed as suffering from minimal brain dysfunction, while others showed no signs of neurological malfunction. A few children had experienced neglect and deprivation in early life. Typically, however, the youngsters were living in fairly adequate homes at the time of the referral to the LD program, and they were not suffering from physical or emotional deprivation. The majority of pupils came from fairly stable and supportive families.

It can generally be said that immature, poorly integrated, poorly controlled, emotionally disturbed children, who may or may not be diagnosed as having minimal brain dysfunction, and who are eight to ten years old, can benefit greatly from a period of time in LD classes. They usually can return to regular classes after two to five years of special education *provided they are of normal intelligence, have no serious deficits in auditory perception, language development, and memory, are not achieving more than one year (or at most two years) below grade level, are non-acting-out youngsters, and come from a reasonably stable and supporting home.* The child's developmental and medical history and medical diagnosis have little or no relationship to his ability to return from the special classes to regular classes.

TYPICAL ADMISSION DATA FOR LONG-TERM LD PUPILS:

The children in this category tended to have difficulty in adjusting to school from the outset. They were usually too immature, socially and emotionally, to hold their own, even in kindergarten. They were either referred to the LD program straight from kindergarten or after one or two unsuccessful years in the first grade. They were most often between five-and-one-half and eight years old when they came to the LD classes. Most of them were of low average or borderline intelligence (IQ scores between 70 and 90) and were characterized by either considerable immaturity or malfunction in the areas of control and integration. That is, they were not only extremely hyperactive, distractible, and had a short attention span, they also had problems in visual-motor perception *and* in auditory perception. The children tended to show marked deficits in language development and/or in the ability to recall and sequence sounds and symbols. They usually had failed to acquire any academic skills in regular classes prior to their referral to the special classes. The behavior of these long-term LD pupils varied greatly as did their developmental and medical histories and their medical diagnoses. Some of them were quite aggressive and hostile, others were withdrawn and extremely anxious—but all of them were more-or-less able to function in small special classes without constant close supervision and one-to-one instruction.

It can generally be said that a child will remain in an LD program for a long time if he can function as a member of a group in a small special class, even though he might have been unable to hold his own in the regular primary grades, and is of dull average or borderline intelligence. Such a pupil characteristically shows marked immaturity in inner controls and in emotional and social development, has serious malfunction in visual-motor and auditory perception and/or in language development and memory, and possesses little or no academic skills at the time of referral to the special classes.

TYPICAL ADMISSION DATA FOR LD PUPILS
WHO HAD TO BE REFERRED FOR HOSPITALIZATION:

These youngsters tended to fall into two main groups. One group consisted of younger children who were so severely disturbed or impaired that they could not relate to adults or peers and could not even follow simple directions. They were unable to function even in small group situations and required constant close supervision. They could learn, if at all, only in a one-to-one situation. The referral records usually stated that the children could not be tested and had never been able to adapt to a regular public school class. These youngsters were also quite unable to adjust to the public school LD classes. The autistic children are representative of the group. Such children need a more specialized and more intensive educational and treatment facility than an LD program in a public school can provide.

The admission data of the second group of youngsters who could not benefit from the LD classes revealed poor integration and considerable overloading of pathology in the developmental, social, and emotional areas. They also showed severe deficits in school achievement. Their academic functioning was, in most cases, three or more years below their grade level. Low intelligence was usually not one of the main factors that contributed to the children's difficulties in school. Their IQ scores ranged anywhere from borderline to superior. These pupils exhibited very poor visual-motor perception and language development. In fact, their entire integrative ability was characterized by severe malfunction and immaturity. In addition, the referral records of these children revealed that in early life they had experienced much deprivation and instability at home. The home situation was frequently still quite inadequate at the time of the follow-up study. Deprivation and unstable family relationships were common. These very vulnerable children lacked the kind of stable and supporting parental figures they so desperately needed. As a consequence many of these youngsters had developed extremely poor self-concepts, while their attitudes towards adults, peers and the school were negative and hostile. The pupils had become discouraged long ago, and lack of motivation for learning only increased their lack of achievement and their asocial, disruptive classroom behavior.

These pupils were usually unable to adjust to the special classes. They were aggressive, explosive, and delinquent. Some showed strong sociopathic tendencies and could not be reached or controlled in the classroom. Others were so anxious and emotionally disturbed that they lost control of themselves and suffered from psychotic episodes or serious mental disorders. All of them needed a period of intensive residential treatment and care and could not be educated in a public school special class. Some of the youngsters had a long history of mental illness and prior hospitalization.

In general it appears that children cannot benefit from public school LD classes if they cannot adjust to and function in group situations, and if they require constant close supervision and a one-to-one teaching situation. A child who cannot be tested individually by a skilled clinician is a poor candidate for an LD class. So is an extremely vulnerable youngster who lives in a highly unstable, emotionally disturbed family situation, who indulges in acting-out behavior, and/or who has a history of mental illness. *A child's need for referral to a hospital is determined by his background, his integrative ability and by his behavior rather than by his level of intelligence, his achievement level, or his diagnostic classification.*

TYPICAL ADMISSION DATA FOR CHILDREN
WHO WERE WITHDRAWN FROM THE LD PROGRAM:

This group of youngsters had only one characteristic in common—they were all children of middle-class parents who were unwilling or unable to accept their youngsters' special class placement. Otherwise the children varied greatly in age, intelligence, behavior, and in the types of problems which they presented in the classroom. *The essential features in this group were parental opposition to having a child in the LD program and the financial means of sending their youngster to a private school.* Thus it can be predicted that some of the more affluent parents will withdraw their children sooner or later from a public school LD program, especially if the pupils fail to make marked academic progress in the span of one or two years.

Admission Data and Pupils' Status Five Years After Entry

TYPICAL ADMISSION DATA FOR CHILDREN WHO WERE TRANSFERRED TO DIFFERENT TYPES OF SPECIAL CLASSES:

These children were usually quite young when they were referred to the LD program and they displayed so many different kinds of handicaps and problems that it was not possible to make a clear diagnosis or determination of which type of class would be best suited for them in the long run. A period of observation in an LD class proved necessary and helpful before correct placement of these children could be made. Such cases will inevitably be referred to an LD program and are well served by it, even if only temporarily.

Chapter 4

The Actual Progress of the LD Pupils

Chapter 3 discussed the relationship between the admission data of the LD pupils and their status five years after coming to the special classes. Now the actual progress of the children during this timespan will be investigated in detail. Once again the LD pupils will be discussed in the same groupings as before; that is, the forty-two children who returned to regular classes, the seventy-one long-term LD pupils who remained in the special classes for five or more years, the twenty-six boys and girls who were referred for hospitalization, the twenty-three youngsters who were either withdrawn from the special classes or who were transferred to different types of special classes, and the fifteen pupils who moved.

PROGRESS OF THE FORTY-TWO LD PUPILS WHO RETURNED TO REGULAR CLASSES

It is self-evident that parents want their children to do well in school. In our middle-class society it is believed that a son's or daughter's success in school reflects glory on the parents and assures a good future for the child. If, unhappily, a child cannot adjust to a regular public school class and does not progress satisfactorily, the blame for

Actual Progress of LD Pupils

this is often placed, rightly or wrongly, on the parents. Both the parents and the child view themselves as failures. It is not surprising therefore that whenever parents are told that their youngster has to go to a special class they ask: "When will he return to a regular class?"

The return of LD pupils to a regular class is the goal toward which parents and teachers strive and the criterion against which they tend to measure a child's success in special classes. The assumption is frequently made that if the LD pupil can return to a regular class then his problems will have all but disappeared and future success in school is a foregone conclusion. But is this really the case? How much help do LD pupils derive from the special classes? How long do the children have to remain in the program before they can go back to regular classes and how do they fare once they are back in their home schools? The actual progress of the forty-two youngsters who returned to the regular classes, after attending the LD classes, was examined in order to find some of the answers to these questions.

LENGTH OF STAY IN LD PROGRAM
BEFORE PUPILS' RETURN TO REGULAR CLASSES

As a group, the forty-two pupils spent an average of three years in the special classes before returning to regular classes. Five of the youngsters returned after only one year in the LD program, fourteen spent two years in the special classes, nine attended the LD classes for three years, six were enrolled for four years, and eight children left after five years of special education. Were there any significant differences between the pupils who returned to regular classes after only one or two years in the LD program and those who remained in the special classes for three to five years before going back to regular classes?

At the time of their admission to the LD program the forty-two pupils had a mean age of 9 years, mean IQ score of 98, their average performance on the Bender Gestalt Test was on the eight-year-old level, and their average achievement was at the beginning-third-grade level. Chi squares were computed comparing the number of children who remained only one or two years in the special classes with those who remained three to five years and whose age, IQ and Bender Test scores, and achievement was either above or below the group means. The results are shown in Table 15. It was found that the length of a pupil's stay in the LD program before returning to regular classes was related to his level of functioning but not to his age at the time of entry into the program. The children who remained only one or two years in the

Table 15.

Comparison of pupils who returned to regular classes after 1 to 2, or 3 to 5 years in the LD program.

Admission data	1 or 2 years in LD program	3 to 5 years in LD program	X^2	P
IQ scores				
$\geq$ 95	15	8		
$<$ 95	4	15	6.51	.01
Level of Bender Test scores				
$\geq$ 8 years	14	9		
$<$ 8 years	5	14	3.72	.05
Reading (Wd.Rec.)				
$\geq$ grade level 3.1	15	8		
$<$ grade level 3.1	4	15	6.51	.01
Spelling				
$\geq$ grade level 3.1	12	6		
$<$ grade level 3.1	7	17	4.42	.05
Arithmetic				
$\geq$ grade level 3.1	15	11		
$<$ grade level 3.1	4	12	3.05	.10

special classes were significantly more often brighter (X^2=6.51, P. 01), had better visual-motor perception and integration as measured on the Bender Gestalt Test ($X^2 = 3.72$, P .05), and had higher achievement in reading ($X^2 = 6.51$, P .01), spelling ($X^2 = 4.42$, P .05), and arithmetic ($X^2 = 3.05$, P .10) than the youngsters who returned to regular classes after three to five years in the LD program. The children's initial age level did not differentiate significantly between the two groups of pupils.

It appears therefore that a child's intellectual, integrative, and academic functioning at the time of admission to the LD program has a direct bearing on the length of time he will spend in the special classes before returning to regular classes. Does this also mean that the brighter and better-integrated children with higher initial achievement made more actual gains in the LD program than the somewhat slower and perceptually more immature children? Do the children who return to regular classes sooner make a better adjustment to these classes than the pupils who need more time before they can leave the special classes?

Actual Progress of LD Pupils

RELATIONSHIP BETWEEN TIME SPENT IN THE LD PROGRAM
AND PUPILS' ACTUAL PROGRESS

Table 16 shows the mean visual-motor perception, IQ scores, and achievement levels for the LD pupils, both at the time of entry into the program and when they returned to regular classes. The total gain of the youngsters during their stay in the LD classes is presented as is their average yearly gain.

Table 16.

Progress of 42 pupils in LD program prior to return to regular classes.

Years in LD class	N	Time of testing	Age	Bender Test	IQ	Read.	Spell.	Arith.
1	5	Adm. LD class	10-5	8-4	103	6.0	4.4	4.0
		Return reg. cl.	11-5	9-0	103	7.7	5.3	5.1
		Gain	1-0	0-8	0	1.7	.9	1.1
2	14	Adm. LD class	9-11	8-6	102	4.7	4.0	3.8
		Return reg. cl.	11-11	8-10	102	6.4	5.2	5.1
		Total gain	2-0	0-4	0	1.7	1.2	1.3
		Avg. gain/yr.	1-0	0-2	0	.9	.6	.7
3	9	Adm. LD class	8-3	7-0	102	2.9	2.2	2.7
		Return reg. cl.	11-3	9-0	105	5.3	3.7	5.0
		Total gain	3-0	2-0	3	2.4	1.5	2.3
		Avg. gain/yr.	1-0	0-8	1	.8	.5	.8
4	6	Adm. LD class	9-1	7-11	90	3.0	2.5	2.7
		Return reg. cl.	13-1	9-4	90	4.8	3.9	4.9
		Total gain	4-0	1-5	0	1.8	1.4	2.2
		Avg. gain/yr.	1-0	0-4	0	.5	.4	.6
5	8	Adm. LD class	9-0	7-4	90	3.3	2.3	2.8
		Return reg. cl.	14-0	9-5	94	7.0	4.9	5.9
		Total gain	5-0	2-1	4	3.7	2.6	3.1
		Avg. gain/yr.	1-0	0-5	1	.7	.5	.6

The Bender Gestalt Test scores reflect the youngsters' maturation in visual-motor perception and their overall level of integration. The pupils who stayed only one or two years in the LD program revealed, at the time of admission to the special classes, Bender Test scores that were on the level of eight-year-old children. The pupils who remained three to five years in the special classes were functioning, on the average, only at the seven-year-old level in visual-motor perception. By the time both groups of children returned to the regular classes they were all functioning on the Bender Gestalt Test at the nine-year-old level, regardless of the number of years they had spent in the special classes. That is, most of the LD pupils were able to copy the Bender Gestalt Test designs without serious errors by the time they returned to regular classes. The Bender Gestalt Test Record shown on Plate 1 was made by Angelo, a ten-year-old LD pupil, just prior to his return to regular classes (p. 17).

The children who returned to the regular classes after one to three years in the LD program had consistently higher IQ scores than those who remained four or five years in the special classes. The level of the IQ scores for each group of pupils remained quite stable during their stay in the special classes, regardless of the length of this stay. These results concur with Bloom's findings (1964). The average IQ scores neither increased or decreased. While there was no evidence that enrollment in the LD classes improved a child's mental ability, there was also no indication of mental deterioration while he was in the special classes.

The academic progress of the LD pupils showed an inverse relationship to the amount of time the children spent in the LD program. The pupils who remained for only a short time in the special classes showed greater annual gains in their achievement than did the children who remained in the program for a longer time. The five youngsters who returned to regular classes after only one year showed a gain in reading recognition of 1.7 grade levels, while their spelling and arithmetic scores increased by one whole grade level. The children who remained for two years in the special classes showed nearly the same amount of academic progress as the five preceding pupils, but they required twice as much time to accomplish this gain. Table 16 shows that the total academic gain for the youngsters who attended the special classes for three to five years was larger than the total gain for the pupils who were in the LD classes for only a short time. Their total gains in reading were 1.8, 2.4, and 3.7 grade levels respectively. But the average annual gain of the long-term pupils was obviously smaller.

It was found that the overall average yearly progress for the children who remained in the LD program for one year was one grade level; the gain was three-fourths of a year per school year for those who remained in the special classes for two or three years; and for those pupils who spent four or five years in the LD classes, the average annual gain was one-half to one-third of a grade level. These figures are overall average gains. They do not tell us at what rate the children

Actual Progress of LD Pupils

progressed. Do LD pupils learn at an even rate? Do they gradually increase their achievement rate, does it improve as they go along? Or do the children learn in spurts? When does most academic progress occur?

The answers to some of these questions were sought by computing the rate of improvement in reading for the LD pupils of different age levels during their first, second, and third years of enrollment in the special classes. The reading progress during the fourth year in the LD classes was computed for all children as a group since there were too few pupils left in each age bracket to allow for a meaningful breakdown of the data. Table 17 reveals that LD pupils, age seven or older, made

Table 17.

Average annual reading gain of 42 LD pupils.

Year in LD program	All pupils N	Gain*	Age 6 N	Gain*	Age 7 & 8 N	Gain*	Age 9 & 10 N	Gain*	Age 11 & 12 N	Gain*
1st year	42	1.1	4	.6	12	1.0	19	1.1	7	1.9
2nd year	37	.7	4	1.0	11	.8	17	.6	5	.7
3rd year	23	.6	4	1.9	7	.4	10	.3	2	.1
4th year	14	.5								

*In grade levels (average).

their biggest gains in reading during their first year in the LD program. In subsequent years their rate of progress in reading decreased. The children who entered the special classes at age six showed a somewhat different pattern in their reading scores. They were still so very immature when they first came to the LD program that they were only functioning on the pre-readiness level. They were nowhere near ready even to begin to read. During the first year in the LD program they received above all extensive perceptual training, language stimulation, and readiness work. These youngsters did not really begin with formal reading until the following year. Their initial progress in reading was therefore quite slow, but it increased each year thereafter. It is worth noting that the youngest group of pupils that was permitted to progress at its own slow rate actually showed more total reading gains than the older pupils. It is of course realized that the sample in each age group studied was quite small; the findings can therefore only be considered as suggestive.

The seven- to twelve-year-old pupils made most academic progress during their first year in the special classes, whether as a result of the change in program, the added attention or specific help they received, or because of a lessening of pressure on the youngsters. This initial rapid rate of progress is rarely maintained during the next few years in school. This is an important factor to remember. Parents and teachers are usually justly pleased with the initial evidence of progress in a child who enters the LD program, but they then expect that the rate of the youngster's progress will continue without letup. If the child fails to achieve as much during his second or third year in the special classes, the adults are disappointed and begin to pressure him once more, conveying a feeling of failure to the child. As a result the child may again become discouraged and revert to some of his former, undesirable behavior patterns.

Perhaps the initial spurt of progress by the LD pupils can best be understood if it is remembered that children (or adults) rarely function up to the level of their capacity. Pupils who experience constant failure in school, especially, will become discouraged and will not really apply themselves to their work. When such children are placed into a new educational program or are given special attention and help they will regain hope and motivation, and they will increase their effort to learn. The writer is convinced that children want to and will learn—often in spite of themselves—if they are able to do so. A change in the children's school situation and an increase in the youngsters' motivation will result in an improvement in their achievement. Yet, part of this seeming progress may actually be an illusion. It was often discovered that the youngsters had not really learned any new material but were rather producing work that they had learned before and had done in the past but had then "forgotten" as their self-confidence and motivation diminished. This process was reserved in the special class program; as the LD pupils' motivation increased, they began to apply themselves and could again produce the work they had done long ago, eventually achieving more. However, once the LD pupils were really putting forth maximum effort and were functioning up to the level of their capacity, their rate of progress tended to diminish. No amount of training or drilling can speed up children's own rate of maturation and learning. What special education *can* do effectively is to maximize the youngsters' motivation for learning and to help them to make full use of whatever capabilities they have (Ames, 1969).

Returning now to Table 16, it is surprising to find that when the five groups of LD pupils returned to regular classes, they obtained quite similar mean Bender Gestalt Test scores and achievement scores, even though the groups of youngsters had differed considerably from each other when they first came to the LD program, and even though they had spent different lengths of time in the special classes. It almost appears as if LD pupils age nine or older have to reach an independent functioning level equivalent to at least the end of fourth grade or the beginning of fifth grade before they can return to regular classes. The length of time a child will need to spend in the LD classes in order to acquire this level of independent functioning will depend on his age, his maturation in perception and integration, his mental ability, and upon the severity of his learning and behavior problems at the time of entry into the program.

ADJUSTMENT OF FORMER LD PUPILS TO REGULAR CLASSES

At the end of the five-year period covered by the follow-up study, the writer sent out questionnaires to the schools which the former LD pupils attended. In some cases, the questionnaires were followed up by telephone or personal conferences with the children's counselors and/ or teachers. The questionnaires were designed to elicit information about the former LD pupils' adjustment to the regular classes. The teachers were asked to comment on the youngsters' emotional and social adjustment to the school and to peers, on their achievement, and on whether the children were doing satisfactory work within the range of their abilities. Copies of the pupils' grade cards were requested, and, finally, the teachers were asked whether the pupils had been "ready" to return to regular classes when they were sent back from the LD program. Information could be gathered on only forty-one of the forty-two former LD pupils who went back to regular classes. One boy moved away shortly after returning to regular class. His whereabouts were not known. The following discussion is therefore based on data concerning only forty-one of the forty-two former LD pupils. Table 18 summarizes the results from the follow-up questionnaires and conferences.

The regular classroom teachers reported that twenty-four (57%) of the former LD pupils made a good adjustment to the regular classes in either elementary or secondary schools. That is, the youngsters got along well with their classmates, presented no serious behavior problems, and turned out satisfactory work. Six children, or 15% of the former LD pupils, made a fair adjustment to regular classes; they just managed to "get by," while eleven (27%) of the pupils who were sent

Table 18.

Adjustment of 41 former LD pupils to regular classes.

Years in LD program	Total N	Adjustment to regular classes				
		Good N	%	Fair N	%	Poor N	%
1	5	2	40	0	0	3	60
2	13	5	38	5	38	3	23
3	9	5	56	1	11	3	33
4	6	6	100	0	0	0	0
5	8	6	75	0	0	2	25
	41	24	57	6	15	11	27

back to regular classes did poorly in their work, were unable to adjust to the regular class routine, and could not get along with their peers. In fact, three of this last group of children eventually returned to the LD program.

When the former LD pupils' adjustment to regular classes was examined in terms of the length of their stay in the LD program, as shown on Table 18, it was discovered that only two of the five boys who left the LD classes after one year did well in the regular classes. The other three boys failed. Of the thirteen children who returned to regular classes after two years in the LD program, only five, or 38%, made a good adjustment; another five children (38%) made a fair adjustment, and three pupils, or 23%, failed in the regular classes. By contrast, the majority of the youngsters who remained in the LD program for three or more years before returning to regular classes, made a good adjustment after leaving the special classes. Five pupils, or 56% of the nine children who stayed for three years in the special classes, did well in the regular classes; one boy made a fair adjustment, and three children, or 33%, did poorly. All six pupils who returned to regular classes after four years in the program made a good adjustment, as did the six youngsters (75%) who were in the special classes for five years before they went back to regular classes.

Since the present follow-up study covers only a total period of five years, it might be argued that the LD pupils who spent only one or two years in the special classes before leaving them had more time to fail in the regular classes than did those children who returned after four or five years in the LD program. After all, the children who were sent back to regular classes after one year in the special classes spent four of the five years of this study in regular classes, whereas those who stayed in the LD program for five years did not return to regular classes until just a few months before completion of the present research. It is conceivable that some of the late returnees would develop problems in regular classes at a later time.

Of course, former LD pupils have their ups and downs (like other youngsters), but it appears that the pupils' adjustment to regular classes follows a general trend that does not change drastically from one year to the next. The teachers' reports and the pupils' grade cards show that the youngsters who made a good adjustment to the regular classes did so from the very beginning. Former LD pupils who were unable to adjust to regular classes had difficulties all along, while those children who barely got by at no time displayed either very good or very poor adjustment. It does not take much time to find out whether a former LD pupil can hold his own in a regular class.

What then are the determining factors that assure a good adjustment to regular classes by former LD pupils? Some answers to this question were sought by studying more closely the twenty-four former LD pupils who made a successful return to regular classes, the six pupils whose adjustment was only fair, and the eleven children who failed in regular classes after leaving the LD program.

Former LD Pupils Who Made a Good Adjustment to Regular Classes

The twenty-four former LD pupils who made a good adjustment to regular classes revealed several common traits and characteristics. The teachers and school counselors reported on the follow-up questionnaires that the youngsters had been *"ready" to return to regular classes* when they did; the teachers also concurred that all of the children *were working up to the level of their ability and were getting passing grades.* All twenty-four pupils had *positive attitudes toward school and teachers,* and all were *well accepted by their peers.* Most of the children were actively-participating members of their classes, with only a few remaining unobtrusively on the fringes of their peer groups. *None of the youngsters were disruptive, acting-out or noticeably "different" in their behavior.*

Beyond these general characteristics which the twenty-four successful pupils shared, they differed in many other ways. They could be divided into four distinct groups, based on the length of time they had spent in the LD program before their return to regular classes.

SUCCESSFUL RETURN TO REGULAR CLASSES
AFTER ONE YEAR IN THE LD PROGRAM

Two boys made a good adjustment in regular classes after only one year in the special classes. The two had always been hypersensitive, immature, restless, and distractible. Yet, they had been able to hold their own in regular classes up to the time of their referral to the LD program. They were both of good intelligence and lived in stable, middle-class homes. The two boys had never presented any serious behavior problems in school.

It was not until the two boys were given a thorough psychiatric evaluation, in connection with their referral to the special classes, that it was discovered that both of them were suffering from minimal cerebral dysfunction. The two boys, like so many other neurologically impaired children, had gone unrecognized and had gotten by in a regular class until unexpected events or crises occurred that overwhelmed them. Since they were vulnerable, they overreacted and became quite disturbed when they could no longer cope with the situation. The change in their behavior was quite sudden and dramatic.

One of the boys was Harry. Harry had had a traumatic early history and had been removed from his home because of severe neglect and malnutrition. He had been placed into a good foster home when he was just a few months old and had remained there ever since. Harry had been a sickly child. He received much warmth and loving care from his foster parents.

Very wisely, the foster parents started Harry in school a year late. This had been to his advantage as he was small and his birthday was not until November. He therefore entered kindergarten when he was 5 years 10 months old, just a month or two older than many other children in kindergarten. Harry had always been a little "nervous" and restless, but he was an average student and he was well-liked by his peers.

Then, when Harry was eight-and-one-half years old and in the second grade, his behavior suddenly changed. This occurred when he inadvertently found out that the parents he had lived with for as long as he could remember were not his own. He learned that he was just a foster child who could be taken away from his home at any time. This had happened to his "sister," who he discovered, was not his sister at all. This revelation was more than Harry could cope with. He was unable to concentrate on his work in school, was extremely hyperactive in class, and had frequent aggressive temper outbursts. The teacher had reason to be concerned about Harry and to seek help for him.

It is most likely that Harry never would have had to face this crisis

Actual Progress of LD Pupils

if his foster parents had been more truthful with him all along. The foster parents were truly devoted to Harry and did everything in their power to reassure him. They took Harry to the community mental health clinic for psychotherapy. He was also placed on medication to help reduce his anxiety, and to stabilize him so that he would not be quite so hyperactive and explosive. And, finally, he was enrolled in the small, protective LD classes. Harry responded well to this three-pronged attack on his difficulties; he made a rapid and good recovery. Within a few months he regained his former control and was able to work on the very real problem of his identity and inner security.

It is not certain what helped Harry most, but it seems fair to say that the special class placement helped to reduce the pressures on Harry and enabled him to regain his good humor and self-confidence. He needed a period of time in which to work through his emotional problems without having to worry about the demands and pressures of a regular school class. It is also evident that without the supportive therapy and the medication, his progress would have been much slower than it was. The LD classes alone could not have done the job as fast or as well. It is also worthwhile to point out that Harry's achievement improved during his stay in the special class as much as, in all likelihood, it would have improved in a regular class, had he not been so upset; he gained more than one grade level in all subjects. However, the major benefit Harry derived from the LD class was in the emotional area since Harry's problems were primarily emotional ones and he did not have real learning disabilities as such.

Harry's inability to do his work in a regular class had been a direct response to his emotional upset. The severity of this disturbance and the extent of his recovery while in the LD program are vividly reflected on his Human Figure Drawings (Plate 4). Figure a shows the drawing Harry made when he first came to the LD program. He began drawing his figure from the bottom up: legs, body, head. Harry merely piled disjointed and distorted parts on top of each other. They look as if they will come apart at any moment, just as he himself was on the verge of falling apart emotionally. The head of figure a on Plate 4 is bulging, ready to burst, as if it can no longer contain all the mounting fears and anxieties therein. The boy in the drawing has no feet to stand on, and the short, ineffectual arms have no hands. The drawing conveys a feeling of helplessness and imminent disintegration (Koppitz, 1968; chap. 5).

Eight months after making the first drawing, Harry produced figure b, Plate 4. He was now able to express his concerns openly and directly

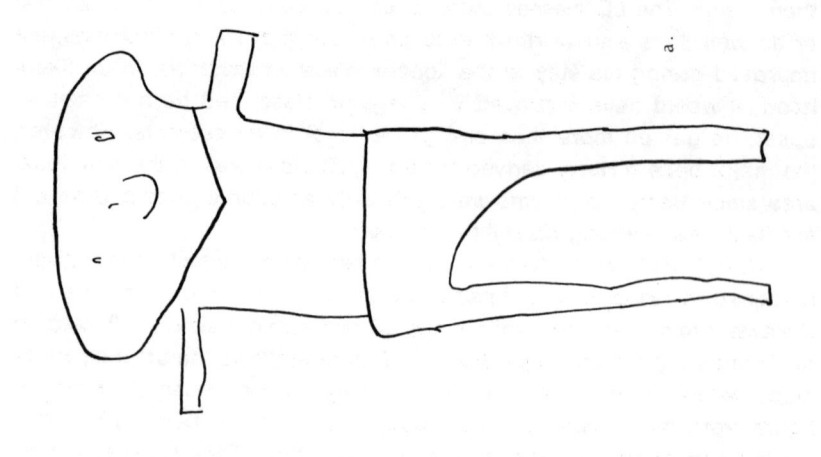

Plate 4.
Harry, *a.*,
CA 8-10;
b., CA 9-6.

Actual Progress of LD Pupils

without being overwhelmed by them. The figure he drew is well-integrated and good in proportions. Harry drew a girl this time and said, "This is my sister, she is a foster—she can go back." The missing hands reveal still some lingering insecurity, but clearly the acute crisis in Harry's life has passed. He was once more an adequately functioning boy. Harry expressed a desire and a readiness to return to a regular class; he was quite willing to continue for a while longer with the supporting therapy and medication.

One year after coming to the LD program, Harry went back to a regular fourth grade class. He was again the same friendly, somewhat restless, sensitive child he had been prior to the crisis; he was able to hold his own academically and was well accepted by his peers. Four years later, at the end of the follow-up study, Harry was still with his foster parents and was still doing well in school. He was no longer receiving therapy but was still on medication. Without medication he was very hyperactive and found it hard to concentrate for long periods of time; with medication his work habits and behavior were quite satisfactory.

The second boy who spent only one year in the LD program before returning to regular classes was Lewis. Lewis had always been a quiet, conscientious, hard-working student. Lewis was one of those somewhat rigid, hypersensitive youngsters with minimal brain dysfunction for whom new situations and changes are difficult. The crisis occurred for Lewis when he had to change from a structured, relatively small elementary school to a larger, confusing middle school. At the same time he had to cope with the added pressures of preparation for his confirmation and with the tensions of pre-adolescence.

He was overwhelmed by the sudden increase in demands at home, by the changes in school, and not least of all by his own awakening impulses. He reacted to all this by withdrawing more and more into himself and by escaping into a world of fantasy. Lewis did not complete his assignments in school, was preoccupied, and seemed to be out of touch with the world about him. It was apparent that Lewis was a very unhappy boy who was in need of counseling or therapy, but his parents were unable or unwilling to get the help their son needed; instead, they increased their pressure on him. The school very wisely decided that Lewis needed immediate assistance and that he could not hold his own in a regular class. He was therefore referred to the LD program when he was just under twelve years old.

At no time did Lewis present any serious learning problems. His achievement was up to his grade level—when he was able to do his work. During the crisis he was, of course, unable to apply himself to school work. Once Lewis was in the LD program, every effort was made to help him regain his emotional balance. He was seen on a regular basis by the school psychologist in preparation for more intensive therapy. The intensity of Lewis' emotional upset is vividly reflected on the Human Figure Drawing he made while in the special classes. The drawing is shown on Plate 5. Lewis referred to the figure on his drawing (himself) as "a nut who wants to commit suicide . . . he is blowing his stack."

The school social worker saw Lewis' parents repeatedly, in an effort to persuade them to reduce their demands on Lewis and to get psychiatric help for him. After many weeks of counseling. Lewis' parents finally agreed to seek help for their son and for themselves at a local guidance clinic. This proved to be most beneficial for all members of the family. By the end of the school year Lewis had improved so much in his ability to handle his emotions at home and in school that he was permitted to return to regular summer school classes on a trial basis. He passed all courses successfully in summer school and returned to a regular eighth grade in the fall.

Lewis continued to be a somewhat quiet and withdrawn youngster, but his work was good and his behavior was appropriate. At the close of the five year follow-up study Lewis was an honor student in high school. According to his psychiatrist, whom he continued to see from time to time, he was "a problem to nobody but himself." When last heard from, Lewis was doing well in college.

Strictly speaking, neither Harry nor Lewis were youngsters with learning disabilities. They were failing in school because they were extremely vulnerable, hypersensitive children who could not cope with specific crises in their lives. The crises and the subsequent emotional upsets might have been avoided altogether if the parents of the boys had been more understanding or aware. As circumstances developed, however, both youngsters had to face situations that were most upsetting and that made it impossible for them to function adequately in regular classes. They needed temporary relief from the demands of regular school classes and required a period of calmness and support in order to find themselves. In this capacity the LD program offered the youngsters a valuable service, but since the boys' main problem was emotional disturbance and not learning difficulties, they received their greatest help from psychotherapy. The LD program played only a supportive, albeit necessary, role in these cases. The difference between attending LD classes or not might have meant the difference between

Actual Progress of LD Pupils 73

"He is a nut. He wants to commit suicide. His girl is making him crazy. He is blowing his stack."

Plate 5.
Lewis, CA 12-3.

The author has transcribed Lewis's description of the drawing at the lower right.

developing a long-term, serious emotional disturbance or going through a relatively brief, intense period of crisis that could be dealt with promptly and from which the children rallied within a year's time.

SUCCESSFUL RETURN TO REGULAR CLASSES
AFTER TWO YEARS IN THE LD PROGRAM

Five children returned successfully to regular classes after two years in the LD program. The five youngsters differed from each other in age (the youngest was nine-and-one-half years old, the oldest one thirteen-and-one-half years old when they left the program), but in many other respects they were quite similar. All five pupils were *primarily* referred to the special classes because of behavior problems in school; none of them could get along with their peers. None of them had *severe* perceptual or learning problems when they first came to the LD classes and none were functioning academically more than a year below their appropriate grade level. However, even though the children were *able* to do the work, they had not been completing their assignments, nor were they putting forth effort in school. The children had sufficient academic skills to work with, but they lacked the ability to apply these skills. All five youngsters had been diagnosed as having minimal brain dysfunction. They were all immature, hyperactive, and distractible and all had a very low frustration tolerance. The mental ability of the five pupils was in the average range (IQ scores 93 to 117).

The five pupils who remained for two years in the special classes belonged to that large group of neurologically impaired youngsters *who require more time than most children to mature socially, emotionally, and perceptually*. Despite often good mental potential, such children are usually nowhere near ready or mature enough to begin formal education when they reach legal school age. Since the law requires that all children begin school at a given age level, it means that these vulnerable, immature children are forced into classroom situations they cannot cope with. Such youngsters then become unduly frustrated and develop behavior and emotional problems.

In most elementary schools, children are expected to enter school at a given date and to progress from one grade to the next at a set speed. Until recently, allowances were seldom made for individual differences in the rate of maturation. A new and positive step in recognizing individual differences between pupils is the introduction of ungraded primary classes, "extended readiness classes," or "pre-first and pre-second grade" classes in elementary schools. Many more such classes are needed for very immature youngsters, starting with "pre-kindergarten" classes or extended Headstart classes during the first year of school. It is essential that children be permitted to progress at their own rates, even if they are slower than average. It is believed that a trend in this direction could help to minimize and/or to prevent many emotional and behavior problems in elementary school children, and could eliminate for many youngsters the need for referral to special classes. This belief is in agreement with that of Lazure and Roberts (1969, p. 137) that *the schools actually contribute to the problems of many pupils by enforcing a "lock-step" grade system.*

All five youngsters who spent two years in the LD program, had failed in regular classes as a result of having attended them long before they were ready to do so. Three of the five children had repeated a grade prior to coming to the special classes. They had already learned that they were "failures," they had developed defeatist attitudes, and, as a result, avoided school work rather than risking more failure. The task facing the LD staff with these youngsters was therefore twofold: first the harm done in the regular classes had to be undone, then the pupils had to be helped to acquire better self-concepts and improved work habits and had to be motivated for higher achievement and for more acceptable behavior. Work on the pupils' attitudes and behavior was just as important as specific training in reading and in arithmetic. It took time to accomplish all this. As a result, the five LD pupils progressed academically little more than one grade level in two years attendance in the special classes. That is, they "lost" a year in the process.

For example, Floyd, a seven-and-one-half-year-old boy, came to the LD program after attending first grade unsuccessfully. He had been much too immature to participate in regular classroom activities and had been unable to follow the teacher's directions or to do first grade work. He remained in the special classes for two years. During the first year of his stay, he was given intensive perceptual and language training and was presented with a readiness program. Floyd was also provided with much time for play with other children and for creative activities. He was permitted to grow and to mature socially without undue pressure. Not until the end of his first year in the LD classes did he begin with reading and more formal academic work. During his second year in the special classes Floyd was almost nine years old, yet he looked and functioned like a seven-year-old child. He had needed two extra years to really come into his own. When Floyd was nine-and-one-half years old, he successfully returned to a regular third grade. He gained immensely from his stay in the special classes even though he "lost" a year while there.

Tom had repeated the fifth grade in regular school before coming to the LD program. After two years in the special classes, he returned to a regular slow-track seventh grade class thereby effectively repeating the sixth or the seventh grade. Or, put differently, Tom needed eight years to complete six grades. In view of the fact that Tom was not only emotionally immature but also physically small, these extra two years in school were essential for his long-range success in later life. It would have been better if his own school had taken his slower rate of maturation into account when he first entered and had, from the outset, programmed a slowly-progressing sequence of classes for him instead of placing him into classes that he could not master, and letting him fail. Tom floundered for several years in the regular classes until he finally rebelled. Only then was he sent to the special classes as a behavior problem.

It is an illusion to think that immature, poorly integrated children with minimal brain dysfunction can "catch up" with other children and make up for "lost" time. The additional time they need to mature and/or compensate for their neurological malfunctioning is not really "lost," of course, and it cannot be "found." A slower rate of maturation must not be considered synonymous with mental retardation. The mere fact that a child requires extra time before he can cope with school work and can hold his own in a large class does not tell anything about how far the youngster will ultimately progress. The long-range success of a child in school will depend only partly on his ability; of equal importance are his attitudes. The *prevention* of emotional and behavior problems contribute greatly to a child's final success or failure in school. It is well worth an extra year or even two in school, if needed.

All five youngsters who returned to regular classes after two years in the LD program had been considered behavior problems before coming to the special classes. Yet, once they were in the special classes they showed no acting-out behavior. The LD program provided for them a curriculum that was geared to their needs, it relieved them of the pressures they had been under before, and it eliminated the competition with more mature and more capable classmates. The special classes offered the youngsters emotional support and encouragement. The children experienced, often for the first time, the joy of success. They no longer had any need to rebel in school.

SUCCESSFUL RETURN TO REGULAR CLASSES AFTER THREE YEARS IN THE LD PROGRAM

The five children who returned successfully to regular classes after three years in the LD program were not unlike the five youngsters who went back to regular classes after only two years in the special classes. They too suffered from minimal brain dysfunction and were hypersensitive, restless boys and girls of average intelligence who were not more than one year below grade level in their academic achievement. But they were, at the time of admission to the special classes, even *more* immature, *more* poorly controlled, and *more* emotionally disturbed than the preceding group of youngsters. Only one of the five children had a serious reading disability. Whereas the needs of the previous group of pupils probably could have been met by a slower-moving regular class at the primary level, the five children here under discussion definitely needed more help than a regular class could offer. They required temporarily a small protective class and intense, prolonged help with emotional, social, and perceptual problems.

The case of Terry, one of the five pupils who returned successfully to regular classes after three years in the LD program, will help to illustrate the point. Terry had "failed" kindergarten. According to his kindergarten teacher's report he had been hyperactive, distractible, unstable, irritable, and aggressive. In kindergarten Terry had displayed poor emotional control and had had frequent temper outbursts. He had bitten other children and the teacher. His attention span was short and his fine motor coordination was extremely poor. Terry had been diagnosed as suffering from minimal brain dysfunction. He was a bright child with good language ability and good visual perception. He learned easily and retained what he learned. At age six, Terry obtained an IQ score of 110 on the Stanford-Binet Intelligence Scale. Terry's WISC scores a year later were: Verbal IQ 104, Performance IQ 108, Full Scale IQ 107. All of his WISC Subtest scores were in the average range and there was little scatter between them.

Terry had no serious learning disabilities as such, but he could not work independently and he could not complete his assignments in kindergarten. Terry still required a highly structured learning situation and much individual support in order to perform even simple school tasks. In a one-to-one setting he could perform almost up to his age level as can be seen from his Wide Range Achievement Test scores shown on Table 19. His spelling scores were consistently the lowest and reflect his poor written expression. Learning problems were clearly *not* the main reason for his need for the LD program. In almost any regular class there are children whose achievement is no better and often far worse than Terry's was, yet they get along without difficulty and are not referred to special classes.

Table 19.

Terry's progress during three years in the LD program.

Terry's age	Wide Range Achievement Test scores		
	Reading	Spelling	Arithmetic
6-4	1.0	1.0	1.5
7-1	1.8	1.5	2.5
7-5	2.2	1.9	2.5
8-4	2.8	2.2	2.7
9-1	4.0	2.6	4.7

Terry had, above all, poor inner control and poor fine muscle coordination. He was also a perfectionist who set high standards for himself, but because of his short attention span, his impulsivity, and his difficulty in coordination, he could rarely if ever turn out work that satisfied him. Terry had a very low frustration tolerance level and was easily disgusted with himself. When angry, he destroyed his own work and that of his classmates. Terry resented other children, especially his siblings, who could achieve more in school than he did. His self-concept was entirely negative.

While Terry was in the LD program, his teachers tried not only to improve his academic skills but also put much emphasis on helping him to control himself better, on strengthening his ability to cope with frustrations, on building up his self-esteem, and on improving his fine motor coordination and work habits. It was a big task that required much time, patience, and skill.

Terry's progress in the LD program was uneven. He had good periods, during which he made major strides forward; and he had periods of regression when he faced a personal crisis at home. Terry's emotional states and gradual maturation while in the special classes are reflected on his Human Figure Drawings. Plate 6 shows five of these drawings. When Terry was 6 years 5 months old, just after his transfer to the LD program, he drew a poorly integrated boy, figure *a*. He displayed his feelings of inadequacy by omitting the boy's arms; the heavy neck revealed his valient effort at controlling himself. At age seven, Terry

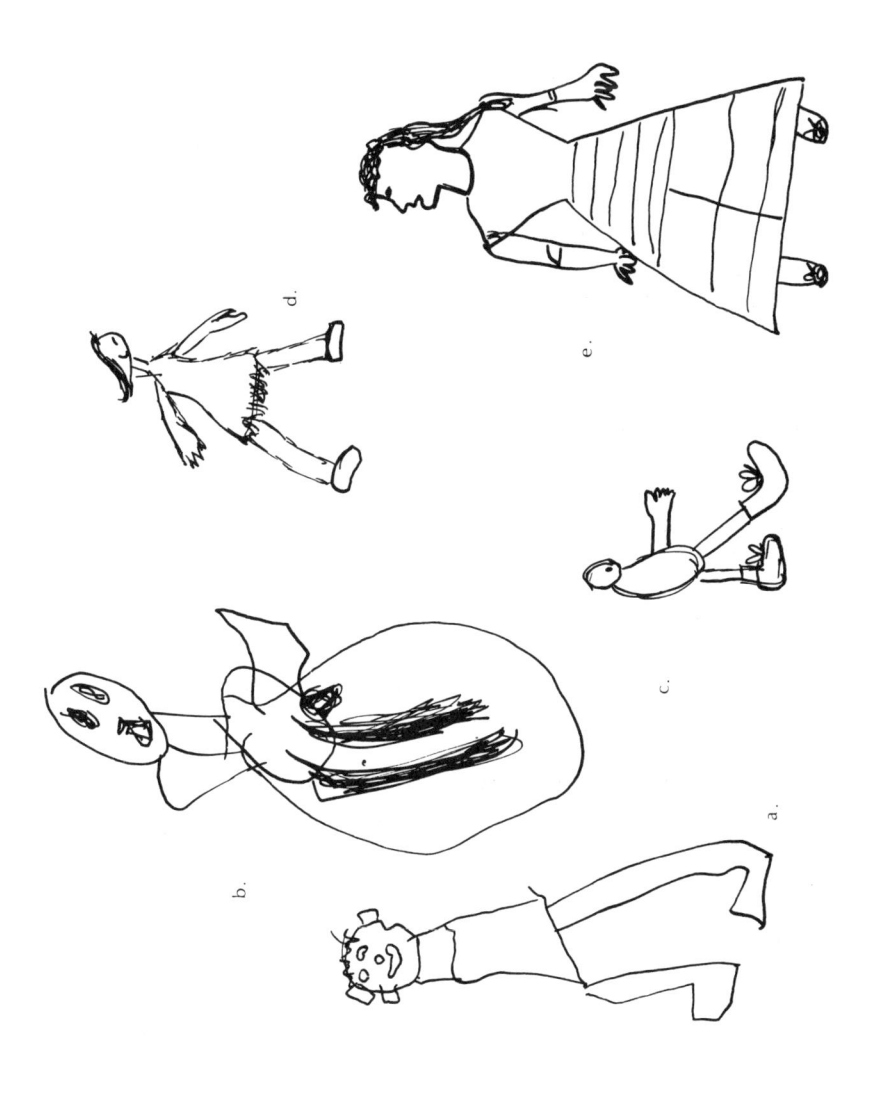

Plate 6.
Terry's progress in the LD program.
a., CA 6-5;
b., CA 7-1;
c., CA 8-10;
d., CA 9-1;
e., CA 9-6.

went through a traumatic period at home that coincided with the birth of a sister. Figure *b* on Plate 6 shows Terry's acute anxiety, and an increase in impulsivity, disorganization, and aggressiveness. By the time Terry was eight years old his behavior and achievement had improved, but he was still immature and impulsive. He still lacked self-confidence, as can be seen in figure *c* on Plate 6. Terry worked very hard on figure c; he erased and redrew the figure several times and was still unhappy with the results. He finally got disgusted, ripped up the paper and threw it into the wastepaper basket, from which it was later retrieved. Terry could not be persuaded to make any more drawings on that particular day. It was apparent that Terry was not yet ready to cope with the stresses and demands of a regular class.

Terry did not really come into his own until he was nine years old. At that time he drew a girl (figure *d,* Plate 6) who is striding forward with confidence. The drawing still shows some impulsivity and poor integration, but the figure is complete and relatively well-proportioned, and, what is more important, it pleased Terry. Figure *e* on Plate 6 was drawn just after Terry's return to regular classes. The drawing reflects his new found self-confidence and his greatly improved integration and control. The figure is appropriate for a child of his age. His attempt at drawing elbows and feet from the front reveals Terry's intelligence. By this time, Terry was functioning academically, socially and emotionally on the fourth grade level and was able to hold his own successfully in a regular fourth grade class with an understanding teacher who made some allowance for his vulnerability.

It is unlikely that Terry would have progressed as well as he did if he had not been placed into a special class. If Terry had remained in a regular class during the primary grades, his emotional and behavior problems would most likely have increased to the point where he might have had to be excluded from school altogether, or where referral to a residential treatment center would have become necessary. It was also evident that just one or two years in a special class would not have given Terry enough time to overcome his emotional problems and to gain the maturity and self-confidence necessary for success in a regular class. Terry required three years to allow for maturation to take place and to learn how to control himself and to compensate for his minimal brain dysfunction. The LD program provided for Terry a protective and supportive school setting in which he could progress at his own rate and could maximize his strengths. All of this did not just happen by itself. Terry had exceptionally fine, dedicated, and skilled teachers to help him throughout his stay in the special classes.

Actual Progress of LD Pupils

The greatest contribution the LD program made in Terry's case was that it *prevented an increase* in his problems and that it kept his problems from interfering with his academic progress. All the effort of the LD staff could not have produced such good results if Terry had not had good mental potential, if his perception and language ability had not been well developed, and if he had not been able to retain what he learned. Finally, part of the credit for his success in the LD program must also go to Terry's very interested, cooperative, and supportive parents.

SUCCESSFUL RETURN TO REGULAR CLASSES AFTER FOUR OR FIVE YEARS IN THE LD PROGRAM

Some LD pupils needed more than three years in the special classes before they were able to hold their own in regular classes. This was particularly true when the boys and girls were not only extremely immature and poorly integrated but also had only modest mental ability. The six children who remained for four years in the LD program and the six who stayed for five years in the special classes before returning successfully to regular classes all scored in the Low Average to Average range on the WISC. Their IQ scores ranged from 85 to 97. As a group they had been unable to cope with the demands of regular, large classes. They were anxious and confused youngsters who needed the protection of smaller, less pressured classes in which they could mature and progress at their own slow pace. The regular school curriculum did not make allowance for these immature pupils. They were not acting-out children, they were rather clinging and attention-seeking, or they were quiet and withdrawn. These youngsters did not really have specific learning disabilities or severe emotional problems; their main difficulty was immaturity and mental slowness. They were, above all, slow learners.

When these slow learners were enrolled in regular classes they developed feelings of inadequacy and anxiety which further added to their burden. If these children had been placed into slower-moving, smaller classes from the time they first entered kindergarten, they would probably never have "failed" and would never have been referred to the LD program. They needed more time than most children, especially in the primary grades. All twelve slow learners ultimately "lost" a year or even two in the special classes before they were ready to return to regular slow-track classes in the middle school.

A case in point was Guy. He was said to have been a normal, well-functioning boy until age three, when he suffered a brain injury due to a fall on his head. He was born in October, which meant that he was one of the youngest children in the class when he entered kindergarten. He was small, very immature, restless, distractible, poorly coordinated, and had immature visual-motor perception, but he was a friendly and cheerful child who received much warmth at home. If anything, he was given too much affection and was somewhat overprotected by his parents. In kindergarten, he was unable to follow the teacher's directions and could not keep up with his classmates but since Guy presented no behavior problems and was well-liked by his peers, he was passed on to the first grade and then on to the second grade. By the end of the second grade Guy increasingly showed signs of frustration. He was still only functioning on the first grade level. That is, his achievement was a year below that of most of his classmates. He had become extremely restless, impulsive, and silly. At times he withdrew and seemed to be "out of it." At this point, Guy was referred to the LD classes as a brain-injured child with learning disabilities.

Guy was a brain-injured child but, in truth, he did not really have learning disabilities. He actually was doing as well as could be expected of a not-quite eight-year-old boy with an IQ of 85 and a mental age of six-and-one-half. Guy was really a slow learner who was showing emotional problems because more had been demanded of him than he was able to produce. As soon as he came to the LD classes, he relaxed and his good behavior returned. Once again he was his former cheerful self. He adjusted well to the special classes and was popular with the other LD pupils. During the next four years Guy made slow, but steady, progress in all areas. This progress was reflected on his Human Figure Drawings, shown on Plate 7. Gradually Guy matured and became less distractible and better-integrated and coordinated. He became an enthusiastic baseball player and joined the Little League. At age eleven Guy drew himself (figure *d,* Plate 7) with a baseball hat, a baseball mitt and a ball. His attitude toward school was positive.

When Guy was almost twelve years old he returned to a regular slow-track sixth grade. During his stay in the LD program Guy had brought his reading level up to the end of the fourth grade and his arithmetic to the beginning of the fifth grade level. Thus, Guy had covered three grade levels in four years of special class attendance. He had "lost" one year but had gained confidence and good work habits. During that time he had also matured sufficiently to cope with a big class. At the end of the five year follow-up study his middle school teachers reported that Guy was "friendly, pleasant, cheerful, quiet" and that he "was doing satisfactory work."

Plate 7.
Guy's progress in the LD program.
a., CA 8-1;
b., CA 9-0;
c., CA 9-11;
d., CA 11-1.

From the foregoing discussions of the twenty-four LD pupils who returned successfully to regular classes after one to five years in the LD program, it appears that the special classes served a variety of functions. For some children the special classes offered a haven in a time of crisis, for others they provided primarily a protective setting where the children could be helped to resolve their emotional problems and could develop positive attitudes toward school, peers, and above all, toward themselves. The LD classes were able to meet individual children's needs and could offer them the experience of success. Some children had never had this experience before. For many youngsters, the LD program served as a nonthreatening environment in which the boys and girls could grow and learn at their own pace until they could return to regular classes.

It should be emphasized here once more that all the youngsters who returned successfully to regular classes had much going for them. They were all of at least low average or average intelligence, none had *severe* learning disabilities, none were *grossly* deprived or acting-out youngsters, and most of them had interested and supportive parents.

Former LD Pupils Who Made A Fair Adjustment To Regular Classes

The six pupils who made a fair adjustment to regular classes after leaving the LD program differed greatly from each other, but they could all be described as "atypical" or "different," even in comparison to the other LD pupils. They were youngsters who cannot be easily categorized, who do not fit into established groupings of children. While in the special classes, they were social isolates and were not accepted well by their peers. It is doubtful whether these children really benefitted a great deal from their stay in the special classes. The LD program was not really able to meet their particular needs.

The six youngsters were returned to regular classes not because they were thought to be well-adjusted and well-functioning pupils, but rather because it was felt that continued attendance in the LD program would serve no purpose. It was hoped that these six children might possibly be able to hold their own in regular classes despite their many problems. It is probable that the very specific needs of these six youngsters could have been best met in small private schools. Or perhaps they were destined, even at best, to go through life as "square pegs" who never quite fit into round holes. Some people may always have to get along as best they can, outsiders on the fringes of society.

Actual Progress of LD Pupils

The six children under discussion here were all of average or better-than-average intelligence. Their IQ mean score was 108. None of them had severe learning problems. They all came from middle-class homes. What set them aside from others was their behavior and their attitudes, especially their difficulty in relating to other children.

One of the six was Frederick, who was simply, "too good for this world." It may be significant that Frederick always insisted on being addressed as "Frederick;" he objected to being called "Freddy" or "Fred." He never unbent or relaxed long enough to just enjoy himself; life was a serious matter for Frederick. He was a rigid, perfectionistic, slow-moving, compulsive youngster of normal intelligence. Due to minimal brain dysfunction he had poor visual-motor perception, problems in sequencing, and difficulties in oral expression. He was eight years old when he was referred to the LD program. He could not keep up with his school work and had difficulty getting along with other children.

Frederick's family recently had moved from the deep South. They were members of a fundamentalist religion which set them apart in their neighborhood. The parents were very strict and were achievement-oriented. They had excessively high expectations for their son. They were unable or unwilling to accept the fact that Frederick had a real learning problem. The parents blamed Frederick's slow progress in school on his first grade teacher and on the children in his neighborhood. The children had beaten Frederick up when he had first arrived. Since that time he had not been allowed to associate with them. Frederick also blamed his problems on others and never missed a chance to express his disapproval of his peers.

Frederick just *had* to be perfect in all he did; he kept emphasizing his "superiority" and delighted in pointing out the shortcomings of his "bad" classmates. Needless to say other children did not react kindly to this. He fared no better with the other LD pupils than with the neighborhood children. Since Frederick was unable to stand up for himself, his classmates made his life miserable and reinforced his feeling of being "picked on." The LD pupils were possibly even less tolerant of Frederick than the children in the regular classes had been.

His parents were strongly opposed to Frederick's special class placement. Neither the parents nor Frederick felt that they had any problems (after all, "it was all the other people's fault"); they therefore saw no need to modify their ways or attitudes. Since Frederick would not or could not change, there was really little reason for prolonging his stay in the special classes. He was a diligent worker who was really achieving up to the level of his capacity. He could be expected to do this also in a regular class. Frederick was therefore returned to a regular class after two years in the LD program.

According to the follow-up reports from his high school teachers Frederick was "just getting by" academically in a slow-track class. His social adjustment was poor; he still complained a great deal that others "picked on him." Frederick's needs would, most likely, have best been met in a small private school run by his denomination.

Another atypical child was Sharon. She was a bright, eleven-year-old girl who suffered from petit mal epilepsy. The petit mal was only partially controlled, and as a result of this affliction Sharon often lost her train of thought. She had difficulty following class discussions and easily became confused. She did not understand much of what was going on around her although she had no problem reading and comprehending printed material and books. Even when she blanked out momentarily she could always go back to the printed page in the book where she had left off. Print stays put and does not change from minute to minute. Sharon's achievement in school was good as long as she could rely on books. She read well and copiously. But her overall functioning in school was quite uneven and her social adjustment was very poor. Most of her peers merely tolerated her. She made them feel uneasy since she was so unpredictable. Sharon was no behavior problem in the usual sense. She was referred to the LD program because it was feared that she would not be able to cope with the big regular middle school. Sharon's adjustment to the LD class was good and her academic progress was excellent. Her main difficulty was her lack of social understanding and her poor social judgment. She missed out on much that other children learn through observation and experience. She led a rather sheltered and restricted life at home, which made her extremely naive and gullible for a child of her age. She was easily influenced by some of the more acting-out and disturbed children in the LD program who set a bad example for her. At that time, the program did not yet have protective, academically-oriented special classes in a regular middle school or high school. While Sharon was in the LD program, the choice of classes was limited, especially at the secondary school level. By the time Sharon was thirteen, the LD staff and her parents were concerned about the suitability of the special classes for her. It was jointly decided that after two years in the LD program Sharon should be sent to a small private school for girls where the pressures would be fewer than in regular school and where the other children would be, hopefully, more considerate of her.

Unfortunately, it turned out that the parents could not get the finan-

Actual Progress of LD Pupils

cial assistance they had hoped for. Without it they could not afford the tuition of the private school. Sharon was thereupon returned to a regular high school where a modified program was worked out for her. At the end of the five year follow-up study Sharon was reported to have been showing "fair" achievement. She still suffered from petit mal and her peers, considering her "peculiar," avoided her.

The other four youngsters who made only a "fair" adjustment to regular classes after leaving the LD program were also unusual. All of them were doing passing work, according to their teachers, but had poor peer relations. They were all outsiders. Three were erratic, hyper-talkative, restless, and annoyed other children, but they were not aggressive or acting-out youngsters and were therefore tolerated by other children and by the school. One exceedingly bright but schizoid boy was planning to go to college. He had a good chance of succeeding. He could not relate to people, but he did not bother them. He could and did relate to books and was a hard worker.

Former LD Pupils Who Made a Poor Adjustment to Regular Classes

Eleven youngsters, or one fourth of all LD pupils who returned to regular classes, made a poor adjustment after leaving the LD program. The teachers and high school counselors reported on the follow-up questionnaires that the eleven former LD pupils did poor work—if any at all; the youngsters did not get along with their peers, and they were uncooperative or hostile toward adults. None of the children participated in school activities and all of them were regarded as "unreliable" and unstable. With one exception, the teachers stated that the former LD pupils had *not* been "ready" to return to regular classes when they did.

Why then were these children sent back to regular classes? Why did the screening committee (p. 7) recommend that the youngsters be transferred from the small, protective special classes to large, demanding regular classes? Could not the pupils' failure have been foreseen and prevented? In what way did the eleven former LD pupils who failed in regular classes differ from the twenty-four children who did well in such classes?

The answers to these questions are neither simple nor clear-cut. Many factors enter into a decision to return an LD pupil to a regular class, and many factors contribute to the child's good adjustment or failure after he has been transferred. A comparison between the former

LD pupils who succeeded and those who did not succeed in regular classes showed no significant differences in the children's age or in their IQ and achievement scores while they were in the LD program. Thus, lack of mental ability or lack of academic skills were not the reason for the poor adjustment of the eleven youngsters.

A review of the case histories of these children reveals that most of them had been aggressive and acting-out youngsters or had had serious emotional disturbances prior to coming to the LD program. Most of them came from unstable homes and at least three of them had suffered severe deprivation in early life. All of them had extremely low frustration tolerances and were very poorly integrated children, but most of the youngsters were of good intelligence and their learning disabilities were not severe. It was evident that all eleven pupils had benefitted greatly from enrollment in the special classes. While in the LD program they had shown not only academic gains, they also made a good emotional and social adjustment. Even so, they remained quite vulnerable and they had periods of ups and downs.

How was the decision reached to return these children to regular classes? Ideally, the decision to return an LD pupil to a regular class should depend solely on whether or not such a transfer is in the best interest of the child. In reality, many factors enter into the picture. The following four case histories are given to illustrate why the children were returned to regular classes and why they failed.

Alex came to the special classes during the first year of the program's existence. He was a very anxious, restless, and withdrawn boy with minimal brain dysfunction. He was nine years old at the time and had high average intelligence. Alex was poorly coordinated, had serious malfunction in visual-motor perception, and was a very disorganized child. He had always been a social isolate at home and in school. He was tormented and teased by his peers because of many nervous mannerisms. He was nicknamed the "termite" because of his tendency in class to chew up several pencils each day. Alex was hypersensitive and could not tolerate pressure or frustration; when he feared failure he withdrew.

His adjustment to the LD program was excellent. In the small, protective class Alex was able to relax. He even began tentatively to reach out toward others and showed good academic progress. In reading, Alex achieved a gain of two years in a mere eight months' time. His teacher was justifiably proud of him. The screening committee, including the writer, was also duly impressed by Alex' progress and went along with the teacher's recommendation to return the boy to a regular class in the fall. Completely ignored was the fact that Alex was still an outsider in his class and that he was still regarded as "odd" by his classmates. He was still hypersensitive and quite fragile. In a flush of pride and ignorance, the LD staff assumed that just because Alex had been able to bring up his achievement in the small, structured special class, he would also be able to function in a big regular class.

By way of explanation—but not as an excuse—it must be pointed out that the decision to return Alex to regular classes was made early in the history of the LD program when the staff had much enthusiasm but, as yet, little experience. It was a poor decision and one that should not have been made. The screening committee erred by overemphasizing the importance of academic achievement, especially in reading, and by underestimating the significance of a child's emotional and social adjustment and of his inherent vulnerability. Prior to coming to the LD program, Alex had had a *long history* of problems in the community and in school. His difficulties did not just develop suddenly; they were deep-seated and of long duration. Alex was not merely reacting to a specific crisis as had been the case with Harry and Lewis.

After returning to a regular fifth grade class, Alex once again, became anxious and was unable to keep up with his school work. As the pressures on him mounted he regressed in his behavior until he resembled once again the withdrawn, schizoid boy he had previously been. He just could not cope with the large, competitive regular class. All the gains he had made during the year in the special classes disappeared in a few weeks' time. Finally, at Alex's own request, he was permitted to return to the LD program. In that setting, Alex was again able to do well and progressed steadily. The case of Alex demonstrates that some hypersensitive children need long-term education in small, protective classes even when they are of average intelligence and can function academically up to grade level. These children are so fragile that they simply cannot get along in big regular classes. The experience with Alex shows the danger of placing a child in a class only or primarily on the basis of his achievement, while ignoring his social and emotional adjustment.

Furthermore, it can be stated with certainty that it is a mistake to return to regular classes any nine-year-old LD pupil who has a *long history* of difficulty in school and in the community, after only *one year* in the special classes, even if he did make good progress while there. Such a child cannot possibly overcome all his problems in one short year. That child will need at least one year to correct some of his major problems and another to consolidate his gains; most LD pupils with longstanding problems need considerably more time than even that before they are ready to return to regular classes.

Another child who came to the LD program during its first year of operation was Miles. He was a brain-injured, hypersensitive, and emotionally disturbed boy of low average intelligence with serious perceptual problems. He was aggressive with peers, defiant with adults, and disorganized and explosive in the classroom. Miles was nine years old when he came to the LD program. He remained there for five years.

At first, Miles' progress in the special classes was slow and uneven, but gradually his behavior and his achievement improved. By the end of his fifth year in the LD program, Miles was ready for a more meaningful prevocational high school curriculum. He was growing restless and wanted new challenges, new teachers, and new activities. Unfortunately, at that time the LD program did not have a comprehensive high school program for the LD pupils. The special classes were unable to meet Miles' needs at this time. He was then fourteen years old; his academic functioning was at the beginning fifth grade level. Most fourteen-year-old children have graduated from elementary school and have gone on to a middle school or a high school. Miles had remained through the five years in the same school. He was ready to leave and he wanted "out." One of the reasons he had worked as hard as he had, had been his desire to "earn" his way out of the special classes—he desperately wanted to go back to a regular high school.

The screening committee concurred that Miles was doing as well as he could do and that a prolonged stay in the LD program, as it then existed, would be self-defeating for Miles. He would only get discouraged and would lose his desire to work and to learn. The LD program was not really able to offer Miles anything new or challenging. Yet, there was also a consensus among the LD staff that Miles was a poor candidate for a regular high school. Miles was still emotionally too unstable and mentally too limited to make it on his own in a big, regular high school class. The screening committee was caught in a dilemma.

A meeting was held with Miles, his parents, the LD staff, and representatives of the regular classes. It was decided jointly to take a chance and to let Miles return to a regular slow seventh grade on a modified schedule. This was done for lack of any better alternative. It was felt that with the help of the school counselor, Miles just might be able to hold his own. It was a gamble, and the gamble failed. Miles could not function in the large regular class. He regressed in his behavior and could not attend to his work. He again became disorganized and struck out at his peers. Before the school year had ended, Miles had to be removed from the regular class and was sent to a residential school.

Had the screening committee been wrong in returning Miles to a regular class? Under the circumstances, no other decision could have been reached. There are times when one has to take chances. It was *certain* that Miles was finished with the LD program, as it existed then. It would have been foolish and harmful to forcibly retain him in the special classes. Not only would Miles have gained nothing, he probably would have lost all the progress he had made during the preceding five years. In addition, he would have become a very disruptive and negative influence in the LD program. In other words, it appears that Miles' failure was unavoidable at the time because no suitable public school program existed that could meet his needs. Fortunately, since then, the LD program has expanded and now offers a comprehensive middle school and high school program including both academic subjects and vocational training for LD pupils. There can be no doubt that one of the most essential parts of any LD program is the high school curriculum. With an LD program ranging from kindergarten through high school there is no reason why youngsters like Miles could not be retained in the LD classes throughout their primary and secondary education and, after graduation, be placed into jobs.

Sometimes the screening committee returned LD pupils to regular classes when there was every reason to expect that the children would be successful in this venture, but then unexpected events occurred in the children's home that changed the situation. Such factors are usually beyond the influence or control of the school. This is what happened in the case of Ruth.

When Ruth came to the LD program she was an eight-year-old girl of normal intelligence with brain dysfunction. She had both behavior and learning problems. In her three years in the LD classes she made good academic progress and improved her relationship with peers and authority figures. She had good mental potential and, in view of her rate of progress in the special classes, her long range prognosis appeared to be good. This was especially true since her unstable parents agreed to get counseling help for themselves and for Ruth. The parents were most cooperative with the LD staff and were interested in helping their daughter. Ruth returned to a regular fifth grade; a modified program was worked out for her to meet her particular needs.

Ruth returned to the regular class with great hopes and all went well for a few weeks. Unforeseen, serious illnesses of Ruth's mother and sister changed the family picture. As the home situation deteriorated, new and unexpected pressures and responsibilities fell on Ruth. *If* she had been a strong, well-integrated child without serious learning problems, then she probably could have coped with the family situation while maintaining herself in a regular class; or *if* she had only had to deal with the demands of the regular class while receiving support and encouragement from the parents, then she also would have succeeded in school. Since, however, she was a brain-injured, vulnerable child with learning problems and poor integration, she could not cope with *both* the demands of the regular class *and* the emotional tensions and conflicts at home. It was too much for Ruth.

She found it difficult to concentrate, failed in her work, found it hard to conform to school rules, and provoked fights with peers. Ruth reverted to her earlier delinquent behavior pattern and acted out her frustration and anger. Ruth was one of the three former LD pupils who failed in regular classes but who did well once they were permitted to return to the LD program. In the protected, structured special classes, Ruth was able to regain her inner control and could again apply herself to her work.

A few LD pupils were returned to regular classes as a result of political pressure. In such cases the decisions to return the youngsters were made at the top administrative level. The opinion of the screening committee and the welfare of the children were ignored. This is always a very regrettable but, it seems, at times unavoidable circumstance.

One such case involved LeRoy. LeRoy was an eight-year-old boy of low average intelligence. He had suffered from severe deprivation and neglect in infancy and early childhood. At age six he was removed from his totally inadequate home and was placed into a good foster home; he had been there for two years when he was referred to the LD program. The foster mother had done wonders for LeRoy, but even she could not undo all the harm and damage he had suffered during his first traumatic years of life. LeRoy was well-coordinated and was an excellent athlete, but he had severe learning disabilities. He was also explosive, aggressive, and had serious problems in interpersonal relationships. He revealed a marked impairment in impulse control and showed gross malfunction in visual-motor perception and sequencing.

The foster mother was unable to recognize or accept the fact that **LeRoy was a child with minimal brain dysfunction and with deep-seated** emotional problems. She believed that love and hard work could overcome whatever difficulties LeRoy "occasionally" exhibited. She was unalterably opposed to LeRoy's placement in a special class. As far as

Actual Progress of LD Pupils 93

the foster mother was concerned, the LD program was just a "dumping ground" for children who misbehaved and who could not be handled in regular classes. The foster mother was a strong force in her community and was politically very active. She was determined to get LeRoy out of the LD program and back into regular classes. For two years the LD staff was able to hold her off, largely because LeRoy was obviously making good progress and was happy in the LD program despite the foster mother's misgivings. But then, as happens so often (p. 63), LeRoy's achievement began to level off. At age ten he was still only reading on the second grade level while his arihemtic achievement was on the fourth grade level. He was also still explosive and unstable. LeRoy had very low frustration tolerance, got mad easily, and bullied younger children.

When LeRoy did not show any marked academic improvement during his third year in the special classes, the foster mother blamed his failure on the LD program and carried her demand for his return to regular classes to the top school administrator. The matter began to take on political overtones. It was deemed best to give in to the foster mother for the sake of the child who was caught in the middle. LeRoy was beginning to show increased signs of stress and was actually regressing in school. The best the LD staff could do, under the circumstances, was to work out a modified program for LeRoy in a regular class. He was placed into a slow sixth grade and was given each day two gym periods, remedial reading, arithmetic and a token program of other subjects—but even this modified program proved to be too much for LeRoy. Despite his keen desire to succeed and to please his foster mother, he was in real trouble almost immediately. He could not get along with his peers and he was unable to do any work in school.

The progress LeRoy had made during his three years in the LD program was quickly lost. He regressed in his behavior to the point where he became uncontrollable at home and in the community. Ultimately, LeRoy had to be removed from his foster home and was placed into a residential treatment center. Could this have been avoided? It is difficult to see how the LD staff could have prevented these events from taking place. If LeRoy had not been returned to a regular class his foster mother would have brought court action against the LD program. The feelings of all concerned would only have become more bitter and intense. Even if one could have *forced* the foster mother to leave LeRoy in the special classes, he would not have been able to benefit any longer from this experience. The foster mother's totally negative attitude toward the LD program had by then been transmitted to the child. The

LD staff had obviously not been successful in changing the attitude of the foster mother. There came a point where there really was no choice left but to return LeRoy to regular classes, regrettable as it was. The school can usually deal with problems affecting a child in the classroom, but it is powerless against forces that are beyond its scope.

It appears therefore, that some failures by former LD pupils in regular classes could have been avoided, others not. Faulty judgment and lack of experience by the LD staff can be corrected and the curriculum of the LD program can be altered and expanded to meet the needs of all LD pupils; but unexpected illnesses, family upheaval, and political pressures, all of which influence a child's functioning in a regular class, are outside of the school's control. Because of this, there can never be an absolute assurance that former LD pupils will succeed in regular classes. Some failures may be unavoidable.

Chapter 5

*Progress of
Long-Term LD Pupils*

Seventy-one pupils remained in the LD program for the entire five-year period of the follow-up study. Most of these children continued in the special classes even beyond that time. These seventy-one youngsters were evaluated when they first came to the LD classes and each year thereafter. Table 20 shows their mean IQ and achievement scores, both at the time of admission to the LD program and five years later. The mean WISC scores for all seventy-one pupils at the time of admission to the special classes were: Verbal IQ 87, Performance IQ 89, and Full Scale IQ 87. That is, all the mean IQ scores were in the low average range. Five years later, the mean IQ scores were still in the low average range; they were 87, 87, and 81, respectively. The changes in mean IQ scores during the five-year period were minor and statistically not significant. It appears therefore that long-term LD pupils, as a group, maintain their level of mental functioning while attending special classes— they neither gain nor lose significantly in IQ points.

When the seventy-one LD pupils first came to the special classes, their mean CA was eight years, while their average MA was on the seven-year-old level. Their average achievement, as measured on the Wide Range Achievement Test, was on the end-of-first beginning-of-second grade level. Their achievement level was therefore almost equivalent to their mental age level. At the end of the five year follow-up study the seventy-one children had an average CA of 13 years and a

Table 20.

Progress of 71 long-term LD pupils.

N	Time of testing	Age	IQ mean scores Verb.	Perf.	F.S.	Mean Achievement Test scores Read.	Spell.	Arith.
71	Adm. LD class	6 to 12	87	89	87	2.0	1.6	2.2
	5 yrs. later	11 to 17	87	87	81	3.7	3.0	4.1
	Gain or loss		0	− 2	− 6	1.7	1.4	1.9
14	Adm. LD class	6	83	84	84	1.0	.8	1.0
	5 yrs. later	11	84	80	80	3.1	2.6	3.2
	Gain or loss		+ 1	− 4	− 4	2.1	1.8	2.2
19	Adm. LD class	7	89	91	88	1.4	1.2	1.6
	5 yrs. later	12	88	89	89	3.5	3.0	3.8
	Gain or loss		− 1	− 2	+ 1	2.1	1.8	2.2
17	Adm. LD class	8	90	90	90	1.9	1.7	2.2
	5 yrs. later	13	88	90	88	3.6	2.7	3.8
	Gain or loss		− 2	0	− 2	1.7	1.0	1.6
8	Adm. LD class	9	91	92	87	2.7	2.2	2.7
	5 yrs. later	14	88	86	86	4.7	3.4	4.7
	Gain or loss		− 3	− 6	− 1	2.0	1.2	2.0
7	Adm. LD class	10	91	90	89	2.9	2.1	2.7
	5 yrs. later	15	85	92	87	4.6	3.5	5.0
	Gain or loss		− 6	+ 2	− 2	1.7	1.4	2.3
6	Adm. LD class	11 & 12	80	89	81	1.8	1.7	2.8
	5 yrs. later	16 & 17	88	86	86	2.8	2.5	4.2
	Gain or loss		+ 8	− 3	+ 5	1.0	.8	1.4

mean MA of 10 years. Their average achievement scores at the time were at the end-of-third grade beginning-of-fourth grade level. It appears that the seventy-one long-term LD pupils "lost" a year in their work. At the end of the five-year period they were functioning more than a year below their mental age level. The total average gain for the group was only 1.7 grades in reading, 1.4 grades in spelling, and 1.9 grades in arithmetic. That means the average achievement gain was only three to four months for each year the LD pupils spent in the special classes.

It was shown on Table 8 that the age at which all 177 LD pupils were admitted to the special classes was significantly related to their status five years later. Furthermore it was found that youngsters age 8 to 10 made more progress in the LD classes than did pupils who were either younger or older than 8 to 10 years. Since the majority of long-term LD pupils were 6 and 7 or 11 and 12 years old when they first came to the LD program, it might be assumed that their poor achievement was in part related to their age. This hypothesis was checked by computing the gains and losses for long-term LD pupils of different age levels. The results are shown on Table 20.

Contrary to expectations, the children's age did not appear to be a significant factor in the limited academic progress of the long-term LD pupils. The gains in achievement were almost identical for all age levels from 6 through 10 years. The gains ranged from 1.7 to 2.1 grade levels in reading, 1.0 to 1.8 in spelling, and 1.6 to 2.3 levels in arithmetic. There was no indication that the 33 children who were 6 and 7 years old when they came to the LD program, did less well than the 32 pupils who were 8 to 10 years old. Only the 11- and 12-year-old youngsters showed somewhat less gain than the other children. In five years of special education, the six 11- and 12-year-old pupils progressed only one grade level in reading, less than a year in spelling, and 1.4 levels in arithmetic.

The admission age of the long-term LD pupils also bore no relationship to the gains or losses in IQ scores during the five year follow-up period. None of the mean IQ changes for children of different age levels were statistically significant. The greatest improvement in IQ scores occurred among the 11- and 12-year-old LD pupils, the very ones who had shown least academic gain.

The results on Table 20 indicate that the age of the long-term LD pupils was not the main factor in determining their intellectual and academic gain or loss. The records of the 71 long-term LD pupils were therefore more closely examined in order to find other characteristics that might account for their slow progress in the special classes. These investigations revealed four distinct groups (to be discussed separately) among the long-term LD pupils that differed greatly from each other. They were:

Group A: Dull children
Group B: Children with poor reasoning and good memory
Group C: Children with specific learning disabilities
Group D: Children with emotional and behavior problems

Table 21.

Progress of four groups of long-term LD pupils.

Group*	N	Time of testing	Age Mean	IQ Mean	Read.	Spell.	Arith.
A	18	Adm. LD class	8-5	77	1.3	1.2	1.6
		5 yrs. later	13-5	72	2.6	2.4	3.1
		Gain or loss		− 5	1.3	1.2	1.5
B	9	Adm. LD class	7-6	81	2.1	1.7	1.6
		5 yrs. later	12-6	80	5.7	3.9	4.1
		Gain or loss		− 1	3.6	2.2	2.5
C	21	Adm. LD class	7-11	91	1.4	1.3	2.1
		5 yrs. later	12-11	90	2.4	2.3	3.9
		Gain or loss		− 1	1.0	1.0	1.8
D	23	Adm. LD class	8-4	94	2.4	1.4	2.3
		5 yrs. later	13-4	96	4.8	3.5	4.5
		Gain or loss		+ 2	2.4	2.1	2.2

*A: Dull children.
B: Dull children with good memory.
C: Children with specific learning disabilities.
D: Children with primarily emotional and behavior problems.

Group A: Dull Children

Group A included 18 youngsters whose major handicap was limited mental ability. These children had difficulty with abstract concepts; they could not think well. Of course, they had other problems as well, but all of these other difficulties were secondary in importance to their difficulties in reasoning. All 18 children showed evidence of minimal brain dysfunction or brain injury and all had varying degrees of emotional and behavior problems. As a group, these children were extremely immature and their overall functioning was either on the borderline or retarded level.

Table 21 shows that the average admission age of the 18 dull children was eight years five months (Range 6-2 to 12-6). Their average achievement when they came to the LD program was on the readiness level (Range .0 to 2.4). Five years later their average achievement was still only at the mid- to end-of-second grade level. In five years they had made only slightly more than one year of progress in their school work. At this time, they were functioning six years below their CA and two years below their MA.

The mean IQ score of the 18 dull pupils was 77 or borderline; their IQ range was from 62 to 87. The large special education department of which the LD program was a part also included special classes for educable mentally retarded children (EMR classes). The 18 dull long-term LD pupils acted just like retarded children and were, in fact, moderately retarded. Why then were the 18 dull children not enrolled in the EMR classes?

In the state in which the youngsters lived, a child is not considered legally mentally retarded, nor is he eligible for the EMR classes, unless he has an IQ of 75 or less. A child with an IQ of 77 or with a "high" IQ of 82 is therefore not regarded as retarded. The folly of using arbitrary IQ cutoff points to determine whether a child is or is not retarded has, of course, been long recognized by psychologists and educators.

Many children with IQ scores of 78, or even 84 or 89, may indeed be retarded; that is, their test scores may be relatively high because of good memory. These youngsters may nevertheless be quite dull and unable to *think,* whereas many children with IQ scores of only 69 or 73 may be able to think quite well may not really be retarded. They may be scoring poorly on the IQ test because of specific language or memory deficits or because their backgrounds lack certain test-related experiences. It is apparent that *a specific IQ score* is a poor criterion for identifying mentally retarded boys and girls.

At the end of the five year follow-up study, it was clearly established that the 18 dull children were moderately retarded youngsters, but this had not been as obvious when they first came to the LD program. Since all of the children had multiple problems and suffered from minimal brain dysfunction as well as from varying degrees of emotional and behavior problems, it was not certain to what extent their functioning was really impaired or only depressed. It is most difficult to make a valid assessment of a young child with multiple problems and it is almost impossible to arrive at a meaningful differential diagnosis for such youngsters without prolonged periods of observation and evaluation. The possibility always exists that, in time, some of the children might improve suddenly and show a marked increase in their mental functioning. Unless one is absolutely sure of a child's evaluation or test results, it is always wise to give him the benefit of the doubt when major decisions regarding his school placement are to be made.

The only thing that was certain about the 18 dull children when they entered the LD program was that they could not hold their own in regular classes and that they needed special help. All else was uncertain. For this reason, most of the younger children were placed into so-called "observation classes" within the LD program. Here observations, diagnostic teaching, and testing were used to obtain, over the course of many months, a meaningful assessment of the children's ability. To begin with, the youngsters had to be helped to be comfortable in school and to be able to function emotionally, socially, and perceptually at the actual level of their maturation and development. Particular care was taken to evaluate the degree of scatter and unevenness in the children's functioning and their rate of progress. Truly dull or retarded children tend to show an overall slowness or dullness and their rate of progress is extremely slow. The immediate spurt in achievement these youngsters sometimes show after admission to the LD classes is usually misleading and of short duration. It is the long-term progress that is important.

As time went by, it became quite apparent that many of the children in the observation class were truly dull and would require a long-term, low-level educational program that had to lead to vocational training and ultimately to a work-study program and a job placement. Several of the 18 dull LD pupils could easily have been transferred to classes for educable mentally retarded children if it had not been for their "high" IQ scores, their behavior, and—not least of all—for their parents.

Some diagnostic labels are more socially acceptable than others. Many parents prefer to be told that their child is "emotionally disturbed" rather than "brain-injured." Others are able to accept a diagnosis of "minimal brain dysfunction" but reject any suggestion that the youngster might be mentally retarded. Again others are quite willing to admit that their child is a little slow, but resist the idea that he has "learning problems" or "perceptual malfunctioning." Unfortunately there is still too often a stigma attached to having a mentally retarded child. Some parents fight hard in order to have their child placed into a class for brain-injured or emotionally disturbed pupils rather than into a class for slow children, even if it means that their child will be woefully misplaced. A truly dull child can be just as badly misplaced in a class for children of normal intelligence with specific learning disabilities as in a regular class. Once again, it must be emphasized that a child's success in a special class depends to a large extent on the cooperation and support of the parents. Sometimes a child must first be enrolled in one type of special class before being transferred to another type of class, more suitable to his needs, until the parents are ready to accept such a change.

Experience with the dull children in the LD program showed that many of them really needed slow classes but could not be transferred to the existing EMR classes because of their IQ scores, their behavior, or their parents' attitudes. The solution to this dilemma was to reorganize and broaden the LD program. Theoretically, the LD classes had been set up to serve only children of "normal intellectual potential." In reality, it was found that many youngsters who were obviously not of "normal intellectual potential," but who were not eligible for the EMR classes, also needed special classes. It was recognized that the categorization of pupils into retarded versus nonretarded was arbitrary and meaningless.

Just as the initial division of special classes into those for emotionally disturbed and those for brain-injured children had been found untenable and was eliminated (p. 4), so the division between EMR and LD classes was done away with. Instead, classes were set up for *slow* children with learning disabilities. These Slow LD (SLD) classes were designed for children with learning disabilities whose *main* problem was poor reasoning—who were dull children regardless of their diagnoses, IQ scores or behavior. These classes took the place of the EMR classes and included many of the LD pupils, such as the 18 long-term pupils here under discussion. The SLD classes were and are an integral part of the learning disability program and extend from the kidergarten level through high school and vocational school.

The significant feature of the SLD classes was the recognition that dull children are not *just* dull, but that they usually also have emotional and behavior problems and that they need many of the same types of services needed by the LD pupils who are of normal intelligence. The difference between the youngsters in the LD and SLD classes is largely one of degree and not of kind. There is considerable overlapping between them; most characteristics and problems of youngsters with learning disabilities exist in both groups but in varying degrees. The class placement of an LD pupil should always be made on the basis of his needs rather than his IQ score.

The SLD classes tended to be somewhat larger in size than the LD classes. They usually had 10 to 12 pupils, compared to 8 to 10 children in the LD classes. The SLD classes fulfilled a great need for many slow learners who could never before be properly placed. In the past some children had always been too bright or too dull or too disturbed to fit into any of the existing classes. The SLD classes were also well-accepted by the parents, especially when they were located in regular elementary or middle schools. The creation of the SLD classes was one of the most successful innovations of the LD program to date. It is hoped that this idea will catch on and will be widely copied by other school districts.

The case of Adam is presented here as being characteristic of the 18 dull, long-term LD pupils. Adam was referred to the LD program after an unsuccessful year in kindergarten. His kindergarten teacher reported that Adam was extremely immature and had poor comprehension, poor concentration, and very poor coordination. He was highly distractible, anxious, and vague, and revealed very immature visual-motor perception. Furthermore Adam could not retain what little he learned. He also had difficulty relating to other children and showed serious emotional problems. Adam suffered from a mild case of cerebral palsy; he had little use of his left arm. On the Stanford-Binet Intelligence Scale Adam obtained an IQ of 75.

Adam's parents refused to believe that Adam was dull and rejected outright any thought of placing him into an EMR class; but they were willing to enroll him into an LD class, since Adam had been medically diagnosed as brain-injured. They were certain that daily exercises and tutoring sessions would help the boy to catch up with other children. He was six years old when he entered the LD program; however, he was so immature that he more closely resembled a four-and-one-half-year-old nursery school child. Since Adam also had emotional problems it was indeed difficult at that time to say with certainty whether the 75 IQ score was a valid measure of his ability or not. Adam was therefore placed into an "observation class" in the LD program. After one year in this class, Adam was still quite unable to write his name, to count, or to recognize any letters. His social and emotional functioning was barely on the five-year-old level. His achievement was still on the pre-school level, despite the special training in school and the tutoring he received at home.

As was mentioned before, one sign of mental retardation is a lack of progress or extremely slow maturation and change. On Plates 8 to 12 are shown five of Adam's Bender Gestalt Test records, made between the ages of six and ten. These Bender protocols reveal not only Adam's extremely poor organization and integration, his weak inner control, and his difficulty with details and numbers; but above all they show his very slow rate of maturation in visual-motor perception and his slow mental

Progress of Long-Term LD Pupils 103

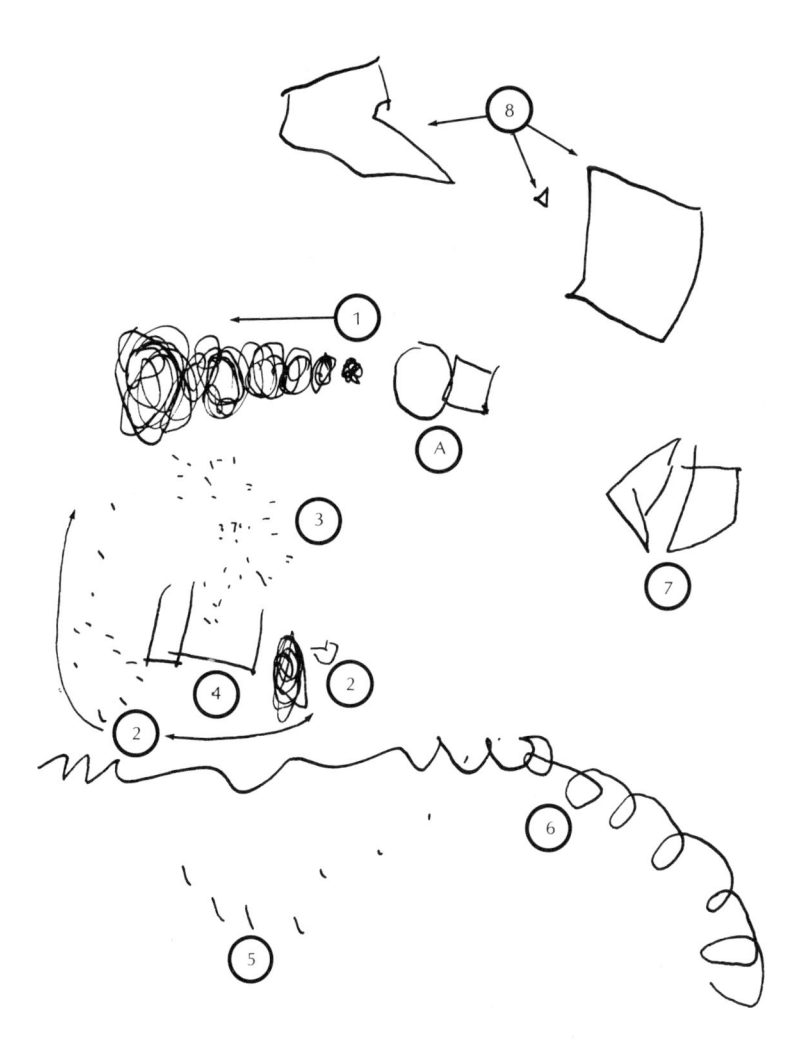

Plate 8.
Adam, CA 6-1.

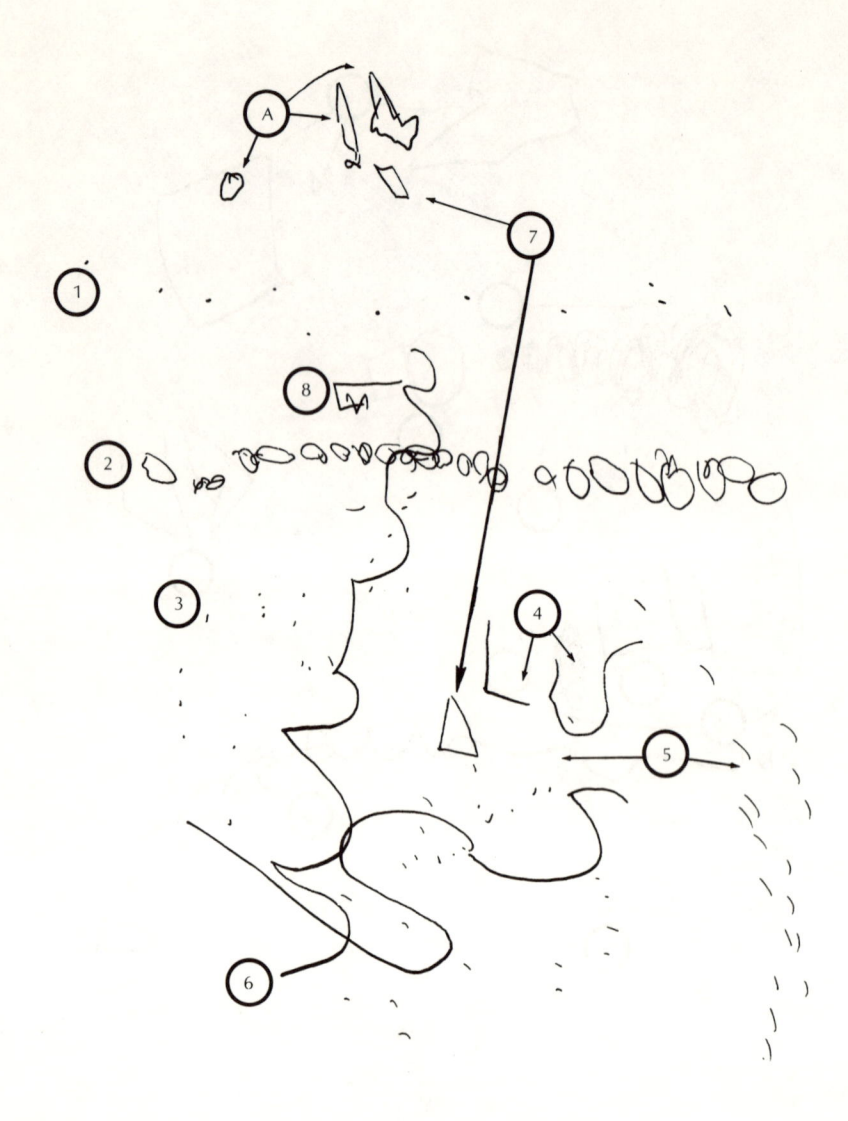

Plate 9.
Adam, CA 7-0.

Progress of Long-Term LD Pupils 105

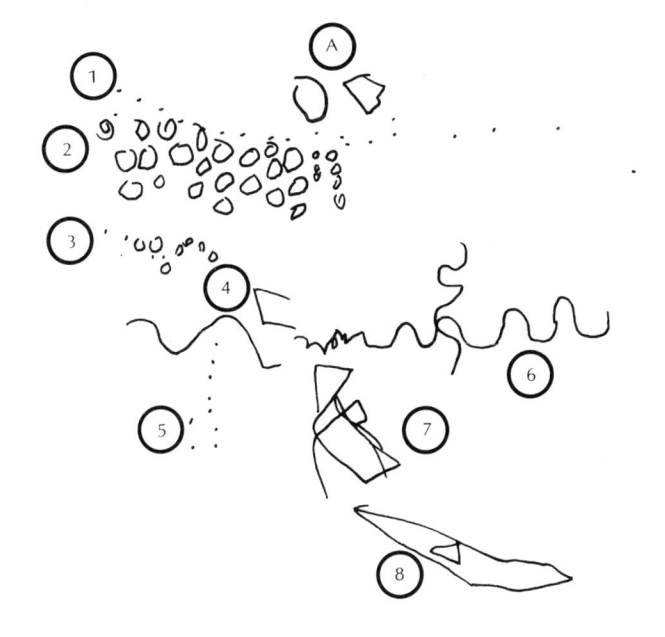

Plate 10.
Adam, CA 8-2.

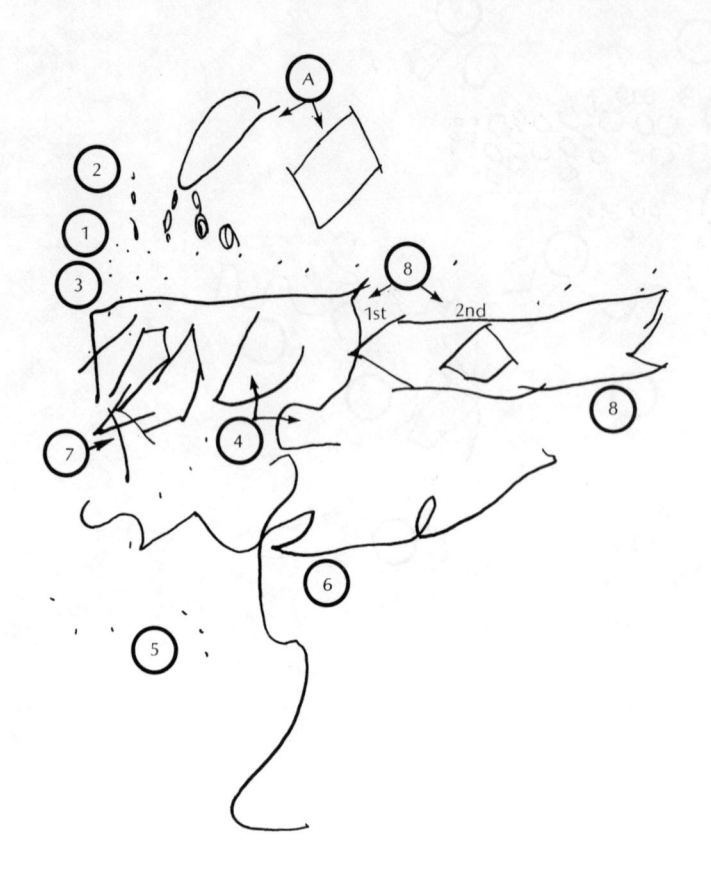

Plate 11.
Adam, CA 9-2.

Progress of Long-Term LD Pupils

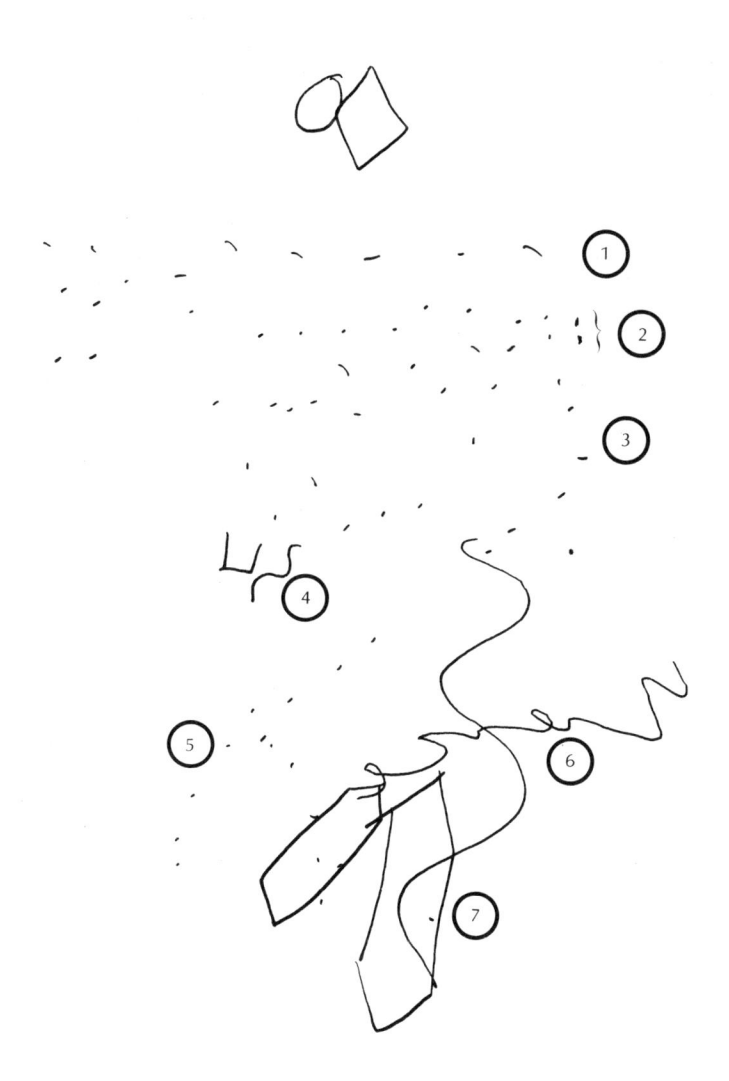

Plate 12.
Adam, CA 10-4.

(Figure 8, not reproduced here, was drawn on a separate sheet.)

development in general. At age six, Adam's Bender Test record (Plate 8) resembled that of a four-and-one-half-year-old child. Five years later Adam's Bender Test protocol (Plate 12) still was very immature and was similar to the records of anxious six-year-old children. On the basis of his five Bender Gestalt Test records alone one might conclude that Adam was a moderately retarded child (Koppitz, 1964; p. 114).

Table 22 shows Adam's successive IQ and Wide Range Achievement scores during his five years in the LD program. At the time of admission Adam's CA was 6-1, his MA was 4-8, and his achievement level was practically zero. At the end of the follow-up study, his MA was 7-2 and his achievement level was end-of-first grade in arithmetic and beginning-of-second grade level in reading recognition. That means in five years Adam's mental age had increased by two-and-one-half years, as had his reading. His arithmetic was lagging only slightly behind. Adam's overall functioning was, in effect, just equivalent to the level of his mental ability. Figure 1 displays the data from Table 22 in

Table 22.

Adam's progress in the LD program.

CA	MA	IQ Score	Wide Range Achievement Test Scores		
			Reading	Spelling	Arithmetic
6-1	4-8	75	.0	.0	.4
7-0	5-1	—	.7	.3	.5
8-2	5-9	72	1.2	1.2	.5
9-2	6-4	—	1.4	1.5	1.4
10-4	6-11	67	1.9	1.6	1.4
11-4	7-2	63	2.5	1.8	1.8

the form of a graph and shows the widening gap between a normal child's rate of mental growth and Adam's rate of development. Since Adam's average mental gain per year was only six or seven months, it was inevitable that his IQ scores would decrease gradually, even though his mental age increased. One characteristic of dull children is their lack of discrepancy or their evenness of functioning in different areas. Figure 1 reveals that Adam was doing as well as could be expected. There was no marked discrepancy between his achievement scores in reading and arithmetic and both were right up to his level of mental ability. It can therefore be concluded that Adam's slow progress in

Figure 1.
Adam's progress in the LD program.

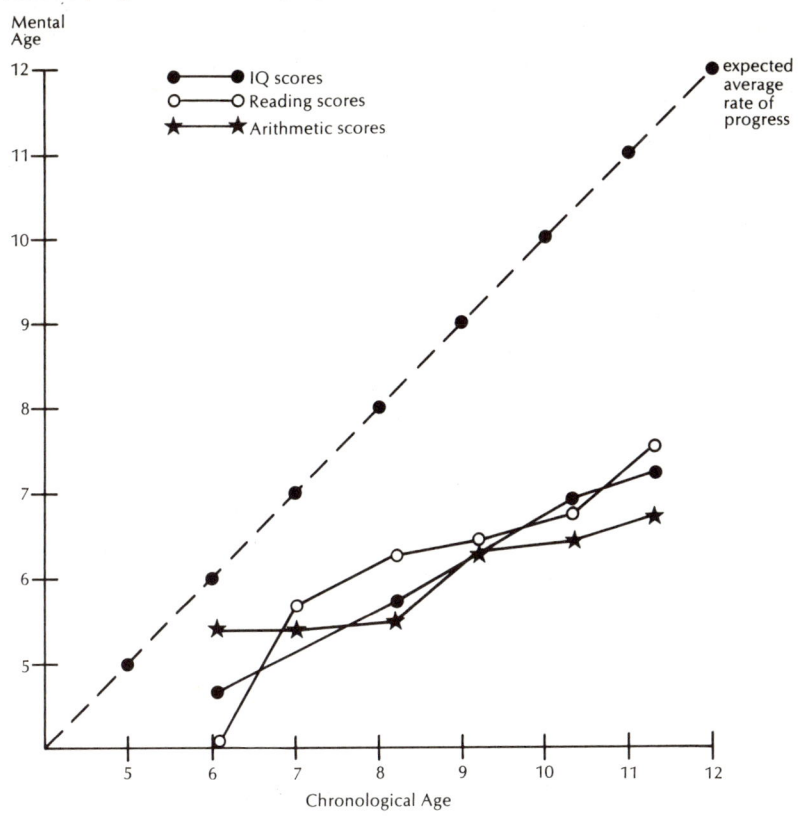

school was due neither to emotional disturbances nor to specific learning disabilities, but was the result of an overall mild retardation. Neither tutoring, nor perceptual training, nor optometric exercises could overcome his limited capacity and could not alter the fact that Adam was a dull child.

After two years in the "observation class," the LD staff was in agreement that Adam would benefit from placement in a SLD class with other dull children with multiple problems. Adam's parents had no objection to such a placement—as long as it was not a class for "retarded children." A class for "slow children with learning disabilities" was less threatening to them. Adam adjusted well to the SLD class. He became less anxious and disturbed. His academic progress was steady but very slow. Not until he was ten years old and had been in the LD program for four years were the parents reluctantly able to concede that Adam would most likely not be able to go to college. They even admitted that Adam was a little slow. Adam was twelve years old when his parents acknowledged for the first time the possibility that he might not be able to graduate from high school and would probably never be able to hold his own in a regular class. Prior to that time the parents would not or could not hear what the LD staff had tried to tell them in regard to Adam. It took years of patient and understanding work with the parents on the part of the school social worker, the psychologist, and the consulting psychiatrist to finally get them to be more realistic about their son, and to stop them from pressuring Adam for more achievement.

The LD program provided a valuable service for Adam. His history shows that it is not sufficient for a school system to have special classes only for retarded children and for youngsters of normal intelligence who have learning problems. The slow learning child or the child of borderline intelligence with emotional problems is often overlooked and neglected; yet, he needs as much or even more help than his brighter peer. An LD program should be comprehensive and offer special services for all youngsters who need them, from the dullest to the brightest child, from kindergarten through high school. *The success of an LD program should not be measured by the number of children who return to regular classes but rather by how well the children's needs are met and by whether or not the youngsters are happy, able to function socially, and able to learn up to the level of their ability, no matter what that ability might be.*

Group B: Children With Poor Reasoning and Good Memory

Group B included nine long-term LD pupils who had *poor reasoning* but who were *able to retain* much of what they saw or heard even when they did not understand it. The pupils in Group B were basically no brighter than the 18 dull youngsters in Group A; what differentiated them from the 18 dull children was their good memory. Good memory is a gift that cannot be taken for granted.

A great deal of school learning and success in later life depends on memory and easy recall of facts, figures, and past experiences. For instance, the ability to read depends to a large extent on recognition and recall of sounds and symbols. A child who cannot remember sounds or symbols will have great difficulty in learning how to read, but just because a pupil can remember something does not necessarily imply that he understands what he recalls. In the case of the nine youngsters in Group B, good memory made them *appear* brighter than they actually were. Since most of them could read fairly well for their ages, parents and teachers usually expected more of these children than they actually could produce. As a result, they were often under great pressure and experienced much frustration. Only when they could no longer keep up with their school work in regular classes and began to exhibit marked anxiety and behavior problems, were the children referred to the LD program.

Table 21 (p. 98) shows that the mean IQ score for the nine pupils in Group B was 81. The range of their IQ scores was from 67 to 92, most of the youngsters scoring in the 80's. Their mean age was 7 years 6 months, with an age range from 6 years 4 months to 12 years 0 months. Their mean achievement scores were 2.1 in reading recognition (range 1.0 to 3.2), 1.7 in spelling, and 1.6 in arithmetic. It was characteristic of Group B that their reading scores were always higher than their spelling and arithmetic scores. After five years in the LD program, the nine pupils in Group B still had a mean IQ score of 80; their mean score in reading recognition was 5.7; in spelling, 3.9, and in arithmetic, 4.1. The average IQ score for this group had remained quite stable throughout the period of the follow-up study. The greatest improvement for Group B occurred in reading. The gain in reading recognition was 3.6 grade levels—a gain that was almost three times as large as that of Group A. The strength of Group B lay in their ability for visual recognition and recall. Their progress in arithmetic was slower since they had difficulty with number concepts and reasoning.

Silberberg and Silberberg (1967, 1968) aptly describe these kinds of youngsters as "hyperlexic." They can read, but they cannot comprehend much of what they read. This fact is often not immediately apparent. The children's early history is sometimes misleading. As toddlers and later in kindergarten these children appear to be "bright" since they can frequently remember nursery rhymes and can count and say their ABC's at an early age. They learn by rote, and if they are well behaved they may even pass the first grade. It often comes as a surprise when they begin to fail in the second grade and cannot keep up with their work in the third grade. After the first grade, rote learning no longer suffices to master the requirements of the classroom. It is not uncommon for the parents to blame the school for making their children "dumber," and teachers and parents may pressure the children for more achievement. As a result, the youngsters not only fail their school work, they also develop emotional and behavior problems. The dull children with good memory were usually referred to the special classes as pupils with learning and emotional disorders.

Most of these long-term pupils made a good adjustment in the LD classes. Relieved of unrealistic pressures and demands, they were soon able to relax and feel comfortable. Their functioning level was usually quite uneven. They did not really "fit" into any one grade level or class group. A special curriculum was worked out for each pupil; each youngster was permitted to progress at his own speed in each subject. Thus a child might be reading on the third grade level, doing arithmetic on the first grade level, and participating in second grade social studies and in group activities. The overall instructional level for the children was based on their mental ages.

A pupil's class placement was determined by his chronological age and by his overall social and emotional maturity. Some of the boys and girls in Group B did well and were happy in SLD classes, others were best placed in regular LD classes. In each case, the decision for the child's class placement was based on the child's welfare rather than on his IQ score. All children in Group B required long-term special education or some type of modified, slow-moving educational program. The children could not hold their own in regular classes. All of them were good candidates for vocational training. The prognosis for these children was fairly good, provided emotional and behavior problems could be avoided or alleviated. Youngsters like the ones in Group B can usually be trained for routine jobs that require little abstract reasoning or decision-making.

The case of Darlene is presented here in detail as representative of Group B. Darlene had always been a good little girl who worked hard and never presented any problems in school. She was eager to please her teachers, but despite all her efforts she could not keep up with her classmates. She lived in an upper middle-class suburb and attended a school where most children were of above-average intelligence. Darlene was extremely concretistic and had difficulty with abstract concepts. She repeated the first grade and had difficulty in the second grade. The one thing Darlene excelled in was visual memory and drawing. Her oral recall was poor, as was her comprehension. Her peers just ignored her. She was too immature and too limited to be of much interest to them. Darlene was a social isolate who clung to adults for recognition and attention.

Darlene loved to read and won much praise because of her reading ability. The fact that she read a great deal but understood little of what she read did not seem to bother her. What did bother her was that she was constantly asked to compete with brighter children who functioned at a level far above hers. As her frustration mounted she began to

Progress of Long-Term LD Pupils

develop somatic complaints and withdrew more and more into a world of fantasy. She became resentful of other children and blamed them for her difficulties in school. She maintained that she really was a good student since she could read, but that others picked on her. Her parents shared her misperception and also thought of Darlene as a capable student. When she was eight-and-one-half years old, Darlene was referred to the LD program.

A complete psychological and psychiatric examination of Darlene revealed that she suffered from both cerebral malfunctioning and emotional problems. She was of low average intelligence. Table 23 gives Darlene's IQ and achievement test scores during her five-year stay in the special classes. When she was admitted to the LD program, she had an IQ score of 85 and a mental age of seven-and-one-half years. Darlene was able to read words on the second grade level, but could not comprehend them. She could add and subtract numbers from one to ten in a mechanical fashion by counting on her fingers, but she had no understanding of number concepts.

While attending LD classes, Darlene continued to improve her reading skill. By age eleven, she could read fifth grade material with ease, even though her level of understanding was on only the third grade level. In three years, her total gain in reading recognition was two years nine months, or almost three years, compared to a gain of only one year in arithmetic. Darlene had learned to carry and to borrow numbers, but could only do the simplest kinds of multiplications. At the end of the

Table 23.

Darlene's progress in the LD program.

			Wide Range Achievement Test scores		
CA	MA	IQ Score	Reading	Spelling	Arithmetic
8-9	7-5	85	2.9	2.4	2.3
9-4	7-9	83	3.6	2.8	2.3
10-3	8-7	—	4.4	2.8	2.3
11-2	9-7	—	5.8	3.3	3.3
12-1	10-3	85	—	—	—
13-3	11-3	—	7.2	3.8	3.8

follow-up study, when Darlene was 13 years old, her skill in reading recognition had advanced to the seventh grade level while her comprehension and her arithmetic achievement continued to lag behind. She was still only able to do by rote simple arithmetic computations on the third grade level. Darlene's IQ scores remained quite stable throughout the five-year period of this study.

Figure 2 shows Darlene's progress in the LD program in graphic form. Most striking in this presentation is the increasing discrepancy between her achievement scores in reading and arithmetic—that is, between her visual memory and her reasoning. The line for the IQ scores on Figure 2 falls halfway between the lines for the reading and arithmetic scores. The IQ line represents most adequately Darlene's overall level of functioning. It can readily be seen what a mistake it would have been to judge Darlene mainly on the basis of her reading skill.

Many children with good visual memory can master the technique of reading despite poor comprehension. Darlene was a dull child who needed a slow-moving class and who could not compete with children of normal intelligence. Remedial reading and special perceptual training were not what Darlene needed. Her biggest problem was limited mental capacity; above all, she had poor reasoning ability. In the LD program, Darlene was placed into an SLD class where she could progress at her own rate without undue pressure and with maximum support. Nothing the school could do could change the fact that Darlene was a slow child. But there was no reason why she also had to be an emotionally disturbed child. In the accepting and therapeutic atmosphere of the LD program, Darlene was able to be comfortable. Her somatic complaints disappeared and she gradually began to reach out toward her peers. Both Darlene and her parents learned to accept her strengths as well as her weaknesses. With the help of the LD staff, the parents set more realistic goals for their daughter. At the time of her last follow-up Darlene was looking forward to vocational training and hoped to work in an office some day.

Darlene's greatest accomplishments, during her five years in the LD program, were her improved self-concept and the establishment of a close friendship with another girl. She no longer had to cling desperately to adults for reassurance and no longer needed to delude herself about her ability. Darlene benefitted greatly from the LD program. Without it, she would have withdrawn more and more and would most likely have become a severely disturbed child and a slave to her somatic ailments. As it turned out, Darlene developed into a happy and healthy girl who was functioning up to the level of her ability and was gaining much satisfaction from her accomplishments.

Figure 2.
Darlene's progress in the LD program.

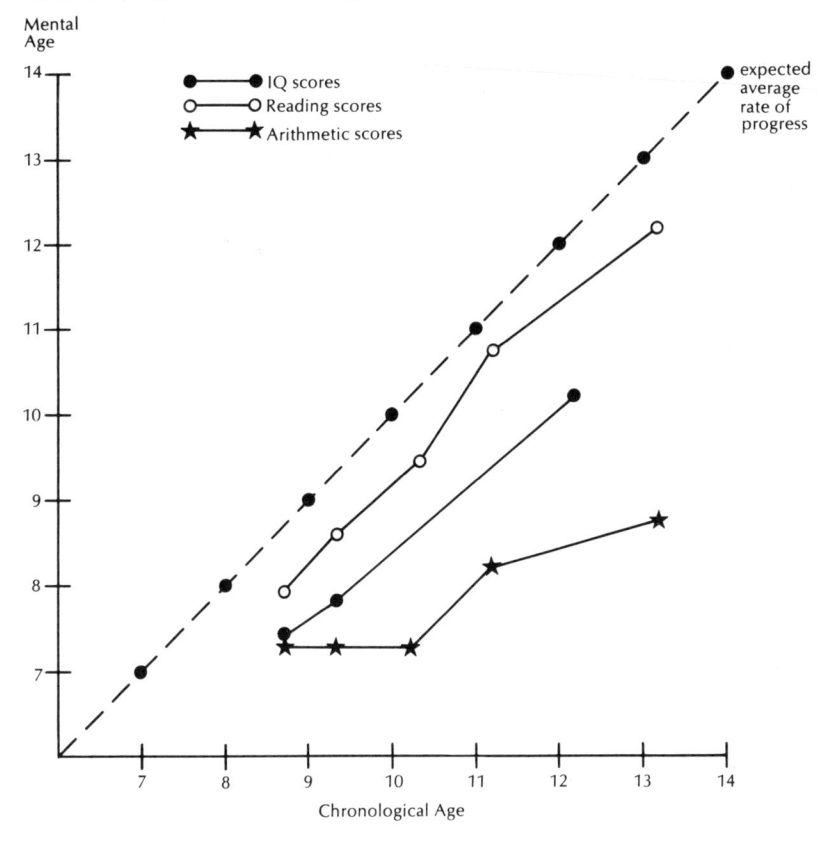

Group C: Children With Specific Learning Disabilities

Group C included 21 long-term LD pupils with specific learning disabilities. They suffered not only from *serious perceptual malfunction but also from severe memory deficits.*

School learning requires all of the following skills: auditory perception, visual-motor perception, reasoning, and memory. Experience with LD pupils has shown that many children are able to compensate, in time, for problems in visual-motor perception *if* they are of at least average intelligence *and if* they have good auditory perception *and* good memory. Similarly, it has been found that bright children with good visual-motor perception and the ability to retain what they have learned can progress in school quite well, even if they have rather poor auditory perception. And finally, it was observed that youngsters with weaknesses in memory and sequencing can still get by in school *provided* they are of good intelligence and have adequately functioning auditory and visual-motor perception. Thus it appears that deficiencies in either auditory perception, visual-motor perception, or memory and sequencing can be overcome and compensated for *if* a child is functioning well in the other two areas and *if* he has average or better than average mental ability.

The picture changes drastically if a child has difficulties in *two* of the areas. That is, if he suffers from malfunction in visual-motor perception *and* auditory perception, or in visual-motor perception *and* memory for sounds and symbols, or in auditory perception *and* memory. Even a bright child has difficulty compensating for more than one major area of deficit, especially if one of the areas is memory. The situation is even more critical if a youngster is deficient in all three areas under discussion.

Children of average intelligence with multiple problems in perception, memory, and sequencing tend to show even less progress in school than retarded children. However, the cause for their poor achievement is often not recognized since their problems are usually not obvious. As a result, these pupils are among the most severely handicapped and the most misunderstood of all children with learning disabilities. When youngsters who are apparently intelligent do not learn, parents and teachers often call them "lazy" or "lacking in motivation" and claim that the children "could learn if they only tried a little harder." In consequence, many teachers and parents begin to pressure the children with extra work and with threats and/or promises in order "to make them learn." However, since the youngsters really are not able to learn, they become more and more frustrated and either give up entirely or strike out at others and develop emotional and behavior problems, in addition to their learning difficulties. When the children's behavior can no longer be controlled in regular classes, the youngsters are referred to the LD program. They are, by then, usually labelled as "emotionally disturbed."

Even in a special class program, the children of average intelligence with specific perceptual and memory deficits are often misfits. They are either placed into classes with dull children (whose academic functioning is correspondingly low) or into classes with other LD pupils of normal intelligence who may also have emotional problems but whose achievement is usually much higher. In the first case, the youngsters with specific learning problems get bored and may become even more disturbed. Being with dull or moderately retarded children only tends to confirm their fears that they themselves really *are* "retarded," which, of course, they are not. In the second case, the pupils may get the kind of stimulation and general education they need, but since they can never keep up or compete with their classmates, they may feel as frustrated as in a regular class and may become totally discouraged.

The twenty-one children in Group C were all pupils with multiple specific problems in perception and memory. Their difficulties resulted from various different causes. In some cases the children were diagnosed as brain-injured or showed medically verified minimal brain dysfunction that could be traced back to prenatal or birth trauma or to other medical causes. In other children, the specific learning disability seemed to be associated with severe early emotional and physical deprivation and neglect. In these children, there was no medical evidence of brain injury. Their neurological examinations and their EEGs were entirely within the normal range. Yet the youngsters showed the types of specific learning problems and the extremely poor inner control which are characteristic of many pupils with minimal brain dysfunction. The children acted just like brain-injured children and required the same kind of education and treatment as brain-injured children (Hallahan, 1970). For practical purposes, they were children with brain dysfunction.

And, finally, Group C also included some pupils who were truly "dyslexic." They had no history of illnesses or accidents and had not suffered severe deprivation or neglect in early childhood. Instead, these youngsters had inherited their learning problems; they suffered from genetically determined dyslexia. In each case, other members of the children's family had similar learning problems. Several of the dyslexic youngsters were somewhat better-integrated than the other children in Group C, but they did not differ from the other pupils in the types of learning problems they presented or in the kind of help they required. It was found that diagnostic labels contributed little to understanding the problems of the 21 children in Group C, while a detailed analysis of their functioning and of their strengths and weaknesses provided a basis for developing a meaningful program for them.

Table 21 shows that the 21 pupils in Group C had a mean age of seven years eleven months (Range 6-9 to 11-8) when they first entered the LD program. Their IQ mean score was average or 91 (Range IQ 78 to IQ 114), while their mean functioning in reading was on the readiness level (Range .5 to 2.4). In arithmetic, their achievement was a little higher. After five years in the LD classes, their IQ mean score was still 90. As a group they had held their own mentally, even though they had progressed only one grade level in reading and less than two grade levels in arithmetic during this time. The lack of progress of these long-term LD pupils is sobering indeed if one considers the amount of effort expended by the pupils and the LD staff, and all the special teaching materials and teaching techniques that were employed to help these youngsters. No wonder that teachers, children, and their parents often get frustrated and discouraged.

The 21 intelligent youngsters in Group C achieved less in five years of special education than the 18 dull pupils in Group A (Table 21). It was apparent that the LD classes were distinctly unsuccessful in raising the level of achievement of the children with specific perceptual and memory deficits. It is certain that laziness or lack of motivation were *not* the causes of the children's poor showing; most of the boys and girls wanted desperately to learn. Neither could lack of experience or lack of skill on the part of the LD staff be blamed for the pupils' failure to learn. Does this mean that the youngsters might have been helped more by a different type of program? Or does it indicate that the children in Group C really *cannot* learn to read and write?

The case of Russell, one of the boys in Group C, is presented here in detail in order to illustrate more fully the problems of these youngsters and how they functioned. Russell entered kindergarten at age five-and-one-half. He was well developed and appeared normal, but he was quite restless, socially and emotionally immature for his age, and he had a severe speech problem. He talked incessantly but his speech was unintelligible. The school referred the parents to the regional speech and hearing clinic, where Russell was evaluated when he was six years old. He was diagnosed as being "probably aphasic" and was given speech therapy twice a week. By age seven Russell had shown little improvement in speech. His speech therapist determined that Russell could not perceive his own speech correctly and that he had extremely poor memory for sounds and symbols. The clinic staff felt that Russell was unable to profit from speech therapy and discontinued their work with Russell.

In school, Russell was hyperactive, hypertalkative, and silly much of the time. Yet, he was a friendly and good-natured child who was accepted by his peers. He also appeared to be of average intelligence and participated in class activities; however, he failed to show any academic progress whatsoever. After attending kindergarten and first grade, Russell was still unable to write his name, knew only a few isolated letters, and could barely count and add numbers from one to five on his fingers. So, after two unsuccessful years in regular classes,

Progress of Long-Term LD Pupils

Russell was referred to the LD program. He was ⟨...⟩ months old at the time. His speech was still quite p⟨...⟩ definitely of average intelligence. On the WISC he obtain⟨ed⟩ of 92, a Performance IQ of 97, and a Full Scale IQ of 94. ⟨...⟩ highly motivated for learning and he was eager to please the ⟨...⟩

Russell's academic progress in the LD program was no bett⟨er⟩ it had been in the regular classes. Table 24 shows that during the ⟨...⟩

Table 24. *Genetic causes*

Russell's progress in the LD program.

			Wide Range Achievement Test scores		
CA	MA	IQ Score	Reading	Spelling	Arithmetic
7-8	7-2	94	1.2	1.0	1.2
8-3	7-10	—	1.6	1.3	2.5
9-4	8-11	96	1.7	1.5	2.7
10-4	10-1	—	1.5	1.5	2.4
11-2	11-2	100	1.9	1.8	3.0
12-2	12-2	—	1.8	2.3	4.2

year follow-up period Russell's gain in reading and spelling was minimal and his progress in arithmetic was slow and uneven. Yet, each year his new classroom teacher would start out full of enthusiasm and would assure Russell that *this year* he would learn to read. And each year Russell would get his hope up and would work hard, only to be disappointed once again. No matter how hard Russell and his teachers tried and worked, they failed to achieve any real success; no lasting improvement in his reading achievement was evident. Why?

Careful evaluation of Russell revealed that he suffered from specific learning disabilities that apparently had a genetic basis. Russell was a "dyslexic" child, as were several other members of his family. Although he acted and functioned like a brain-injured child, there was no medical evidence of any brain lesion. He had apparently inherited minimal brain dysfunction that manifested itself in several areas: Russell had difficulty discriminating sounds, his auditory perception was quite poor; he had a disturbance in both oral expression and written expression; his visual perception was good, but he often could not say or copy without error what he perceived correctly; he had serious difficulty with directionality and time relationships. Above all, Russell suffered from a severe memory

Children with Learning Disabilities

deficit, especially for sequences, symbols, and sounds; he had difficulty in intersensory integration—that is, he could not translate what he perceived in one sense modality into another sense modality. All of this grossly interfered with his academic progress. Some descriptions of Russell's actual functioning in the LD classes will further clarify the nature of his difficulties.

Russell's poor auditory perception was reflected on his performance on the Wepman Auditory Discrimination Test. Even at age twelve, his scores on this test were only on the level of a five-year-old child. For example, he was unable to perceive the differences between "din" and "dim," between "pat" and "pack," or between "thimble" and "symbol." His own speech was slurred and he tended to leave off endings. Even more frustrating for Russell was his expressive disturbance. He could *say* the letters of his name, but he rarely *wrote* his name correctly. If asked to write his name three times he would write it in three different ways, all wrong, even though he *knew* the correct spelling. During the process of putting the letters down on paper, Russell would get confused; he would omit letters, write them in incorrect sequence, or reverse them. He could not retain the correct sound pattern of the name in his head while writing it down.

Russell could never be sure what he would actually do or say, even if his intentions were clear enough. He might say that he was going to *add* two numbers, but then proceeded to *subtract* them. He could not look at the number 17 and just *say* "17," even though he knew that it was 17. He could only *say* 17 in a number sequence. Thus, he had to count to himself "1, 2, 3, . . . 15, 16, 17"; then he could say "17." His disturbance for time and space relationships were often apparent in the endless stories Russell liked to tell. He was always eager to share his experiences, but he was never sure whether the events he described had occurred a day, a week, or a year before. He also got confused about the sequence of happenings and mixed up the concepts of *before* and *after*.

All of this was most frustrating for Russell. It was time-consuming and made him appear stupid. Actually, he was not at all stupid. A little story will help illustrate both Russell's intelligence and his problems in recall: When school started again after the summer vacation, Russell was eager to tell the psychologist about his trip. Full of enthusiasm, he related his adventures on the beach and in the ocean, but when he was asked where he had been, Russell could not remember the name of the place or the state he had visited. Russell obviously *knew* them both, but he just could not recall them. "You know," he said, "where the

Progress of Long-Term LD Pupils

ferry is, where the pilgrims landed." Then he proceeded to draw a perfect map of Cape Cod and Plymouth. When these names were mentioned to him Russell exclaimed excitedly, "Yes, yes, that's it!" He knew quite well where he had been, but his poor memory prevented him from recalling the names although his good intelligence and his ability to deal with visual material enabled him to get his message across by means of a drawing. It is always a sign of good intelligence if a child can compensate for problems.

The extent of Russell's intelligence was also shown on the WISC that was administered to Russell when he was eleven years old. His Full Scale IQ score was 100. Russell's IQ had actually increased by six points, compared with the Full Scale WISC score he had obtained at age seven (Table 24). The distribution of Russell's WISC IQ and Subtest scores is quite revealing:

WISC Verbal IQ: 96
Performance IQ: 104
Full Scale IQ: 100

Subtests and Weighted Scores

Information	7	Picture Completion	12
Comprehension	13	Picture Arrangement	12
Arithmetic	8	Block Design	11
Similarities	10	Object Assembly	13
Vocabulary	11	Coding	5
Digit Span	7		

These test results indicate beyond a doubt that Russell was of average intelligence. They also show that his strength was in the performance area. However, the good Subtest scores in Comprehension, Similarities, and Vocabulary reflect Russell's excellent common sense, his good verbal reasoning ability, and an understanding and knowledge of language appropriate for his age level. All but one of the Performance Subtest scores were very good and reveal his ability in perceiving, analyzing, and dealing with concrete and visual material. He could not copy or reproduce material from memory, but he could manipulate and use concrete material at hand.

Russell's single lowest WISC Subtest score was in Coding. His performance in this Subtest was on the defective level due to his problems in memory and sequencing. The Coding Test is timed for speed and accuracy. Russell could not retain the coding symbols in his head, so he had to return to the key for each symbol before he copied it. This slowed him down a great deal and made him lose points. Furthermore, he was inaccurate in copying the symbols. He made several reversals and sequencing errors for which he was also penalized.

Russell's poor showing on the Information, Arithmetic, and Digit Span Subtests are, of course, also reflections of his serious memory deficit and his difficulty in sequencing. Russell just could not remember specific bits of factual information and was unable to repeat more than four digits in the correct sequence. It was hard enough for Russell to do arithmetic computations on paper—he was utterly incapable of retaining numbers in his head and working with them. Russell's WISC Subtest pattern is identical with that found by Ackerman, Peters, and Dykman (1971) in a population of children with specific learning problems.

In Russell's case, lack of mental ability was clearly not the cause of his learning disability (Black, 1971). His main problems were *poor auditory perception, an expressive disorder, and severe memory deficits.* It was the combination of several areas of malfunction that made it so difficult for Russell to learn. He had no difficulty comprehending what he was taught, but he could not retain it.

His teachers tried many different approaches to reading with Russell, but none proved to be successful. He could neither learn to read by the visual or the phonetic method nor by a combination of these; the tactile and kinesthetic approaches were also of no help. Equally unsuccessful was the color coding method or the intersensory approach.

Russell did well in arithmetic "if his nose was pointed in the right direction" each time he was given an assignment. He understood the problems, but he forgot from one session to the next where to begin and the sequence of steps to follow. Once he was reminded of the process involved, Russell could continue on his own, if given enough time, for the remainder of that period. The next day, however, the procedure had to be repeated all over again. Russell enjoyed most working on projects and carrying out science experiments. He also had a good understanding of social relationships and of practical everyday problems.

Figure 3 demonstrates better than test scores the ever-widening discrepancy between Russell's mental ability and his achievement. Since he was of normal intelligence, his CA equalled his MA. The line formed by his IQ scores runs parallel to that of an average pupil. Russell's achievement line for arithmetic shows uneven and slow gains at first; then, at age ten, a gradual improvement in his arithmetic scores is seen. Russell's reading progress was negligible throughout the five year

Figure 3.
Russell's progress in the LD program.

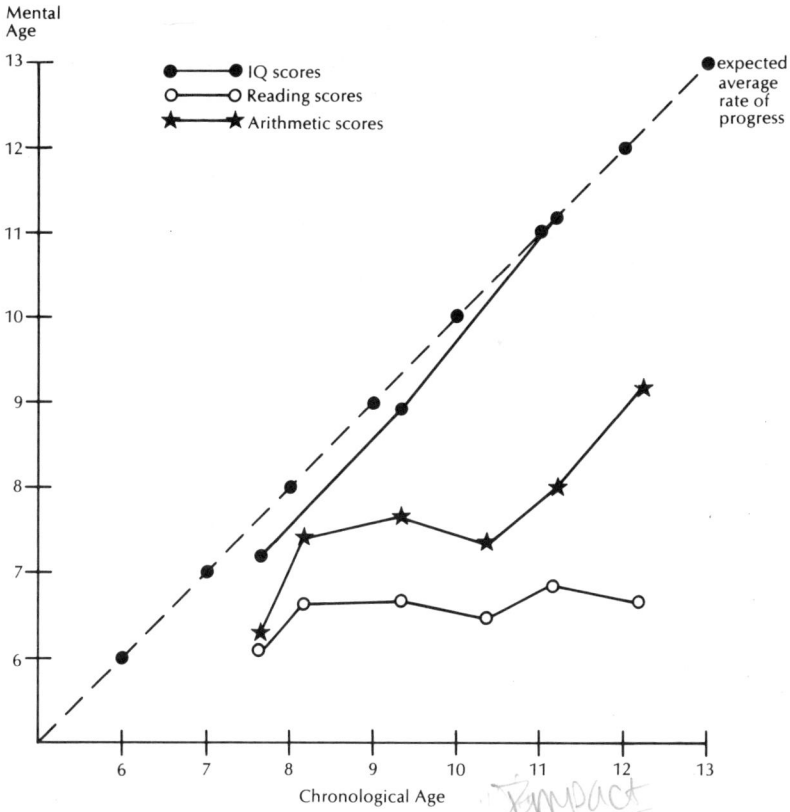

follow-up period as can be seen by the slightly wavering but essentially horizontal line of reading scores on Figure 3. At age twelve, Russell was still completely illiterate.

Russell was painfully aware of his poor achievement and at times became discouraged. He was also sensitive to teasing by siblings and peers. Other children liked him, but they often got tired of his endless stories and jokes, especially since he usually forgot the point of the story or could not remember the punch line. Russell was often frustrated and lonely. He had amazing insight into his difficulties. He told the psychologist that he was aware that he got silly and loud when he felt nervous or when he could not keep up with his peers. He also confided that he loved to tell jokes, but that "... you are the only one who *listens* to my jokes." There were times when Russell was quite depressed and low in spirits, but, amazingly, he always was ready to try again—he never gave up completely. When asked what he wanted most in life Russell replied that he wanted more than anything to learn to read.

It is an unhappy fact that children like Russell may never be able to learn how to read beyond, at best, the second or possibly the third grade level, if at all. This does not mean that one should give up trying to find new and different ways of helping children with perceptual and memory deficits. It does imply, however, that an educational program should be developed for these children that does not rely mainly on the printed word and on reading. Although these youngsters cannot profit from written symbols, they can nevertheless be educated and can be trained for a job. They are basically intelligent human beings and can and should be prepared to lead independent and useful lives. Perhaps the major misfortune of these children is that they were born a century too late or in the wrong place. If he had lived in a preliterate or agricultural society, Russell would not have been considered "atypical" or a child with learning disabilities. He could have held his own in his community without problems.

In a sophisticated, twentieth-century, urban society, children like Russell are grossly handicapped and need a special educational program. There will always be children like Russell in the public schools, but at present very few of them are getting a meaningful education. Most of them are just wasting their time in school since they cannot possibly profit from a regular school curriculum. Even though Russell's academic progress in the LD program was extremely poor he did derive much benefit from attending the special classes. He was placed into a class with other children who had similar problems in perception and memory. Russell learned best from direct experiences and from *doing* things with his hands. He was provided with a curriculum that was mainly experience- and project-oriented. Russell was presented with a general science and social studies program that was taught at his appropriate mental age level but without the use of books. Academic subjects were kept to a minimum. An attempt was made to give Russell a functional reading vocabulary since there was little indication that he would ever acquire sufficient reading skills to be truly literate. When last seen Russell was in a prevocational program. He will continue on to vocational school and a work-study program at the high school level.

In some ways Russell could even be called fortunate among the children in Group C. He "only" had malfunctioning in auditory perception, and in expression and memory. His visual perception was actually good, as was his reasoning. Russell had areas of competence to build on, offsetting some of his weaknesses. Furthermore, he had very accept-

Progress of Long-Term LD Pupils

ing and supportive parents. Other children in Group C were less lucky.

There was Rolf, for instance, who had a serious impairment in both auditory *and* visual perception, as well as a severe memory deficit. He had great difficulty differentiating between similar sounds and between letters that looked alike (for example: *b, p, d, q, n* and *m*). He was unable to associate sounds and symbols since he was never quite sure of the sounds and the symbols to begin with. He had also difficulty integrating what little he did understand and absorb.

Rolf had suffered a brain injury at birth. However, in early childhood he showed no significant developmental delays or abnormalities, other than a general immaturity and infantile speech. His difficulties did not become apparent until he entered school and had to begin to cope with letters and numbers. He was hypersensitive and had a low frustration tolerance. Rolf had great difficulty adjusting to kindergarten and failed to make any progress while there. He was shy, did not understand what was required of him, could not follow directions, and learned nothing. Yet he appeared to be of average intelligence. The WISC was administered to Rolf when he was in the first grade. He obtained a Verbal IQ of 100, a Performance IQ of 100, and a Full Scale IQ of 100. Thus, theoretically, at least, he was an "average" boy. He was definitely not retarded, but still Rolf did not learn.

After an unsuccessful year in the first grade, he was referred to the LD program. His parents could not understand why Rolf failed to make any progress in school since there was "nothing wrong with him." They increased their pressure on Rolf and worked with him every night on his reading and tutored him for long hours on weekends, but it was all in vain. Rolf just could not perceive the sounds and shapes of letters correctly and he could not form associations between them.

In the LD program, the teacher, the reading consultant, and the psychologist went all-out to try to find ways of helping Rolf with his reading. When a visual and phonetic approach failed, Rolf was introduced to a kinesthetic and a tactile approach to reading. Only then was it discovered that he also had a deficit in kinesthetic and tactile perception. Color coding, used as an aid in reading, proved helpful for some of the pupils, but not for Rolf. He was color blind. Rolf never even learned to recognize his own name.

With each succeeding year, Rolf became more discouraged and more withdrawn while his parents became more impatient and more desperate. They were determined to "make" Rolf learn. At the urging of the school social worker, they finally agreed to take Rolf to the county mental health clinic for a complete evaluation. But even after it was found that Rolf had an abnormal EEG, and after he had revealed several positive signs on the neurological examination, his parents insisted that there was nothing "wrong" with Rolf. They rejected the diagnosis of brain injury. The LD staff was not only unsuccessful in improving Rolf's achievement, it also could not prevent an increase in his emotional disturbances. The parents overwhelmed Rolf with their demands to the point where he withdrew more and more into fantasy and began to lose touch with reality.

When Rolf was seven years old, he stated that his biggest wish was "to live all alone in a castle with a high wall and water all around it." By the time Rolf was eleven years old, he had achieved his wish. He lived in social isolation in a world of infantile fantasy. He was a very immature, unhappy, and withdrawn child who was functioning almost like a retarded child. He had not actually deteriorated mentally, but he had failed to gain and to grow appreciably in the intervening years. When he was tested at age ten, Rolf's IQ score had dropped by 18 points; his Full Scale IQ score was only 82. He no longer acted or functioned like a child of average intelligence. When he first came to the LD program he had been primarily a child with learning disabilities. At the end of the five year follow-up period Rolf was still a youngster with severe learning difficulties, but he was also a boy with serious emotional problems.

It cannot be claimed that the LD program had helped Rolf to overcome his learning problems, but it can be stated with certainty that Rolf would have been even worse off if he had not been in a small, protective class. The history of Rolf illustrates how the children in Group C were often doubly handicapped because their difficulties were not obvious. If Rolf had been physically impaired or blind his parents would have made allowances for his handicap, but because they could not *see* his perceptual and memory deficits they refused to believe in their existence. Thereby, the parents unwittingly contributed to Rolf's problems. The combination of *very severe* learning disabilities and serious emotional problems along with an absence of parental support made Rolf's prognosis guarded indeed.

Group D: Children With Emotional and Behavior Problems

Group D included 23 long-term LD pupils who were referred to the special classes primarily because of serious emotional and/or behavior problems. The youngsters also had varying degrees of perceptual and learning difficulties, but these were of secondary importance compared to their extremely poor inner control and their emotional and social maladjustment. The twenty-three children in Group D differed widely in their mental ability. The problems they exhibited could be traced back to both organic and environmental factors. In some cases, the youngsters' behavior was almost entirely the result of their severe neurological impairment, that is, the consequence of marked immaturity, incoordination, and impulsivity. The problems of other children stemmed from a combination of factors. Some boys and girls were so vulnerable, poorly integrated, and hypersensitive that they could not cope with their environmental stresses and strains as readily as non-brain-injured children. When these youngsters were overwhelmed by conflicts and pressures at home and in school they developed emotional and behavior problems. None of the children were "just" emotionally disturbed.

Table 21 shows that the mean age of the 23 pupils in Group D was 8 years 4 months (Range 6-1 to 12-4). Their mean IQ score was 94 or average. However, the IQ scores of the 23 pupils ranged all the way from the Borderline level to High Average, from IQ 69 to 115. A wide range of achievement levels was also found in Group D. It extended from kindergarten to fourth grade, from 0.9 to 4.5 in reading and arithmetic. The average achievement level for the group was at the beginning second grade level.

At the end of the five year follow-up study, the IQ mean score for the pupils in Group D was 96, still normal. On the average, the youngsters had gained a little more than two grade levels in achievement. Of course, some children actually gained more than that, others less. Some youngsters functioned academically right up to their grade level and could have returned to regular classes if it had not been for their persistent behavior problems. In general, the emotional adjustment and the behavior difficulties of the 23 pupils improved considerably during the youngsters' five years stay in the LD program. But enough problems remained to make continued enrollment in the special classes advisable for all 23 children.

Since the children in Group D varied so much from each other, none could be regarded as typical or as representative for the Group as a whole. The case histories of two boys will be given here in detail to illustrate some of the types of problems the pupils presented and to show the progress the youngsters made in the LD program.

The first child was Bruce. He was six years old when he came to the special classes at the request of his parents. They had very wisely kept Bruce out of kindergarten and had enrolled him in a nursery school when he was five years old. Thus, Bruce came to the LD classes without having had the humiliating experience of having "failed" kindergarten. Bruce had been medically diagnosed as brain-injured; his EEG was abnormal and he had revealed many positive signs on a neurological examination. He was a cheerful and friendly child who related easily to adults but who could not play with other children. His peers rejected him because Bruce was too hyperactive and unpredictable. He never stayed put and did not follow through on anything. Bruce rarely stayed with any activity for more than a few minutes. He was *extremely* restless, distractible, uncoordinated, and disorganized. He had an unusually high threshold for pain and suffered from a sleep disturbance. Bruce was also alert, inquisitive, verbal, and he retained whatever he learned or saw. It was literally impossible for Bruce to sit for more than a few minutes at a time without falling off his chair. When he walked, he tripped over his own feet or ran into doors. When he talked, he distracted himself by a chance word he said and rarely completed a sentence or a thought. His thinking was disorganized. Bruce appeared to be a fluid, poorly integrated being in a big, confusing world. He could only function when he was provided with a highly structured situation and a routine he could adhere to rigidly. Since Bruce was so grossly deficient in inner controls, he needed outer controls to give him support and guidance. Any new or unexpected event upset him very much. Despite all this Bruce could and did learn. He learned "on the run," so to speak.

Bruce's difficulties in school and at home were almost entirely the result of his serious neurological impairment. There was no evidence of any significant emotional disturbance. Much credit for Bruce's good emotional adjustment had to go to his remarkable parents. Bruce was fortunate in having a warm, accepting, and stable home and loving and supporting parents. His mother and father had full understanding of his organic involvement and met his needs in a calm, matter-of-fact way. His older sister was also affectionate and protective of Bruce. It is obvious that a child like Bruce would have developed serious emotional problems in a less stable and supportive home. It is as apparent that Bruce could not possibly have functioned in a large regular class without experiencing much frustration and failure.

Table 25 shows Bruce's academic progress in the LD program. When he came to the special classes, he was six years old and was already able to read at the beginning second grade level. He could add and subtract numbers from one to ten even though he had never been in school before. Bruce had taught himself by watching others and by asking questions. He had received no tutoring or encouragement to do

Table 25.

Bruce's progress in the LD program.

			Wide Range Achievement Test scores		
CA	MA	IQ Score	Reading	Spelling	Arithmetic
6-2	6-2	100	2.2	1.7	2.2
6-9	7-3	—	3.1	1.3	2.7
7-5	8-8	117	4.3	2.6	3.5
9-10	10-11	—	5.2	—	5.0
10-10	11-10	109	7.0	5.5	5.9

school work at home. In fact, his parents expressed concern because his mental activity far outstripped his physical and emotional development.

According to his admission data Bruce had obtained an IQ of 100 on the Stanford-Binet Intelligence Scale. The LD staff felt, however, that this was not a valid assessment of his mental ability. His language development was excellent and he appeared to be of above average intelligence. This was also indicated by the Human Figure Drawing Bruce made when he was 6 years 2 months old. The drawing, shown on Plate 13, reveals neurological impairment and a valiant attempt to master extreme impulsivity and disorganization. Such a spontaneous and successful effort to compensate for weak inner control and poor organization is only found on the drawings of bright children. Most youngsters who are as poorly coordinated and as disorganized as Bruce was, draw poorly integrated figures with disconnected parts. Bruce drew his figure instead with one continuous line that even included a bent arm. Only the head of the figure and the watch, the ring, and the necklace were drawn separately. Drawings with continuous lines are done mostly by brain-injured children who are trying to control their impulsivity by setting a firm boundary around their poorly organized personality (Koppitz, 1968; p. 133).

Another way in which Bruce tried to overcome his lack of coordination and his weak inner control was by following compulsive rituals and routines in daily life. Such guidelines helped him a great deal. Furthermore, Bruce had been placed on medication. Without medication, Bruce found it impossible to manage himself and was in constant danger of hurting himself. As it was, he was always covered with bruises and cuts from falling and from running into things.

"necklace"

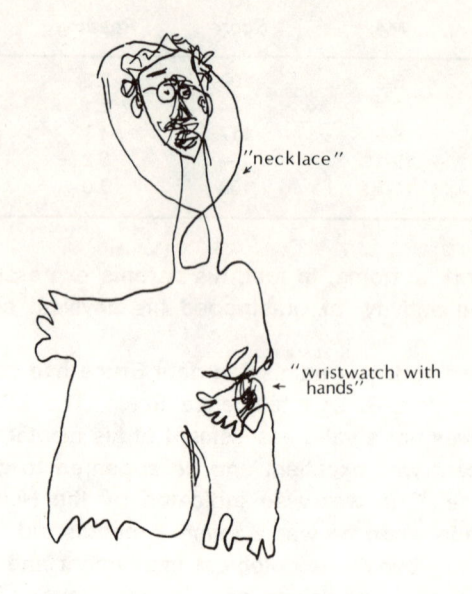

"wristwatch with hands"

Plate 13.
Bruce, CA 6-2.

Progress of Long-Term LD Pupils

When Bruce was seven years five months old, the WISC was administered to him. It was very difficult to test Bruce because of his short attention span and his hyperactivity. It took no less than three sessions to complete the test. Bruce was most cooperative and announced: "I will do everything you tell me to do." He answered all questions and completed all subtests while crawling over and under the table, sitting on and falling off his chair, wiggling and giggling, singing and talking, humming and drumming. At times, I had to physically restrain Bruce and had to hold him on my lap to help him to focus on a given task. This may not be the standard way to administer the WISC, but the results did provide a measure of Bruce's intellectual potential.

He obtained a Verbal IQ score of 126, a Performance IQ of 104, and a Full Scale IQ of 117. Bruce was a child with superior abstract reasoning and verbal ability. His auditory and visual perception were excellent, as was his memory. All the weighted WISC Subtest scores were between 12 and 16 with the exception of the Object Assembly and Coding Subtests. On these two Subtests, Bruce was penalized for his poor fine motor coordination. He just could not manipulate the pieces of the puzzles and the pencil well enough and fast enough to gain credit points although he correctly completed all tasks involved.

During his stay in the LD program, the major emphasis was placed on helping Bruce gain better control of himself. He was provided with a highly structured class situation and was given a stimulating program without pushing him in the academic area. Even so, Bruce progressed well during the five-year period of the follow-up study. When he was not quite ten years old, he was functioning on the fifth grade level (Table 25). According to his teacher's report that year, Bruce "talks incessantly, always asking questions. He absorbs information like a sponge even while he appears to be on cloud number nine. He shows real interest in and a genuine understanding of what he learns." His teacher went on to describe Bruce as immature, overactive, and showing numerous mannerisms. Bruce was said to be "friendly, pleasant and had good work habits, but he was somewhat remote from everyday life. His common sense and social understanding were poor. His abstract reasoning is excellent." By the time Bruce was just under eleven years old, he was reading with comprehension on the seventh grade level and was doing sixth grade arithmetic.

Figure 4 shows that Bruce's mental age and his academic functioning were consistently above average during the entire five years of this study. Unquestionably, he could have been a good student in a

Figure 4.
Bruce's progress in the LD program.

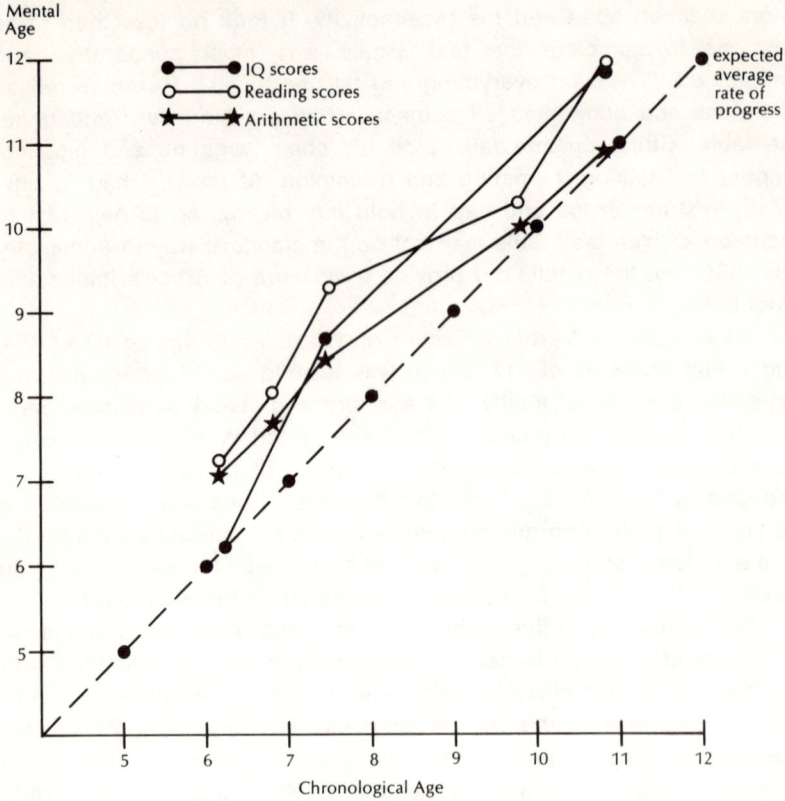

regular class, had it not been for his incoordination and disorganization. He was a very atypical youngster who needed a protective school environment.

As Bruce got older and matured his behavior also improved. He learned in time to stay in his seat and to stick with a thought or task until it was completed. He became less distractible and less hyperactive. He was also no longer as rigid or as easily upset as he had been when he was younger. Bruce learned to adjust more readily to new and unexpected situations. All this was, however, relative. Compared to his own earlier behavior, he had made great strides forward, but, compared to other children, Bruce was still highly unusual and very immature. Even after five years in the LD program, Bruce still required the structure and the support the small special classes could offer. When he was eleven years old, he attended an LD class in a regular middle school and was enrolled in one or two regular classes each day. After *seven years* of special education, Bruce returned full-time to regular classes.

It can be seen that Bruce benefited a great deal from being in the LD program. His history shows that some bright children with good achievement may still need long periods of time in small, protective classes before they can successfully cope with big, regular classes. The greatest service the LD program performed for Bruce was to provide him with the opportunity to develop and to grow without undue pressure at his own uneven rate. In this way Bruce was able to maintain his intellectual curiosity and his joy in learning without having to feel "peculiar" and without being pressured to "conform."

Bruce also demonstrated that a child need not fall behind in his work while attending special classes. He refuted the popular notion that special classes "keep children back" or that they "make children dumber." *A child who can learn, will learn, if given a chance.* The LD classes offered their pupils every opportunity to learn. And, finally, Bruce showed that even five years in a special class may not be long enough to enable some children to get back into regular classes. There should never be anything final about a special class placement. In a well-planned, comprehensive LD program, each child should be routinely evaluated. Some children may be ready for return to regular classes after only two or three years, others may need five, or even seven or eight years, before they can hold their own in regular classes. Again other youngsters may never be able to leave the special classes. The essential thing is that each child is given as much time in the special class program as he needs. No time limit should be placed on the enrollment in an LD program.

Another youngster in Group D was Derek. Just like Bruce, Derek was also a brain-injured child who was referred to the LD program primarily because of his behavior. While Bruce suffered from severe difficulties in motor coordination and in inner controls, he had the good fortune of being bright and of having a stable and supporting home—Derek was not so lucky. Derek was well-coordinated, but he was hypersensitive, rigid, explosive, and had more modest intelligence. His WISC Full Scale IQ score was 90. Derek showed physical and emotional immaturity, poor language development, and malfunctioning in visual-motor perception. He would have been a difficult and slowly-maturing child no matter who his parents had been or what home he had been born into. The fact that Derek was one of ten children of a socially and economically marginal family served only to intensify his problems. Derek needed much support and understanding and a stable, non-threatening environment. Instead he had had to learn to fend for himself at an early age. His mother was well-meaning but unable to meet his needs. She was herself overwhelmed by her family and by the demands of life; she was emotionally depressed and physically worn out. Her mental ability was quite limited. The father, a truck driver, was away during most of the week. On weekends, when he was at home, he spent most of his time drinking and was often abusive to his wife and the children.

Derek was a shy and aloof youngster. He distrusted others and preferred to be alone. When demands were made of him or when he anticipated failure Derek ran away and hid. His attitude toward authority figures and school was negative. He had had to enter school long before he was mature enough to profit from it. He experienced so much failure and frustration in the early years in school that he became discouraged and just gave up. Before long, Derek was not even attempting to do any work, but just sat in his seat, lost in dreams. When pressured to work, he either panicked and ran out of the room or he exploded in a violent outburst. When left alone he was quiet and peaceful; Derek did not look for trouble. He was a social isolate who did not like group activities and could not stand teasing. Derek was small for his age; he was skinny but tough. When other children bothered him, he lost his temper and fought back.

Derek's behavior might be considered primarily a sign of emotional and social maladjustment, but it is certain that Derek would not have developed as many emotional and behavior problems if he had not been a brain-injured child. His siblings, for instance, were all low average students and could cope fairly well with school and with the less-than-ideal home situation. It is also certain that in a different kind of family setting, Derek would have learned to deal with his neurological problems more adequately without necessarily developing major emotional maladjustments. Derek's difficulties were clearly the result of both organic and environmental factors.

Derek spent unhappy years in kindergarten and in the first grade; he then spent two more unsuccessful years in the second grade, entering the LD program on his ninth birthday. He was then a small, pale, bedraggled-looking boy. He was anxious, distrustful, and angry; he did not talk to anyone. Derek was threatened by all school work and did not even attempt to do any of his assignments. He was totally lacking in self-confidence and trust. It took several weeks before his teacher could get close to him and before his achievement level could be established.

As important as academic achievement might be, it was obvious that Derek's attitude and his behavior had to be, at least initially the primary concern of the LD staff. As long as Derek refused to attempt any work whatsoever and as long as he distrusted himself and everyone else, he could not possibly make any academic progress in school. Derek was placed therefore into a specially selected class with a very understanding and sensitive, but firm, teacher. Derek was given gym and woodworking classes which he loved, and other nonacademic subjects. He was only gradually introduced to reading and arithmetic through an individualized program in a one-to-one teaching situation with the help of a teacher's aide. The main goal set for Derek during his first year in the LD program was an improvement in his self-image and in his relationships to others. Accomplishing this goal was a slow and difficult process since no help or cooperation could be expected from the parents.

In addition to emotional and behavior problems, Derek also had learning disabilities. At age nine, his achievement was on the end-of-first-grade level. During the five years of the follow-up study, Derek made slow but steady academic progress. When he was eleven years old he was reading on the beginning-third-grade level and was doing fourth grade arithmetic. By age twelve, his reading had progressed to the end-of-third grade level while his arithmetic skills had advanced to the fifth grade level. By the end of the five-year period, when Derek was thirteen-and-one-half years old, his overall achievement (including reading) was on the fifth grade level. Academically, he was doing as well as could be expected. If it had not been for his behavior, he could have returned at this point to a regular slow-moving middle school class just as Guy had done (p. 82). Any number of pupils in regular slow or ungraded middle school classes do not achieve above the fifth grade level and still get by. In Derek's case, a return to regular classes was unthinkable.

Even though his attitude toward school and toward peers had improved, he was still much too vulnerable, much too unpredictable, and much too disturbed to be able to hold his own in a big, regular class. On his report card the teacher noted: "Derek is still greatly frustrated by all academic work and gives up easily. He is non-conforming and requires constant individual attention in order to complete a task. He rarely attempts to work on his own and never contributes to class discussions or group projects. He is moody and nervous." Obviously, Derek would still need the structure and support of a special class for many years to come. In the long run, Derek will require vocational training.

There can be little doubt that without the special class placement Derek would have been expelled from school long before. Or, if he had been tolerated in school, it is unlikely that he would have learned as much as he did in the LD program. Derek's emotional maladjustment improved in the special classes, but it could be neither entirely corrected nor eliminated because his disturbances were deep-seated and of long duration. It was particularly difficult to help Derek with his emotional problems since they were constantly reinforced by his home situation.

The history of Derek shows how public schools actually contribute to the development of emotional and behavior disorders in some pupils. It is nearly certain that many of Derek's difficulties could have been *prevented* if he had been referred to the LD program (or to some type of special class) at age five or six instead of age nine, after four years of failure and frustration in regular public school classes. Furthermore, it is believed that vulnerable children like Derek who live in unhealthy family situations would benefit from being away from home as much as possible. An effective public school LD program should ideally include dormitory facilities for such children, so that they can stay in school all week and only go home on weekends. Or, at least, the schools should provide an all-day program with after-school recreation and with trips on weekends, in addition to a summer program. The amount of time these youngsters spend at home and on the street should be minimized at all costs. And finally, an LD program should include counseling or supportive therapy for those youngsters who need it and who can use it, but who do not get it in the community. The school usually refers families to the community mental health clinic. Too often, initial contacts are made, but then no follow-through takes place. If a child does not get to the clinic, then the clinic should come to the child; that is, clinic services should be available through or in association with the schools. Derek needed psychotherapy as well as a long-term, slow-moving educational program to overcome his emotional and learning problems. When he was provided with such an educational program he made satisfactory gains in achievement. If he had had counseling too, his emotional problems might have shown more improvement as well.

Chapter 6

Pupils Who Were Referred for Hospitalization

Twenty-six LD pupils proved to be so disturbed that they could not benefit from the special classes. After a careful educational, psychological, and psychiatric examination, the LD staff decided that the needs of these youngsters could not be met in the LD program. The 26 children were given a psychiatric exclusion from the special classes and were referred for more intensive help either to a residential treatment center or to a mental hospital.

In some instances, the exclusion occurred after the youngsters had spent only a few weeks in the LD classes. In other cases, the referral for hospitalization took place only after several years of unsuccessful efforts on the part of the LD staff to help the children. A few pupils made a good initial adjustment to the LD program, but then suffered later from a marked mental deterioration or from a psychotic episode which required hospitalization. Exclusion from the LD program was always regarded as a last resort, to be used only after all available alternatives within the program had been exhausted. The exclusion of a child from school is a traumatic experience for all concerned. Inevitably, the teachers and other staff members feel they have somehow failed, and for the child and his parents it usually means one more defeat and another blow to their self-esteem.

The question arises therefore, "Could the LD program have been modified to meet the needs of these youngsters more adequately?" What were the children like, how did they differ from other LD pupils? Could these children have been identified at the time of referral to the LD program? Should they have been enrolled in the LD classes in the first place? The history of the 26 LD pupils who could not profit from the special classes was analyzed in detail in an attempt to answer some of these questions.

As a group, the 26 pupils, here under discussion, differed markedly both from the long-term LD pupils (p. 95) and from the LD pupils who returned to regular classes (p. 65). With two exceptions, the children who were referred for hospitalization were all boys. It was shown on Table 8 that most of them were either among the youngest (age 6) or oldest pupils (age 11 and 12) at the time of admission. Only ten of the 26 pupils fell into the 7-to-10-year age range. Apparently, some of the six-year-olds who were too disturbed or too impaired to be maintained in regular classes were also too disturbed for the public school LD classes.

Some other children seemed to have been able to just "get by" in elementary school, but to have been unable to cope with the added strain of preadolescence and the transfer to the larger and less structured middle school. The stress proved to be too much for these 11- and 12-year-olds. Crises ensued that brought the youngsters to the LD program, but it appeared that these particular children needed more intensive help than the LD program could offer. Referral to a hospital or treatment center became mandatory. It is quite probable that some of their more acute problems could have been avoided or minimized if these pupils had been referred to the special classes at an earlier time.

The intelligence of the 26 LD pupils who required more intensive help, ranged all the way from "nontestable" to IQ 131 or the superior level (Table 9). Intelligence, as such, had no direct relationship to the youngsters' problems. No child was given a psychiatric exclusion from the special classes because of lack of mental ability.

Almost all of the 26 children displayed very poor performance on the Bender Gestalt Test (Table 10), thereby revealing poor integrative ability, weak impulse control, and poor visual-motor perception. They also exhibited less achievement in arithmetic than any of the other groups of LD pupils (Table 11). In addition, their behavior was more extreme—many more of the excluded youngsters were acting-out and aggressive; more of them were explosive, rebellious, and delinquent. More in this group had experienced severe early physical and emotional neglect, and more were living at the time of the study in unstable and/or deprived home situations or foster homes (Table 13). Yet, none of these factors occurred exclusively among the LD pupils who were referred for hospitalization, nor did any one child in this group reveal all factors. It is also certain that none of these factors by themselves could account for the youngsters' serious disturbances and for their need for more intensive help. It was apparent that the pupils difficulties resulted from a *combination* of several of these factors within the children and in their home environments.

The histories of the 26 LD pupils showed enormous differences among them. There was no "typical" pattern of pathology or disturbance that applied to the group as a whole. However, it was possible to identify at least five distinct smaller groups among the 26 LD pupils here under discussion. The children in each of these five groups were similar in the types of problems they presented and in the types of treatment they required. The five subgroups were:

Group A: Autistic children
Group B: Uncontrollable and violent children
Group C: Children with symbiotic disorders
Group D: Severely disturbed mother-child relationships
Group E: Delinquent and asocial children

Table 26 shows the number of youngsters in each of the five groups of pupils, their placement and treatment after exclusion from the LD program, and their status at the end of the five year follow-up study. Each of the five groups of pupils will be discussed separately.

Group A: Autistic Children

Four of the 26 youngsters who were referred for hospitalization were autistic (p. 21). The writer concurs with Ritvo and Ornitz (1970) that childhood autism is in all likelihood a disease of the Central Nervous System and not something that results from parental rejection or from a pathological parent-child relationship. The four autistic LD pupils came from rather adequate and stable families, in contrast to the other 22 LD pupils who required more intensive psychiatric help. According to the referral data, the four autistic pupils, all boys, had been "different" and unresponsive since birth. None of the four were able to relate to either adults or children in a meaningful way; they could not follow directions and could not adjust to class routines. None of them

Table 26.

LD pupils who were referred for hospitalization.

Group	N	Treatment received	Pupils' status 5 years after coming to LD program
A. Autistic children	4	2 special school 2 hospitalized	2 special school 1 hospitalized 1 Trainable program
B. Uncontrollable, violent children (4 ex-hospital patients)	8	5 hospitalized 2 home tutoring, then hospitalized 1 special school, then hospitalized	1 LD class (successful) 5 LD class (unsuccessful), rehospitalized 1 hospitalized 1 foster home, working
C. Children with symbiotic disorders	4	3 hospitalized 1 home tutoring	1 LD class (successful) 1 special school 1 hospitalized 1 moved
D. Disturbed mother-child relationship	7	3 hospitalized 4 special school	2 regular class 3 LD class (successful) 1 special school 1 moved
E. Delinquent, asocial children	3	2 special school 1 home tutoring	1 special school 1 home, working 1 home, unemployed, on probation

could be tested by experienced psychologists in a one-to-one situation. At home and in school, the autistic children followed their own impulses and inner drives entirely, with complete disregard for the world about them. Two of the boys were unable to communicate verbally, merely letting out loud shrieks from time to time; another one had a limited vocabulary of a few four-letter words, while the fourth boy had adequate language, but used it only to express bizarre, stereotyped ideas over and over again. His verbalizations bore no relation to what was going on around him and he did not respond to direct questions.

The four autistic youngsters required constant close supervision for their own personal safety and for the protection of other children and their work. One child was so aggressive and kicked others so frequently, that he had to wear sneakers at all times while his teacher took to wearning shinguards. The four youngsters could not even function in small groups of only two or three children. None showed an ability to profit from the LD program. It was apparent almost at once that these children were badly misplaced in the LD classes; they required much more supervision and more intense, individual treatment and education than the LD program could offer. Three of the boys were psychiatrically excluded from the LD classes within a matter of weeks. The fourth boy, Reggie, was maintained in the special classes for three years at enormous cost to the other children and to the teachers.

Reggie upset some of the other children very much, but, even worse, some of the other more adequate pupils imitated Reggie's behavior. Furthermore, Reggie demanded so much of the teacher's time that his classmates did not get as much of her attention as they should have received. Despite all efforts, Reggie showed almost no improvement in his behavior or achievement during three years of special class attendance. During this time his influence in school and on his family, especially on his younger brother, was most detrimental. For several years, both Reggie and his mother were seen privately once a week for therapy. This did not bring about any noticeable change or improvement in the child. It took no less than three years before the LD staff finally persuaded the parents to send Reggie to a special school for autistic children, where his needs could be more fully met. One of the other autistic boys was also sent to a special private school, while the two most severely impaired youngsters went to the children's division of the State Hospital.

Why were the autistic children admitted to the LD program to begin with? The decision of the screening committee, myself included, to admit these boys to the LD classes on a trial basis was determined in part by ignorance and in part by humanitarian concern for the parents. It was soon learned, however, that admitting truly autistic children to the LD program benefitted no one in the long run. The parents of one boy even accused the LD staff of hurting their child by accepting him into the program on trial. Their complaint was not entirely unjustified. The parents had been able to locate a private day school for autistic children that was ready to accept their son. When the boy was admitted into the LD program, the parents had to withdraw their application to the private school. When the child was then excluded from the LD classes six weeks later, the opening in the private school had been filled, and they had to wait for several months before a new opening occurred.

None of the parents of the autistic boys were initially able to accept the LD staff's recommendations for placement of their children into residential schools or hospitals. Not until the youngsters were actually excluded from the LD program did three of the parents go ahead and place their children in appropriate programs. In each instance the action was long overdue, and the parents later stated that they wished they had done so much sooner. Placement in a residential school or hospital benefitted everyone in the families, including the autistic children. All the parents reported that they were able to enjoy their children for the first time when they came home for short visits. When the children had lived at home, it had been a constant struggle and strain for everyone in the family that made enjoyment difficult or impossible. By keeping a grossly misplaced pupil in an LD program, one sometimes unwittingly deprives the child of a placement in another school or facility which may be more beneficial for him and for his family.

At the end of the five year follow-up study, two of the autistic youngsters were still in special schools, one boy was still hospitalized, while the fourth boy, Johnny, had returned home after four years in the state mental hospital. At his mother's request, he was enrolled in the program for Trainable Mentally Retarded children. Even though Johnny differed from most of the other children in the program, he was actually functioning on a severely retarded level. Fortunately, he was small for his age and had quieted down somewhat in the intervening years so that he could be maintained in the Trainable Program. Johnny had difficulty following class routines, but according to his teacher, "he gets some satisfaction from being in school." Johnny's extreme immaturity, his lack of integration, and his strong tendency toward perserveration are tellingly revealed on his Human Figure Drawing (Plate 14) and on his Bender Gestalt Test protocol (Plate 15) that he made when he was twelve years old. Both drawings consist of nothing but primitive, disconnected loops and are not unlike drawings made by immature three-year-old children or by severely retarded, emotionally disturbed, brain-injured children of elementary school age. And this was, of course, exactly what Johnny was.

After the experience with these four autistic children, the screening committee admitted no more autistic children to the LD program. It was concluded that *no child (whatever his diagnosis) can profit from the LD classes if he cannot relate to either adults or children, if he cannot function in a small group of two or three children, if he is unable to follow even simple directions or rules, and if he cannot be tested by an experienced psychologist in a one-to-one situation. Any child who requires constant individual supervision and attention, and who cannot*

Pupils Referred for Hospitalization 143

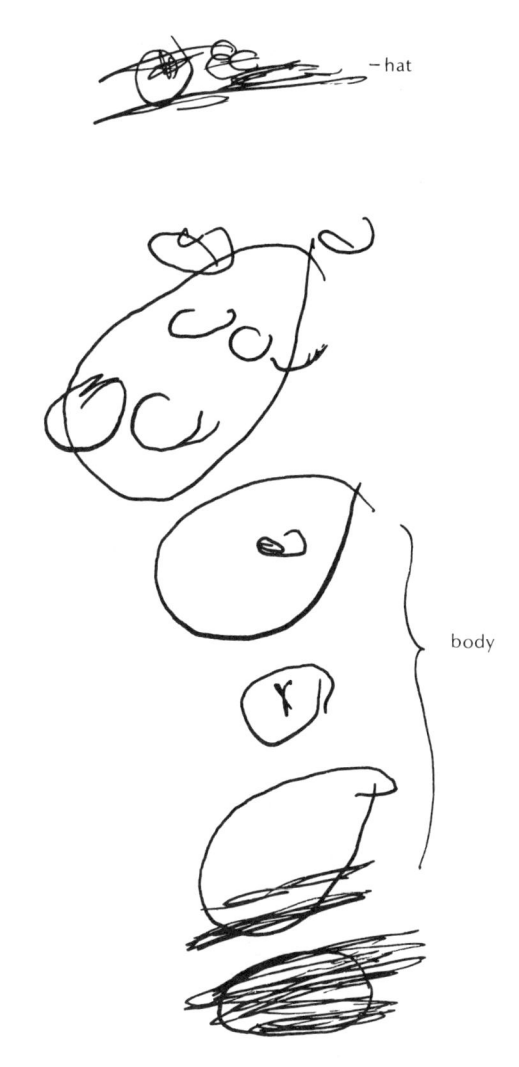

— hat

body

Plate 14.
Johnny, CA 12-1.

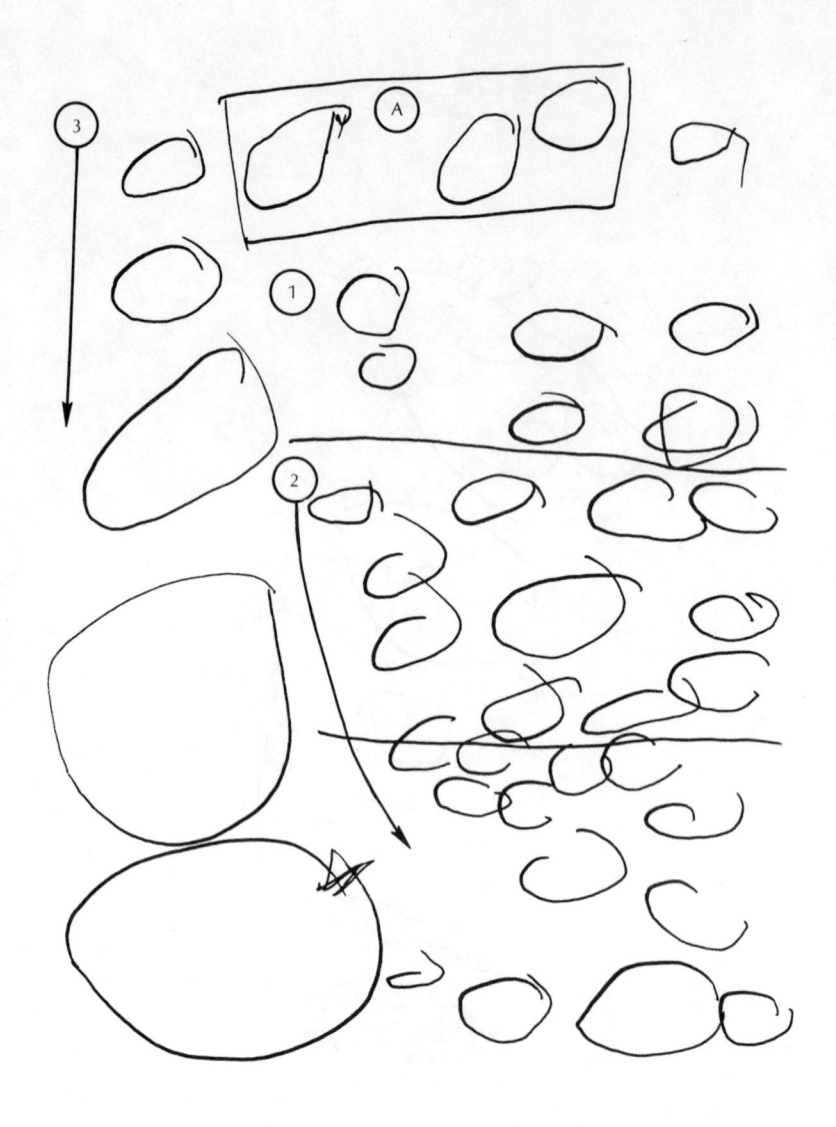

Plate 15.
Johnny, CA 12-1.

communicate with others does not belong in a public school class, not even an LD class. Autistic children, just like any others, are most certainly entitled to an education, but they require special schools and facilities. To date, no "cure" for childhood autism is known and the prognosis for these children is poor. Continued research and experimentation in the treatment and training of autistic children is necessary. But this is outside of the scope of public school LD programs.

Group B: Uncontrollable and Violent Children

Eight children who were excluded from the LD program were either outright psychotic or suffered from psychotic episodes. All of them lost touch with reality, became violent, and could not be controlled at home or in the community. All eight of them were ultimately hospitalized (Table 26).

These eight youngsters—six boys and two girls—were extremely vulnerable and unstable. All of them had suffered from severe deprivation and neglect during the first few years of their lives. Five of the eight were removed from their homes for their own protection and were placed into foster homes. The other three remained in their chaotic and disturbed home situations. All eight children had been exposed to physical abuse, desertion, alcoholism, instability, and mental illness on the part of one or both parents. Three of the mothers were finally institutionalized, after having traumatized their children for long periods of time. Another mother died after years of mental instability.

Prior to the onset of the youngsters' acute mental illness, the eight children had exhibited the type of behavior and learning problems that are characteristic for boys and girls with minimal brain dysfunction. Five of the eight had a history of brain injury, the other three had not been diagnosed as showing brain pathology. It was not possible to find any single cause for any of the children's mental illnesses; it rather appeared that they all were overwhelmed by too many stresses and strains in their total life situation. The youngsters were all acting-out children and all of them seemed to be protesting against the deprivation and maltreatment they had suffered. Their anger and defiance were not unfounded, and, from a logical point of view, not even inappropriate. But uncontrollable violence and bizarre behavior cannot be tolerated by society, especially if it endangers the safety of the children themselves and that of others.

Four of the eight psychotic youngsters had had a long history of mental illness. They had come to the LD program following their discharge from a mental hospital. It is one of the necessary and valuable services of an LD program to provide small, protective classes for children who are returning home after a period of institutionalization, thereby helping the youngsters in their readjustment to the community. Sometimes these efforts are successful, sometimes not. In the case of these four LD pupils, the efforts failed. Within a year or two, all four children had to be returned to the hospital. However, the recurrence of the illness was not related to their school placement. All four pupils were doing reasonably well in the LD classes, but they could not deal with their home situations. As their adjustment and behavior outside of the classroom deteriorated, the pupils also began to act out more in the classroom until they finally could no longer be controlled either at home or in school.

It is not uncommon to find that vulnerable, disturbed children will make good improvement in the controlled, supportive hospital setting (especially if they also receive regular psychotherapy and chemotherapy) only to deteriorate again in their behavior when they are sent home. The unstable, pathological homes they came from usually did not change in their absence. In the home, old conflicts and problems are again brought to life and most of the gains the child made in the hospital are lost. Before long, the youngsters are ready to go back to the hospital. No permanent changes or improvement can be expected until the children are removed from the vicious influences of their homes for long periods of time.

Two of the psychotic pupils, both girls, had seemed remarkably well adjusted when they first came to the special classes. Both had just spent a year in the hospital. But after only a few months at home, they had both become again so disturbed and uncontrollable that they had to go to the hospital for a second time. After a relatively short stay there, the girls again returned home and reentered the LD program. Since no basic changes had occurred in their homes, the youngsters failed again and had to be hospitalized for a third time. It is, of course, possible that the recurring mental illnesses were unavoidable and progressive. Both girls were diagnosed as schizophrenics.

The following three brief case histories of uncontrollable LD pupils will illustrate some of the problems the youngsters presented, and the successes and failures of the LD program in helping them. Pete was a very anxious, small, immature, rather dull, brain-injured boy with extremely poor inner controls and a very low frustration tolerance. He was six years old when he entered the LD program. At that time he was highly disorganized, poorly integrated and coordinated, erratic, and hyperactive. He could not sit still and had frequent violent temper outbursts. It was impossible for Pete to concentrate on any school work and he could not get along with other children. His home situation was chaotic. His mother and father—both heavy drinkers—the father's girlfriend, an assortment of children, and various relatives all lived in two large rooms in a rundown shack. Pete had to fend for himself; he received neither the physical nor the emotional care he needed. He had a past history of convulsions and reported in school that he had "blackout spells" and suffered from dizziness at home, especially when he watched television. Yet, the parents were unwilling or unable to take Pete to a clinic for a thorough evaluation. They rejected the suggestion of the school psychiatrist that Pete might profit from anticonvulsant medication.

Pete was so irrational and unmanageable in the classroom that he had to be temporarily suspended from school. He was placed on home tutoring for the remainder of the school year. By fall, the parents had consented to take him to their family physician who prescribed anticonvulsant medication for Pete. This proved most beneficial. Pete was much better controlled, less erratic, and less explosive in his behavior. He was readmitted to the LD classes. Pete seemed happy in school and did reasonably well for a while, despite serious problems in visual-motor perception and significant learning disabilities.

Then Pete's home situation deteriorated completely. After a period of violent quarrels between the parents, the mother finally chased the father and his girlfriend out of the home. She substituted instead a succession of indifferent, hostile, or abusive "fathers" who took no interest in Pete and his siblings. Some children manage to cope with such situations and are able to seek gratification outside of the home. But a young, hypersensitive, brain-injured child like Pete could not deal with the constant changes and upheavals in the home. Pete needed structure and stability as much as he needed affection, three square meals a day, and a regular dose of medication—he got none of these. He was thoroughly neglected at home and grew increasingly disturbed in school. There was nothing the LD staff could do for Pete. As a last resort, the school social worker called the Society for the Prevention of Cruelty to Children into the case. Pete was removed from his home and placed into a foster home, but it was too late. Despite the efforts of the foster mother and the LD staff, Pete's behavior continued to deteriorate. Pete regressed to the point where he lost touch with reality and had to be hospitalized.

By the time Pete was ten years old his mother had remarried and had settled down to a more stable way of life. While in the hospital, Pete had matured and stabilized. He was permitted to go home again to his natural mother and was readmitted to the LD classes when he was ten-and-one-half years old. By the end of the five year follow-up study Pete had been able to maintain himself successfully in an LD class for a whole school year. He was still on medication. Without it he became extremely restless and disorganized, but with medication he was able to complete his assignments and to participate in class activities. He even showed some slow but steady progress in his achievement. As long as things remain stable at home, Pete will most likely continue in the LD program and will go on to vocational training and the work-study program.

Howard, another brain-injured boy, was referred to the LD classes when he was six-and-one-half years old. Like Pete, he too came from a thoroughly disorganized home with an abusive, alcoholic father. The father deserted the family when Howard was five years old and his well-meaning but ineffectual mother was unable to care for her five children. Howard roamed the streets at will and had little supervision or care. He was extremely explosive, erratic, and aggressive. In contrast to Pete, Howard was of at least average intelligence and had good language ability, and good memory. Despite serious malfunctioning in visual-motor perception, he was able to learn. In the small, well-controlled LD class, with an exceptionally fine, strong teacher, Howard made good academic progress, especially in reading. Arithmetic was hard for him. Outside of the classroom, however, in less structured situations, Howard had frequent violent temper outbursts. As long as he was small he could be physically restrained when he flew into one of his rages. Howard was tall for his age and unusually strong. As he got older it became more difficult to control him.

According to Howard's medical history, he had suffered a brain injury at birth and had had several serious illnesses associated with high fevers in infancy. Since age four-and-one-half, he had suffered from grand mal epilepsy. Howard was on anticonvulsant medicine which his mother administered faithfully. The seizures appeared to be under control; his last major seizure had occurred when he was six years old. In school, Howard was usually cheerful and cooperative in the morning, but by noon his ability to concentrate and to control himself greatly diminished. He became increasingly more restless and more aggressive as the day wore on.

When Howard was eight years old he began starting fights with other children and destroying other people's property. His neighbors began to complain about him. When he was nine years old, he became involved with the law. In school Howard's behavior deteriorated. He became more violent and more difficult to manage. The other children were afraid of him. A complete psychiatric and neurological evaluation and an EEG revealed that Howard's uncontrollable rages were epileptic equivalents. Since they were getting progressively worse, Howard was hospitalized for his own safety when he was ten years old.

In the controlled, stable hospital setting and with the aid of medication, Howard's behavior improved. When Howard was fourteen years old, he returned home and reentered the LD program on a trial visit. This visit was of short duration—after a few weeks it was necessary to send him back to the hospital. Howard seemed to be suffering from a progressive brain disorder.

Another LD pupil who ultimately required hospitalization was Les. Les had lived with his paranoid schizophrenic mother during the first three years of life. Then he was taken from her and placed into a succession of foster homes, but none of the foster homes could cope with the extremely hyperactive and hypersensitive youngster who did not respond to warmth and affection in the way other children respond. Although Les had not been diagnosed as brain-injured, he showed many of the characteristics of a child with minimal brain dysfunction. The traumatic early years of his life had left their mark on Les.

Les was twelve years old when he was referred to the LD program. By then he was a very unhappy, moody, and defiant child who vacillated between periods of depression, when he talked about killing himself, and periods of aggressive acting-out, when he threatened to blow up the school and the foster home. Les' learning problems were relatively minor. He was of above-average intelligence, but produced little or no school work. Les was too upset to be able to concentrate on school work. He needed immediate, intensive psychiatric help. Les was therefore sent to a residential treatment center where he remained for a year. Les' condition continued to deteriorate. Soon, he could no longer be controlled in the open residential school; he presented a serious danger to himself and others. Les had to be referred to a mental hospital.

Hospitalization of youngsters should never be regarded as permanent or final. Many children can and do return successfully to the community after a period of hospitalization. One of the many valuable services the LD program can offer is to accept children who have been discharged from hospitals. There will always be a need for classes for children who are returning from treatment centers and hospitals but who are still too vulnerable to hold their own in regular classes. Every child should have the opportunity to be at home and to attend public school classes of some kind, if there is even a remote chance that he can succeed.

By the end of the five year follow-up study (Table 26), six of the eight uncontrollable, violent LD pupils were still or again in mental hospitals. One child had returned successfully to the LD program while the oldest of the group—by then age 17—had been discharged from the hospital and was living in a foster home. He was working in a store in his community.

Group C: Children With Symbiotic Illnesses

The eight uncontrollable, violent LD pupils who were described in the preceding section had suffered in early childhood from severe parental neglect and deprivation. By contrast, the four LD pupils with symbiotic illnesses, who will be discussed in this section, suffered from a too-close emotional involvement with their mothers. In each of these four cases, the mother was a very disturbed individual who had been unable to recognize her child as a separate, independent human being. Instead the children were treated by their mothers as an extension of their own immature, insecure, and self-centered personalities. The mothers and the children were caught up in one and the same emotional disturbance. All four youngsters were hypersensitive, schizoid boys.

Both the mothers and the children had only a tenuous hold on reality. They lived in their own private worlds. Any move or change on the part of either was a threat to the other. If the child showed any sign of movement toward maturity and independence, the mother would panic; if the mother became more upset or disturbed, the child would also regress in his behavior. The children who were engulfed in such symbiotic relationships could not function on their own, away from their mothers. By necessity, they had difficulty in school. In these cases, the school faced a real dilemma: if the pupils were encouraged to become more independent and if the youngsters began to show an improvement and emotional growth, then the mothers became more upset, whereupon the mothers would keep the children out of school and would try to return them to their former dependent state. Or, even worse, the mothers would become so acutely disturbed that they would lose their precarious emotional balance, and this would in turn add to the child's disturbance. If, on the other hand, the school did not try to change the children's behavior and did not encourage them to grow and to mature, then the teachers and the school staff would be guilty of not fulfilling their job and of contributing to and perpetuating the symbiotic illnesses of the mothers and the children.

The histories of the four pupils with symbiotic illnesses will show the problems involved and why the exclusion of these children from the LD program became unavoidable (Table 26).

One of the four pupils was Brian. When Brian was an infant, his father had had to go overseas with the armed services. During his absence, a very intense, symbiotic relationship developed between the fragile, neurologically impaired child and his emotionally labile mother. When the father returned home after two years abroad, he was regarded as an intruder by both the mother and the son. Brian never did develop a close relationship with his father.

Soon after Brian entered kindergarten, his mother became mentally ill and had to be institutionalized. The strain of having to send her child to school had been more than she could cope with. Brian felt deserted and developed serious emotional problems. He had great difficulty adjusting to school; he was quiet and withdrawn and did not participate in school activities. Since he did not bother others, however, he was passed from one grade to the next. When Brian's mother was discharged from the hospital, mother and son clung to each other more than ever.

As Brian got older, he grew increasingly more negative toward school. He missed no opportunity to inform his teachers how much he hated school. He was only happy when he was at home with his mother.

When Brian was nine-and-one-half years old he was referred to the LD program since he produced no work in school and appeared to be quite disturbed. He was found to be a very vulnerable, poorly integrated, schizoid boy of normal intelligence. His IQ score was 91. He had very poor visual-motor perception, but since his language development and his visual memory were good he had no difficulty reading (when he could be persuaded to do so). Brian was moody, distractible and unpredictable. He was at times completely withdrawn; at other times he was disruptive and defiant. He could not relate to his peers and was distrustful of adults. Most of the time he just sat and indulged in fantasies about his paranoid schizophrenic mother.

As was pointed out before, a child who *can* learn *will* learn, often in spite of himself. Thus it was with Brian. He made good academic progress in the LD program even though he was convinced that he hated school. When he first came, his reading score on the Wide Range Achievement Test was 4.2, his spelling score was 3.3, and his arithmetic score was 2.2. After seven months in the special classes, Brian showed a gain of 1.2 grade levels in reading, .4 grades in spelling, and 1.6 grade levels in arithmetic. Thus, at age ten he was able to read at the fifth grade level and was writing and doing arithmetic at the end-of-third grade level. But his work was sporadic and uneven. Yet, ever so slowly Brian became more positive toward school and a little bit more interested in his work. He derived some satisfaction from his achievement and began to act a bit more mature and independent. This was more than his mother could tolerate.

She restricted Brian to the home after school, did not let him out of the house on weekends, and tried to control his every move and thought. Brian rebelled. A brief struggle ensued between the mother and the son. Then the strain proved to be too much for the mother, her emotional condition deteriorated to the point where she had to be again hospitalized. This was most upsetting for Brian and he too began to regress in his behavior until, finally, he could no longer be contained in the LD class. He lost all interest in school, ran from the school building whenever he was not watched, and retreated into a world of fantasy. His whole being seemed to revolve around his mother. After she was taken away from him, Brian ceased to be able to function in school. Soon he too had to be referred to a residential treatment center for his own protection.

It is not certain whether the mother would again have become acutely ill and required rehospitalization in any event, or if this was entirely the result of Brian's move toward independence and greater maturity. It is difficult to see how the boy could have been kept from learning and maturing while in school. However, a closer contact with the mother should have been maintained by the LD staff. It should also have been recognized from the outset that Brian had a serious emotional problem that necessitated more intensive treatment and help than the LD program could offer.

Another child in Group C was Jody. Jody was an obese, infantilized, twelve-year-old boy of high average intelligence (WISC Full Scale IQ 115). He had suffered a brain injury at birth and had been a sickly infant. According to the family physician, Jody was in good physical health, aside from being overweight, when he came to the LD program. His emotionally disturbed mother was unable to tolerate any separation from Jody. Her need to be close to her son was intensified by her husband's frequent absences from home. The father's work included much travelling and long periods away from his family. The mother made constant excuses to keep Jody at home. If he showed the least sniffle, headache, or scratch, the mother would keep Jody out of school. She succeeded in turning him into a real hypochondriac and a totally passive, dependent semi-invalid. His absences exceeded his presences in school. When the LD staff insisted that Jody had to come to class and charged him with truancy, the mother's precarious emotional equilibrium broke down. She became extremely agitated and disturbed. Jody, in turn, developed many somatic symptoms and became so tense and anxious that referral to a residential treatment center was recommended. Jody was given a psychiatric exclusion from the LD program. When steps were initiated by the school for Jody's referral, the mother panicked. She packed up her family and moved secretly to another state to avoid any possible separation from her son. Since she left no forwarding address, a follow-up of this case was not possible.

The third LD pupil with a symbiotic disorder was Milton. His whole family—mother, father, older sister, and Milton—had an extremely close relationship and maintained a delicate emotional balance among themselves. All four were exceedingly bright but labile. They lived a very secluded, quiet life and did not bother anybody. Both parents held jobs that did not involve much interaction with other people. The sister was quiet and hardworking. She was a superior high school student.

Milton had minimal brain dysfunction due to a serious illness with high fever in infancy. He was poorly coordinated, hypertalkative, and had very poor visual-motor perception. He had always been regarded as "unusual" by his peers, and they avoided him. In the small, structured elementary school he had been able to hold his own, after a fashion, and was a fair student. His achievement bore no relationship to his very superior intelligence (IQ 138). Milton's serious difficulties began when he entered middle school. He was threatened by the large school and could not function in the less structured, (for him) confusing environment. New situations and changes were hard for Milton.

Like many children with neurological impairment, Milton was basically an impulsive, poorly integrated boy who had learned to control his impulsivity by means of compulsive and rigid behavior. He was extremely fastidious and compulsive about his dress, about his language, and about his actions. Milton was so mannered and rigid in his behavior that he became the laughingstock of his classmates. They taunted him unmercifully and called him a "sissy" and a "mama's boy" and worse. Milton responded to his tormentors with verbal aggression and with frequent violent temper outbursts. He had a very low frustration tolerance and could not stand to be teased. When faced with too much inner stress and frustration, Milton's rigid, compulsive behavior gave way to impulsiveness and explosiveness. For his own protection, Milton was transferred to the LD program when he was twelve years old.

Milton's adjustment to the LD program was good. He felt comfortable in the supportive, small classes and was able to relax. In fact, he felt so at ease that he decided to join the other "regular" LD pupils in his class and tried to be like them. Milton deliberately changed his immaculate, formal attire (he always wore a white shirt, tie, and jacket), his utterly correct language, and his very proper, compulsive behavior. He began to imitate the rather sloppy appearance, the often-vulgar utterances, and the more boisterous, sometimes aggressive behavior of his classmates. Milton succeeded remarkably well in his efforts. He became more outgoing, more casual, and more independent. He even gained the respect of his peers and was included in their games. Milton was very much pleased with himself.

But what was regarded as "progress" in school was viewed as a threat by Milton's emotionally unstable mother. She could not tolerate seeing her "baby," "her little boy" grow up. She desperately tried to maintain her hold on Milton. The conflict that developed between the mother and the son upset the entire delicate family structure. In the past, Milton's compulsivity had served as an effective defense against his impulsivity and against his poor inner control. When he relaxed his defenses and changed his behavior, he became much more vulnerable. As long as he was in the protective LD class where he received encouragement and support, he could function well and was happy, but outside of school, when he was on his own, Milton was suddenly quite defenseless. He could no longer barricade himself behind his rigid compulsivity. The conflict with his mother produced intense anxiety and much strain. Milton could not cope with the situation and lost control of himself. He suffered a psychotic episode at home and violently attacked his mother. He also lost control in school and attacked his teacher. Milton was hospitalized for a period of observation. When he was able to leave the hospital, he was placed on home-tutoring for the remainder of the school year. At home, Milton was again quiet, restrained, and docile. Once again, the family balance had been restored. A year later, Milton was enrolled in a private school for children with emotional problems.

In Milton's case, the LD staff had been at fault in encouraging his desire to change and to become independent without any concern for or consideration of his family situation. In a special class program, it is essential to know not only each child's problems but also his home situation and the interrelationships of the various family members. In some instances, a child should be slowed down and stopped from

Pupils Referred for Hospitalization

changing too drastically or too quickly if such a change would upset a precarious family balance and would result in an intensification of problems for the child and for his parents. Whenever a marked change occurs in a child during his stay in the LD classes, it is important to discuss such changes with the parents and to offer them guidance and help in coping with the new situation. There was too little of this done in Milton's case. Whatever contact the LD staff had with the parents was too limited and occurred too late to be effective.

The fourth of the LD pupils in Group C was Dan. Dan was an eight-year-old, hypersensitive, anxious, and neurologically impaired youngster of dull average intelligence (IQ 87). When first seen, Dan drew a picture of a boy inside a block of ice standing out in the rain. This drawing is shown on Plate 16. The picture vividly reflects Dan's actual situation. He was indeed trapped or frozen in the tight embrace of his emotionally unstable mother. He could not move on his own. The falling rain on the drawing symbolizes the acute anxiety that overwhelmed Dan, but he was helpless; he could not "get out of the rain," so to speak. For three years Dan remained in the LD program. He was a tense, withdrawn, unhappy youngster who tried hard to please adults. Dan was a social isolate and his peers rejected him. His attitude toward school and learning was positive, and Dan took pride in his reading ability. However, Dan suffered from severe malfunctioning in visual-motor perception and his achievement in arithmetic was defective.

Gradually, as Dan got older, he began to be a little more outgoing in school. At home Dan began to rebel against his mother's restrictions and infantilization of him. He displayed violent temper outbursts and bizarre behavior at home. No such behavior occurred in school. Dan's mother was profoundly disturbed by her son's change in behavior. The father remained as aloof and ineffectual as he had always been. Fortunately, Dan's mother was an intelligent woman with good insight into the seriousness of her own and her son's problems. She had enough wisdom and strength to seek professional help for herself and for Dan. She even consented to placing Dan into the children's division of the mental hospital temporarily, while she herself sought psychotherapy. This move proved to be most beneficial to both mother and son.

When Dan returned home almost a year later, he reentered the LD program. He was still quiet, hypersensitive, and somewhat withdrawn, but he appeared to be much less unhappy and did much better in his school work. Dan even got along better with his peers. His mother, in turn, was less possessive and controlling of Dan. She had become involved in community activities and no longer centered all her energies

Children with Learning Disabilities

"boy going to be six years old, walking in the rain. It is so cold he is in an ice cube. These are the raindrops."

Plate 16.
Dan, CA 8-8.

The author has transcribed Dan's description of the drawing at the lower right.

and attention on her son. The total home situation had improved; even the father became more involved with Dan. Inevitably, there was still and probably always will be a very close relationship between Dan and his mother, but it was no longer excessively close or pathological. Dan continued to gain in independence and progressed well in the LD program. He will go into the vocational training program in the years ahead.

The long range prognosis for children with symbiotic disorders appears to be uncertain. As was shown on Table 26, the status of each of the four youngsters in Group C differed at the end of the five year follow-up study: Dan had returned successfully to the LD program; Milton did well in a private school for children with emotional problems and after graduation from there he went on to college. Brian still remained in the hospital; the whereabouts of Jody were unknown.

The histories of the four youngsters described above indicate *how extremely important it is for a child's teacher and for the clinical staff of the LD program to be aware of the pupils' whole family situation and of the children's relationship with their parents.* It is essential to know to what extent the children's problems are part of a family problem and to what degree the pupils' difficulties are their own. A child who is disturbed because he experienced too much neglect and rejection at home will require different handling in school from one who got too much of the wrong kind of affection from his parents. If a symbiotic relationship between a mother and child exists (or between a father and child), then the school has to proceed with great caution and should not permit the child to move or change too rapidly.

The LD staff, especially the school social worker, should give the parents maximum support and should try to gain their confidence. Any marked changes in the child's behavior may be interpreted by the mother as a hostile act or as a conspiracy of the school against her. The change in the child has to be explained to the parents. Close contact with the parents of LD pupils is essential at all times. In some instances, problems within a family may interfere with the pupil's progress in school, but the situation may be too involved and deepseated for the school to handle. The best an LD staff can do in such cases is to encourage the parents to seek professional help for themselves and for the child.

Group D: Severely Disturbed Parent-Child Relationships

The seven LD pupils in Group D suffered from severe disturbances in their relationship with their parents. Whereas the eight uncontrollable youngsters in Group B had been emotionally deprived and neglected, the pupils in Group D were not so much neglected as rejected by their parents. Just like the four children with symbiotic disorders in Group C, the seven boys in Group D had a very intense emotional involvement with their parents. But where the former had been too closely attached to their mothers, the latter were caught in a negative—or at least in a highly ambivalent—bind with their parents. Over the years, a vicious cycle had developed in the parent-child relationship that colored the children's interpersonal relationships and attitudes outside the home also and affected their progress in the LD program.

The case histories of the seven pupils in Group D showed that both the parents and the children had contributed to the unhealthy family relationships. Most of the youngsters had been "difficult" (Thomas, Chess, and Birch, 1970) since birth. The parents too were unstable individuals and/or were involved in marital strife. By and large, however, the children did not really develop serious emotional and behavior problems until they started school.

All seven pupils in Group D had minimal brain dysfunction and all had learning disabilities. They were all immature and unable to adjust to the demands of regular school classes. Their achievement was poor. The parents were both concerned for and disappointed in their children. They began to pressure their youngsters for good behavior and for better achievement. This created much anxiety and feelings of inadequacy in the children since they could not possibly produce what was expected of them. Constant frustration and failure made the children discouraged and negativistic. This, in turn, increased the parents' displeasure and led to their rejection of the youngsters. Some parents then felt guilty and began to overindulge their children; some mothers were quite inconsistent and vacillated between periods of overt rejection and periods of indulgence of their children. Subconsciously, the parents usually *knew* that their children really had problems and that they themselves were contributing to these problems, but they just could not admit this to themselves. Instead, the parents became more punitive toward the children, while the children became more and more frustrated and angry.

By the time the pupils were referred to the LD program, they presented serious emotional problems in school and showed little or no motivation for learning. They were angry and negativistic youngsters whose achievement was extremely poor and who could not get along with other children or with adults. All attempts to help the children with their learning problems were unsuccessful as long as the children persisted in their hostile attitude toward themselves, toward others and toward the school. A change in attitude depended mainly on a change in the parent-child relationship. As long as the vicious cycle in the home continued, no real change could be brought about in the pupils' attitude and behavior in school.

In time the boys' behavior and adjustment in school got worse rather than better. A temporary separation of the children from their parents appeared to be the only way to break the severely disturbed parent-child relationship that existed. Initially, the parents were entirely opposed to any such suggestion by the LD staff. It was not until the pupils were finally excluded from the LD classes that the parents agreed to a temporary separation from their children. Only then were they willing to place their youngsters in either a residential school for children with emotional problems or in the children's division of the state hospital. Once this was accomplished, the parents were able to say that they wished they had done so earlier. In each instance, the parents and the children both benefitted from this separation.

As indicated on Table 26, by the end of the five year follow-up study, two of the seven pupils in Group D had been able to return to regular classes after one or two years in a residential school. Three youngsters returned successfully to the LD classes and showed good improvement in their attitude and achievement. One child, who was excluded after three years in the LD classes, was still in the hospital two years later. It is probable that his hospital stay would have been much shorter if he had been sent there two years earlier. The seventh boy in Group D moved to an unknown location after one year in a residential school. No follow-up report could be obtained for him.

In each case, the separation of the parents and the children was the key to reversing the vicious cycle. In the more neutral and stable setting of the residential schools or the hospital, the children were able to control themselves; their behavior and attitudes improved. They also benefitted from therapy and from the medication that some of them received. The more the children improved, the more pleased the parents were. Parental disapproval and rejection gradually changed into approval and acceptance. There is no stronger motivating force for a child than his parents' approval. As the children showed gains in their behavior and achievement, the parents began to accept them more fully. This process took time, of course; there were many ups and downs in the parent-child relationships. Yet, the overall results of the temporary separation of the youngsters and their families were extremely successful.

In retrospect, it appears that the LD staff's efforts to keep youngsters whose relationships with their parents were severely disturbed in the special classes as long as possible before excluding them, were not always in the best interests of either the children or the parents. An earlier insistence on a separation of the parents and the children might have resulted in more benefits sooner for all concerned. The case of Leo is presented here to illustrate this point.

Leo was the youngest child and only son in his family. He had three older sisters. Leo was just six years old when he was referred to the LD program. He was an aggressive, hostile, and immature boy of normal intellectual potential. He suffered from severe malfunction in visual-motor perception and in auditory perception. Leo had been medically diagnosed as being brain-injured. His parents were both rather unstable and neurotic individuals. They were quite ambivalent in their relationships to each other and to Leo. They were very inconsistent in the treatment of their son.

The parents took it for granted that their children would be good students and were deeply disappointed when Leo "failed" kindergarten. One day they would work with Leo after school in an attempt to help him with his school assignments—they would even try to bribe him with money and toys to get him to do better in school—only to punish him the next day for his failure to learn. Marital problems further complicated the situation at home. The parents used Leo as a pawn in their quarrels with each other. If the home situation had been totally negative, Leo would at least have known where he stood. Then he could have been angry with his parents without having to feel guilty about it, but the parents' unpredictable outpourings of love and disapproval, of help and rejection, and of reward and punishment was confusing and was more than Leo could cope with. He reacted to this inconsistency with violent temper outbursts, rages, destruction of property and theft from the parents. In school, he was extremely negative, aggressive and destructive. Leo did very little work in class. His poor showing in school led to more rejection and punishment by the parents who then felt guilty about their feelings toward Leo. Once again they indulged him until a new incident evoked a new round of hostility and anger.

It took no less than three years of intensive work on the part of the school social worker, the principal, the teacher, the psychologist, and the consulting psychiatrist to convince the parents that Leo required psychiatric treatment, that he could not be helped in school as long as he remained at home and as long as the parents did not change their attitudes and actions regarding their son. Finally, after Leo was suspended for the third time from the LD classes, the parents consented to sending Leo to a hospital and they sought counseling help for themselves.

The results were remarkable. The parents volunteered later that they wished they had followed the recommendations of the LD staff earlier. The family relationships improved greatly after treatment was started. For the first time, the parents were able to enjoy Leo. When he came home on weekends he was a different child; he was much calmer and more stable in his behavior than he had ever been before; he also seemed much happier. He even looked better. Formerly, Leo had been pasty and pudgy in appearance. He now developed into a slim, good-looking youngster. When he was discharged from the hospital a year later, he came into a changed family situation. The parents had modified their attitudes toward each other and toward Leo. A fresh beginning could be made by the whole family. Leo returned to the LD program in the fall of that year.

LD staff members who had known Leo and his family for several years could not help but wonder how long this change would last. How long would it be before Leo and his labile parents would regress to their former state? To everyone's delight, at the end of the five year follow-up study a year later, Leo was still holding his own in the LD class. His attitude toward school was positive and his peer relationships were reasonably good. He was, of course, still a very vulnerable child and still had serious learning problems. Despite average intelligence, at age twelve, Leo was functioning barely on the second grade level in reading. The long range prognosis for Leo is guarded. It is certain that without a temporary separation from home Leo could not have done as well as he was doing at the end of the follow-up study. It is also probable that he would have done even better if he had been sent away to a residential school earlier and for a longer period of time.

Another boy in Group D was Claude. Claude had been extremely aggressive and hyperactive in regular kindergarten and first grade. He learned nothing. He was seven years old when he came to the LD program. He had low average intelligence and a severe language problem. He was also a very hostile and frustrated boy who resented his bright older brother. Claude projected his anger onto his peers. His parents were well meaning but older people, set in their ways, who regarded Claude's failure to learn as a sign of "laziness" on the part of the boy and as a sign of incompetence on the part of the school. They would not or could not accept the fact that Claude had severe learning problems due to neurological impairment. It meant nothing to them that Claude had been a premature baby who had weighed less than four pounds at birth, nor that he did not begin to say words until he was three years old, and did not talk in sentences until he was five years old. The parents rejected the medical diagnosis of brain injury and disregarded the abnormal EEG. They *knew* that there was nothing wrong with Claude; after all, he looked normal, he could reason, he was well-coordinated, and he was clever with his hands. It was obvious to them that Claude was not retarded. Therefore, he was just plain lazy and there was no reason why he could not talk better if he only tried harder. That was the whole story as far as the parents were concerned.

The parents were entirely unable to understand or to accept the idea that a child might not be able to learn to read because of poor auditory perception or because of problems in sequencing and in the association of sounds and symbols. The parents kept pressuring and punishing Claude so he would learn better, and Claude kept rebelling and became more and more defiant and aggressive. The vicious cycle continued. The parents would not even consider the idea of getting psychiatric help for Claude or counseling for themselves. They had no confidence in the school or in the recommendations of the LD staff. The LD staff finally decided to force the issue after two years of frustration, and suspended Claude from the special classes because of his extremely aggressive behavior. Only then were the parents willing to send him to a residential school for children with emotional and learning problems.

Once Claude was out of the home his behavior changed almost overnight. He was much happier and got along better with other children. Even his visits home on weekends were harmonious and the parent-child relationship improved greatly. Claude remained in the private school for two years. Then the tuition of the private school was raised to such a level that the parents could no longer afford it, even with the help of state aid. Claude returned home and reentered the LD program. He was by then a friendly, more mature eleven-year-old boy and was well-liked by his peers. He still had serious learning problems. His academic progress, especially in reading, had been very slow. However, by now even the parents had begun to recognize that Claude really *did* have learning disabilities and that he was not "just lazy." They even admitted that it was not all "the school's fault." They were finally able to accept their son as he was and were satisfied that he would receive vocational training in school and that he could become self-supporting some day. It is unlikely that the parents would have reached this level of acceptance if Claude had not gone away to the residential school. The parents did not trust the public schools, but when the expensive private school could not "make" Claude learn any better, they were willing to acknowledge that he really *could* not learn any better.

Group E: Asocial and Delinquent Children

The three LD pupils in Group E were excluded from the special classes because of aggressive and asocial behavior in school, on the school bus, and in the community. All three were acting-out youngsters with serious character disorders. They did not know right from wrong and were unmanageable in the LD program. Since the children received no supervision or control at home, it was believed that placement in a residential school was essential for the youngsters' own future welfare and for the protection of the community.

All three pupils were boys, and all were between eleven-and-one-half and twelve-and-one-half years old when they first came to the LD program. In many ways these three boys resembled other LD pupils. All three were poorly integrated, restless, hyperactive, and explosive youngsters with low frustration tolerances and serious malfunction in visual-motor and/or auditory perception and in abstract reasoning. They were all of low average intelligence. All three came from socially and economically deprived families and had to fend for themselves at an early age. The mothers of these boys were limited mentally and emotionally unstable. The children never received the love and care and supervision they needed. They were emotionally as well as physically deprived and neglected.

The three delinquent pupils did not come to the LD classes until they were preadolescent. By that time they were well set in their ways. Their emotional and behavior disorders were so extreme by then that, by comparison, their learning disabilities were of less significance. After seven years of nothing but failure in regular classes, including time out for suspensions and repetition of grades, the youngsters had developed deep-seated and thoroughly negative attitudes toward school, toward teachers, and toward learning. There was little the LD program could offer these boys that was of any interest to them. Their attendance in the special classes was poor. When they did put in their appearance they made no attempt to cooperate with the teacher or to work on their assignments, but they never failed to be highly destructive and disruptive influences on the other LD pupils.

Emotionally, the three asocial boys were very immature. Like infants, they wanted what they wanted, when they wanted it, without regard for others. When they did not get what they wanted, they flew into a rage and became abusive and destructive. They were only out for themselves and were hostile toward peers and adults alike. Nothing seemed to impress them. They were apparently devoid of guilt feelings and anxiety. They never admitted to being wrong and showed no desire to change, willingness to delay their pleasure, or to work for their gratification.

Finally all three boys were excluded from the special classes. The mothers of two of the boys went along with the recommendations of the LD staff and placed their sons into residential schools for boys. The third mother refused to do so. Her son was given home-tutoring instead. At the end of the five year follow-up study (Table 26), all three youngsters were seventeen or eighteen years old. By then one of them, the brightest of the three, was still in the residential school and was doing quite well. The dullest of the three asocial boys had become a school dropout at sixteen and had become involved with the police. At age seventeen, he was living at home, was unemployed, and was on probation. The third boy had also dropped out of school at age sixteen and also lived at home. However, he was holding a job in the community, when last heard from.

The experience with the three asocial, delinquent preadolescent boys showed that these kinds of youngsters do not belong in an LD program even though they have learning disabilities. A poorly integrated child of low average intelligence who has been exposed to continuous neglect and deprivation at home has little chance of benefiting from the special classes unless he is sent to the LD program at a very young age. If such a child comes to the special classes early enough, the LD program might be able to provide at least one area in the youngster's life that is positive and supportive. Perhaps, however, even that would not be enough. For many deprived and neglected children the only solution may be to have dormitories associated with the public school LD program where the pupils can live during the week so as to cut down as much as possible their exposure to their homes and neighborhoods, without actually taking the children from their families. The youngsters would still go home on weekends and holidays.

Once such children are nine years old, or even eleven or twelve years old, and once they have developed a real character disorder, the LD program can do little to help them. Then, more drastic steps are indicated in order to reach the children. *Delinquent, acting-out youngsters with character disorders should not be admitted to an LD program.* Whenever it can be predicted with a high degree of certainty that a child cannot benefit from an LD program and that he will have to be excluded from it sooner or later, it is not only unwise but also unfair to admit him to the program in the first place. Under such circumstances, admittance to the LD program and subsequent exclusion from it will only add to his failure experience and will delay the referral of the child to a more appropriate school or treatment center.

Chapter 7

Pupils Who Were Withdrawn and Those Who Returned

PUPILS WHO WERE WITHDRAWN FROM THE LD PROGRAM

Seventeen LD pupils who appeared to be well-placed in the special classes were withdrawn from the LD program by their parents or by the local school districts that sent the children to the LD program in the first place. The reasons for withdrawing the youngsters varied. Table 27 shows who withdrew the pupils, the types of classes they were transferred to, and the youngsters' adjustment at the end of the five year follow-up study.

Thirteen of these 17 LD pupils were withdrawn by their parents. The parents of nine boys took their children from the LD classes primarily because they were unable or unwilling to admit that their children had learning and/or emotional problems. In each case, the parents had been opposed to the special class placement of their son from the outset. A child's adjustment to the special classes is, of course, strongly influenced by his parents' attitudes toward the program. As might be expected therefore, the adjustment of the nine boys to the LD program had not been exceptionally good. None had shown any marked improvement in his achievement or in his behavior. The children objected as much to their placement in the program as their parents did. The lack of

Table 27.

Pupils who were withdrawn from LD program.

N	Pupils withdrawn at request of:	New class placement	Adjustment to new class placement
8	parents	home school, regular class	2 good 5 poor 1 poor, returned to LD program
1	parents	private school then home school, regular class	1 poor
3	parents	private school	3 good
4	school district	home school, special class	3 good 1 poor, returned to LD program
1	child	school dropout, home pregnant	
17			

significant progress or change in the youngsters only increased the determination of the parents to get their children out of the LD program, to free them from the "stigma" that they felt was attached to special class placement.

The parents of three other children, also all boys, were initially quite agreeable to having their youngsters in the special classes. They were aware of their sons' difficulties in school, but after one or two years, when their children's behavior and learning problems did not totally vanish, they became disillusioned with the LD program. Perhaps some of them had been unwittingly encouraged to have unrealistic or false hopes as to what special education could accomplish for their youngsters. Or perhaps the parents' expectations were unduly raised by the spurt in achievement that the pupils displayed when they first came to the LD classes. As was shown earlier (p. 63) this initial rate of improvement is seldom if ever maintained in subsequent years (Silberberg and Silberberg, 1969). Or, in time, the parents might have realized some of the negative aspects of having a child in the program (e.g., criticism by relatives, teasing by other children, different school placement from the child's siblings and friends, riding a different school bus from other neighborhood children, etc.). These are real problems and have to be dealt with. Some parents begin to feel that the disadvantages of special class placement might outweigh the obvious advantages of such placement. And, finally, there is the common fallacy that is frequently voiced by parents and children after the youngsters have been in an LD program for a year or more: They claim that the children's difficulties at home and in the community are the *result* of their going to a special class, when in reality the children were referred to the LD program *because* they had problems not only in school but also at home and in the community. Children and parents tend to forget the difficulties that existed prior to the youngsters' enrollment in the special classes.

The LD staff put forth a great deal of effort to change the attitudes of dissatisfied parents and children. These efforts were not always successful. The parents of the twelve LD pupils here under discussion were adamant in their desire to get their sons out of the LD program and back into regular classes or to some socially more acceptable private school. Parental pressure can be very strong indeed, and eight of the home school administrators yielded to the parents' wishes. Contrary to the LD staff's recommendations, the children were withdrawn from the special classes and were returned to regular classes. In most cases it was possible for the LD staff to help in working out a modified program for these children in their home schools.

Four other boys were sent to private residential or day schools for children with learning disabilities. It is much easier for many parents to say that their son or daughter is going to a private school than to have to admit that their child is in a "special class" in a public school. Too often the term "special class" is still equated in the minds of the general public with "mental retardation." If the private school is able to meet the child's needs and if the parents are able to afford the tuition without undue hardship for the rest of the family, then there may be actually an advantage in sending the child to such a school. For if the private school placement meets with the parents' approval, this fact alone will reduce the pressure on the child and will enable him to get the maximum benefit from school attendance.

All four children who were enrolled in private schools showed good progress. That is, they did as well academically as they were able to do, and their behavior improved markedly, especially while they were away from home. One family was forced to withdraw their child from a private school after one year when the school's tuition was raised. The boy returned to a regular class in his home school on a modified schedule.

Thus, ultimately nine of the twelve pupils who had been withdrawn by their parents from the LD program attended regular classes. How did they fare in these classes? In retrospect, one could have predicted the success and failure of these nine boys. Their progress in the regular classes was quite consistent with that of the former LD pupils who had been returned to regular classes on the recommendations of the LD staff (p. 65). It again was found that *the children's behavior and their attitude toward school, their work habits, and their ability to get along with adults and peers were more important for a satisfactory adjustment in regular classes than their achievement.*

Two of the nine LD pupils who returned to regular classes at their parents' insistence made a good adjustment. They were friendly, quiet, non-acting-out boys who were much loved and accepted by their parents *as they were.* In both cases, the parents recognized not only the youngsters' problems but also their assets. The parents did not believe that their children would benefit from a prolonged stay in the LD program. As it turned out, the parents were correct in their judgment.

One of the boys, Jimmy, was only 5 years 9 months old when he came to the LD program after an unsuccessful year in kindergarten. He was much too immature and shy to get along in a regular class. Jimmy had low average mental ability (Stanford-Binet IQ 86) while most of the youngsters in his school were of above-average intelligence. When Jimmy entered kindergarten he was one of the youngest children in his class and one of the dullest ones. His mental age was only on the four-year-old level. He was in no way ready for a big public school class. Above all, Jimmy needed *time to mature.* He showed no specific learning disabilities or serious emotional problems. Rather, Jimmy displayed an overall developmental lag. He had been slow in learning to walk and talk. He was small in build and could easily pass for a child one or two years younger than his chronological age. Jimmy got along well with his younger brothers and was well liked by other younger children in the neighborhood. The parents insisted that there was nothing "wrong" with Jimmy other than his being very immature. Jimmy came from a close-knit family and the parents wanted him in the same school with his brothers.

Jimmy spent two years in the LD classes where he was permitted to grow and develop at his own rate. He was given much perceptual and motor training, language stimulation, and the opportunity to interact and to play with other children who were on his own level. Jimmy was happy in school and did well. When he first came to the LD program he was functioning emotionally, socially, and academically on the prekindergarten level. Two years later he looked and functioned like an immature six and a half year old boy. When the parents began to push for his return to regular classes Jimmy also began to voice misgivings about being in the LD program. He wanted to go to his brothers' school.

It is entirely feasible that there would have been no need to refer Jimmy to the LD program if his parents had kept him out of school for one more year and had sent him instead to a nursery school, and/or if the school had had a prekindergarten and prefirst grade class for immature children like Jimmy, but since this had not been the case, referral to the LD classes served a valuable function for Jimmy. Without the small, protective, low-pressure LD classes Jimmy might readily have developed serious emotional and behavior problems since he could not possibly hold his own with his peers. He had already become quite shy and timid after only one unsuccessful year in kindergarten. Jimmy's shyness and unhappiness are vividly reflected on the Human Figure Drawing he made when he first came to the LD classes. Plate 17a shows a pathetic boy who has withdrawn into himself; the poorly integrated figure has neither mouth, nor nose, nor any legs to stand on, he just balances himself on unattached clumpy feet.

In the LD classes Jimmy quickly lost his timidity, as can be seen by the cheerful grin on his second drawing, shown on Plate 17b. There was a consensus that Jimmy was a good candidate for return to regular classes, but there was no agreement as to when this should take place. The LD staff recommended that Jimmy remain a total of three years in the LD program before returning to regular classes. The parents were unwilling to wait that long. They withdrew Jimmy after only two years in the LD classes.

Jimmy was seven years nine months old when he entered a regular first grade class. Thus, in effect, he "lost" two years while in the LD program, but since he was small and immature, Jimmy looked no different from other first graders, nor was his behavior and his achievement markedly different from that of other dull average pupils in the first grade. By the end of the five year follow-up study, Jimmy was 10 years 6 months old. He had completed three successful years in regular classes and was a well-adjusted third grader. He was popular with other children, loved school and his teacher, and was getting passing grades in all subjects. There is no doubt that Jimmy will continue to hold his own in regular classes, for he has a pleasant personality, a good attitude toward school and work, just enough ability to get by, and, above all, a stable and supporting home.

There was, in fact, nothing an additional year in the LD program

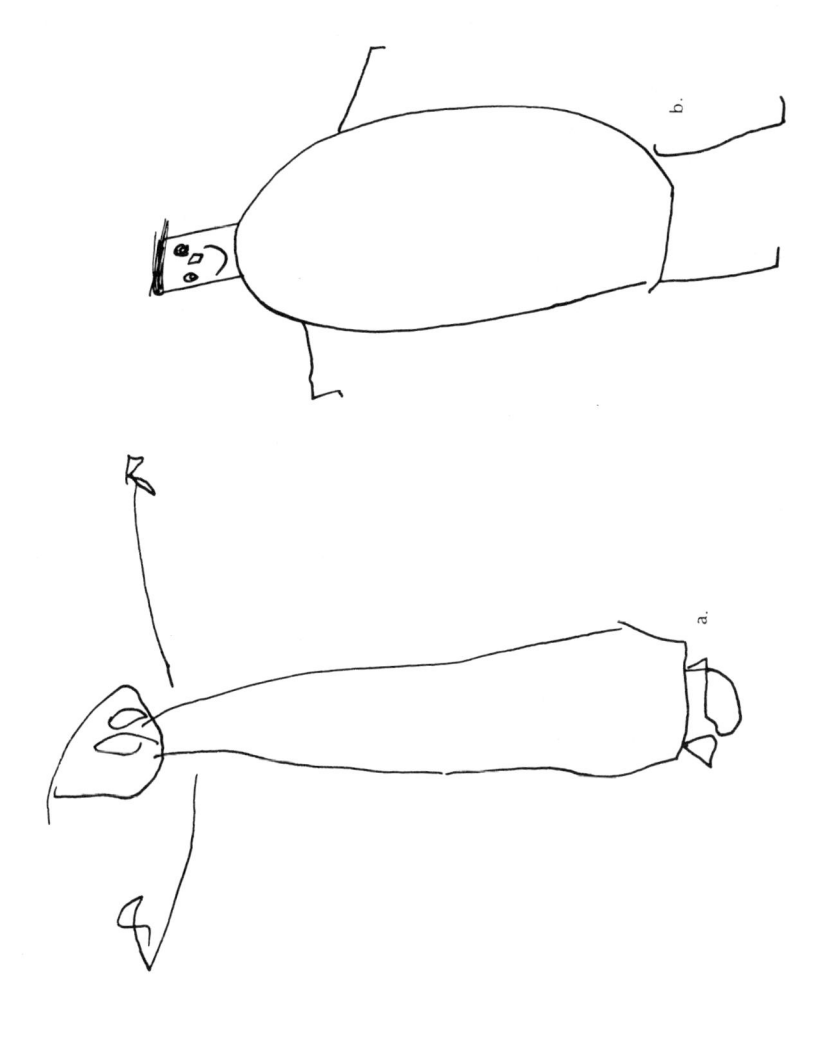

Plate 17.
Jimmy.
a., CA 5-11;
b., CA 7-5.

could have done for Jimmy that he did not get in the regular first grade. A major part of Jimmy's success must be credited to the parents' wisdom. They were willing to let Jimmy reenter the regular classes at the first grade level where he was comfortable, even though he lost two years by doing so. Most parents would have insisted that he go into a second or even a third grade class. Jimmy could not have succeeded in a regular second or third grade; he needed at least two extra years to compensate for his developmental lag. His parents were willing to give him this extra time.

The second youngster who made a good adjustment to regular classes after being withdrawn from the LD program by his parents was Vincent. Vincent was an attractive, outgoing, talented boy of average intelligence (WISC IQ score 100) with a severe reading disability. He was referred to the LD program when he was twelve years old. Despite years of remedial reading and tutoring in elementary school, he was still only reading on the second grade level. His teachers and the principal hoped that the LD program might be able to help Vincent with his reading since the home school had been unsuccessful in its efforts. Vincent had much difficulty keeping up with his assignments in middle school. He was beginning to show signs of frustration and anger and started to develop, for the first time, serious behavior problems in school.

Vincent and his parents, both artists, were bitterly opposed to the special class placement. The parents accepted Vincent's reading problem along with his artistic talent as part of his family inheritance. Two of his uncles, his father, and one of his brothers also had reading problems. However, their difficulties were less severe than Vincent's. The parents considered Vincent "a chip off the old block" and expected him to follow in his father's footsteps. They rejoiced in his creative ability and were not overly concerned about his poor academic achievement and lack of reading ability.

While he was in the LD program, Vincent spent most of his time lobbying for his return to regular classes. He did not interact with the other LD pupils; instead, he maintained close ties with his crowd in the middle school. During his year in the LD program Vincent was given intensive reading instruction. These efforts were no more successful than previous reading instruction had been. Vincent had poor auditory discrimination and could not associate sounds with symbols. He had much difficulty with the sequencing of sounds and with oral and visual recall of symbols. Vincent showed little or no academic gains during his year in the special classes, while he lost out, during this time, on many activities in regular middle school that he liked and had done well in the past.

It was difficult to demonstrate that Vincent had derived any real benefit from being in the LD program. Yet, the LD staff (I include myself) recommended that Vincent spend another year in the special classes. Whether out of optimism or ignorance, the staff still hoped that somehow they would be able to help Vincent overcome his reading problem. In those early days of the LD program no one was as yet willing to admit the awful truth that some children *cannot learn to read even when they have normal intelligence, high motivation for learning and when they are receiving expert reading instructions. (p. 124).* Vincent rebelled. Neither he nor his parents were willing to accept the LD staff's recommendations.

The parents withdrew him from the special classes and reentered him into a regular eighth grade class. A modified program was worked out for Vincent. He was given ample opportunity to develop his talents and soon distinguished himself in the art and drama departments of the high school. Vincent presented no serious behavior problems and was well liked by adults and peers. By the end of the five year follow-up study Vincent was still only reading on the third grade level, but he had won a special prize for his art work and was awarded a scholarship to an art school after his graduation from high school.

The case of Vincent illustrates what can be done for a dyslexic child within a regular school program *provided* the school is willing to work out an individualized curriculum for the youngster and *if* the pupil is of average intelligence, has specific talents that offset his learning disability, presents no serious behavior problems, and has the full acceptance and support of stable, understanding parents. Unfortunately, not many children with severe learning disabilities are blessed with as many assets as Vincent had.

Jimmy's and Vincent's parents insisted that their children could hold their own in regular classes and did not need special class placements. They were willing to make concessions to achieve their goals. Jimmy's parents were willing to let him "lose" two years in school, while Vincent's parents did not expect Vincent to be a good scholar and accepted the fact that he could not read. Under those circumstances the children were indeed able to hold their own in regular classes and the parents decision to return them to their home schools was correct.

The judgment of the other parents who withdrew their children from the LD program was less accurate. As the LD staff had predicted, these youngsters did not do well in regular classes. The main difference between Jimmy and Vincent and the other seven LD pupils seemed to be that the latter had not only learning problems, but also had severe emotional and behavior problems. All seven had difficulty getting along with their peers and none had a positive attitude toward school and toward school work. In addition, none of them had as much talent as Vincent had to counterbalance their disabilities; nor were any of them as small and appealing as Jimmy had been, a factor which had made it easy for him to win approval despite modest endowment. Furthermore, the seven children were not as fully accepted by their parents as were Jimmy and Vincent. The parents' insistence that the youngsters be returned to regular classes was at least partially based on a denial of their children's problems. In some cases, the parents themselves were emotionally disturbed; they viewed the special class placement as a persecution of their youngsters. It is therefore not surprising that these seven children did not do well when they were returned to regular classes.

On the follow-up questionnaires that were sent to the teachers and counselors in the regular classes, six of the seven former LD pupils were described as hostile, defiant, uncooperative, and unwilling to do their work assignments. Of these children, four were very disturbed youngsters who continued to be a disruptive influence on the classroom throughout the period of the follow-up study. The other two pupils had been difficult to manage in the regular classes for two or three years, but eventually they settled down and made a fair adjustment in school as they got older. It is probable that these painful and frustrating years in the regular classes could have been avoided if the children had been permitted to remain one or two years longer in the LD program before returning to regular classes.

The seventh child was a hypersensitive, severely disturbed, brain-injured boy who regressed so badly in the large, demanding regular classes that he had to be excluded from his home school. His behavior had become bizarre and he was beginning to act out his frustration in violent attacks on other children. Despite the parents' objections, the local school referred this youngster back to the LD program. The child appeared to be happy to be back again in the protective and "safe" LD classes. His behavior improved again at once and he was once more able to do his work. The child's failure in the regular classes did not come as a surprise. It had been predicted by the LD staff and the likelihood thereof had been repeatedly pointed out to the parents. But the parents *insisted* on returning their son to the regular classes in spite of the warnings. Some parents cannot hear what they do not wish to hear. Sometimes children have to suffer and fail before their parents can finally be persuaded to do what is best for their child.

As indicated on Table 27, four pupils were withdrawn from the large cooperative LD program when the local school districts decided to set up their own LD classes within their home schools. Thus in effect, the four children were transferred from one LD class to another. Three of these youngsters were non-acting-out children and did not have serious behavior problems. They were mainly immature, restless, and had marked perceptual difficulties. These three pupils did as well in the new LD classes in their home schools as they had done in the special classes of the cooperative LD program. In fact, for these three children, the transfer to the new LD classes was to their advantage. Whenever possible a child should remain in his home school, regardless of whether he is in a regular class or in a special class.

Arnold, the fourth child who was transferred to a special class in his home school, was unable to adjust to this class. The school district he came from was small. The administrators soon discovered that they did not have enough children with learning disabilities in their district to enable them to make good class groupings at the elementary school and the middle school level. As a result, each of the new LD classes included youngsters with a three-to-four year age span and with a wide range of different types of learning and behavior problems. This diversity created many unnecessary and unforeseen problems. Arnold could not cope with the poorly controlled and confusing LD class. He deteriorated in his behavior and achievement. Arnold was a hypersensitive, schizoid, eleven-year-old boy who needed a calm, well-structured class. It was decided, therefore, to return Arnold to the cooperative LD program where there were many different types of LD classes from which to choose. The large number of pupils in this program made for a better and easier grouping of children in the special classes.

The seventeenth and last child who was withdrawn from the LD program was Georgia Mae. Georgia Mae and her family had moved up from the deep South when the girl was twelve years old. She had received little formal education prior to her entry into the LD program. Georgia Mae was a socially and emotionally deprived youngster who displayed serious perceptual malfunction and language deficits, as well as severe behavior problems. She was defiant, explosive, and restless. But Georgia Mae was also a friendly and likeable child. She lived with her mother, two older sisters, several of the sisters' offspring, and two younger brothers. She had experienced much instability at home and was exposed to considerable sexual acting-out on the part of her sisters. Georgia Mae's attendance in school was uneven, but when she got to school she seemed to enjoy it. She remained for four years in the LD program. Then in late summer, when Georgia Mae was just sixteen, she became pregnant and dropped out of school. At the end of the five year follow-up study Georgia Mae was at home awaiting the birth of her baby.

PUPILS WHO LEFT AND THEN RETURNED TO THE LD PROGRAM

It was shown earlier (Table 6), that 71 boys and girls, or 40 percent of all LD pupils involved in the follow-up study, remained in the special classes continuously for five or more years. This means that 106 (60%) of the pupils left the LD program for one reason or another during the five years following their admission to the special classes. Just because a child left the LD classes, however, did not necessarily mean that he left them for good and that he would not return to them at a later date. In the preceding chapters it was repeatedly mentioned that children were readmitted to the LD program.

In all, seventeen pupils who had left the LD program for a full school year or more returned to the special classes at a later time. Table 28 shows why the youngsters left the LD program and the rea-

Table 28.

Pupils who left and then returned to LD program.

N	Reason for leaving LD program	Reason for returning to program
2	Family moved away	Family returned to district served by LD program
10	Phychiatric exclusion, referral for hospitalization	Discharge from hospital or treatment center
3	Returned to regular classes on recommendation of LD staff	Failed in regular classes
1	Withdrawn by parents, returned to regular class	Failed in regular classes
1	Transferred to special class in home school	Failed in special class in home school
17		

sons for their return to the special classes. In some cases, the pupils' return signified improvement and progress on the part of the children; in other cases, it reflected failure.

The return of two boys might be regarded as a vote of confidence in the LD program. The families of these youngsters had had to move, for business reasons, out of the area served by the LD program. In both cases, the parents had been very satisfied with the education their children were receiving in the special classes. The parents had regretted that they had to move. When the opportunity presented itself to relocate again, they made a special effort to come back into the school district where they had lived before so that their sons could benefit once again from the LD program.

Ten of the seventeen youngsters who returned to the LD program had been excluded earlier from the special classes since they required more intensive treatment than the LD program could offer. All had been referred for residential psychiatric care. After spending a year or more in mental hospitals or in treatment centers, they were readmitted to the LD classes. The return of these pupils was greatly welcomed and was considered a sign of the children's improvement and recovery. Hopefully, all pupils who had to be excluded from the LD classes for psychiatric reasons will improve in time sufficiently to return to the LD program or to regular classes. No withdrawal or exclusion from the LD classes should ever be regarded as final.

Five of the ten ex-hospital patients made good adjustments to their homes and to the LD program. The other five youngsters readjusted fairly well to the special classes, but they could not make a go of it at home and in the community. Within a matter of weeks, these five children left the LD program for a second time and again had to return to the hospital (Table 26).

Three of the 42 LD pupils who had been sent back to regular classes on recommendations of the LD staff failed and were returned to the LD classes. These children had done well in the special classes, but they were still too vulnerable to cope with the demands of regular classes. In one case, the principal of the child's home school referred the boy back to the LD program. The other two youngsters requested themselves that they be allowed to return to the small, protective LD classes (p. 89). These three children never should have been sent to the regular classes in the first place—they never should have left the LD program.

Seven pupils who were withdrawn from the special classes by their parents, against the staff's recommendations, did poorly in the regular classes. (p. 174). Six of these youngsters were left to flounder as best they could in the regular classes, but one child became so disturbed and disturbing that he had to be excluded from his home school and had to be sent back to the LD program despite his parents' objections.

Once this youngster was back in a small LD class, he settled down again and presented no serious behavior problems. His work also improved again significantly.

Four pupils were transferred from the cooperative LD program to newly organized LD classes in the youngsters' home schools. One of the four children failed in these new classes (p. 175). He was grossly misplaced in the special class he had been put into, and was therefore sent back to the LD program. The large number of pupils in the cooperative LD program made it possible to achieve appropriate class groupings and allowed for a greater diversity of special classes than could be had in any one small school district. In the cooperative program, more children with many different types of problems could be more effectively educated.

The seventeen youngsters who returned to the LD program (Table 28) make up 10 percent of all 177 LD pupils in the follow-up study. The 71 long-term LD pupils, plus the 17 youngsters who returned to the special classes add up to 88 pupils, or just half of the 177 pupils. It appears, therefore, that a public school LD program must be prepared to provide long-term special education for at least half of all pupils who are referred to it. In the present study, "long-term" means only five years. Subsequent experience with the LD program has shown that most of these youngsters remain for more than five years in the special classes. In fact, the majority stayed in the LD program for the remainder of their secondary education. They either graduated from an academically oriented LD class located in a regular high school or they received vocational training in the LD program and went onto a work-study program and a job after graduation from the program.

It is a fallacy to think that one or two years of special education at the elementary school level will be able to solve the problems of most children with learning disabilities. In fact, there is reason to believe that any child whose problems *can* be solved in one year in a special class probably did not need to come to a special class to begin with. His problems could probably have been dealt with by means of a modified schedule in the regular classes or with the help of a resource room and/or counseling. The value of a one or two year LD program is debatable. If such a short-term program is set up, then the choice of the pupils has to be *highly selective* (p. 67); otherwise it is doomed to failure. What is needed is a *comprehensive public school LD program that serves all children with learning disabilities from kindergarten through high school*. The most important parts of such a program are the primary grades and the vocational training and high school classes. Children with learning disabilities need to be identified early and need to be educated and trained so that they can take their place as contributing members of society.

Chapter 8

Summary and Implications of Five Year Follow-up Study of LD Pupils

In the preceding chapters, the results of the five year follow-up study of LD pupils were presented in detail. As stated in the introduction, the purpose of this investigation was to explore the characteristics of children referred to the LD program and to discover what actually happened to the youngsters during the five-year period following their entry into the special classes. At this time, the main points of the findings will be summarized and conclusions and implications will be drawn from them. Based on the conclusions of the follow-up study, some suggestions will be made for ways of expanding and modifying LD programs in public schools. It is believed that such changes would make special classes more effective and more efficient in helping children with learning disabilities. And, perhaps even more important, such changes would help to prevent and minimize learning and emotional problems in many or most public school pupils.

Purpose of LD Classes and Selection of Pupils For These Classes

The administrators of the thirteen local school districts served by the cooperative LD program here under discussion differed markedly in their attitudes toward the special classes. This attitude determined to a

Summary and Implications of the Study

considerable extent the function ascribed to the LD classes and the selection of the pupils for them. Some administrators thought that LD classes had a primarily remedial function—that is, the purpose of the classes was to correct learning and behavior problems so that the pupils could "catch up" with their peers and could return again to regular classes. Others considered the LD classes a "last resort," a place where you could "dump" pupils who did not learn and who could not be managed in a regular classroom. They viewed the value of the special classes mainly in terms of relieving regular classes of trouble makers and disruptive pupils. And, finally, there were those administrators who recognized the LD classes as a place where pupils could get help *before* they developed serious secondary emotional and behavior problems.

Actually, the LD classes performed, to a certain extent, all of the functions that were ascribed to them. They did help some children to overcome their learning problems suffciently so that they could return to regular classes. They also aided regular classes by freeing them of disruptive pupils, and the special classes most certainly helped to prevent an increase or development of emotional and behavior problems in many youngsters.

Originally, the LD classes were designed to serve only children with supposedly "normal mental potential," but by the time the follow-up study was completed, the LD program was enrolling children whose intelligence ranged from borderline all the way up to superior. The LD classes provided special education for all children with learning disabilities who needed it. The program extended from kindergarten through high school. It was recognized before long that many, or even most, LD pupils required not just one or two years but rather long-term special education (Table 20).

If the purpose of the LD program is restricted to returning children to regular classes, then the selection of pupils for these special classes has to be highly selective (p. 67). Only 17 percent or 30 of the 177 LD pupils were able to return fairly successfully to regular classes. The LD program helped these particular youngsters by giving them extra time in which to mature and to learn, and by reducing the pressures and competition they had had to cope with in regular classes. Almost all of the pupils who returned successfully to regular classes "lost" a year in the process. They did *not* catch up in their work and their problems did not just disappear. Instead, the youngsters learned to compensate for these problems. The pupils were helped to function up to the level of their ability. The learning problems shown by these particular children were, for the most part, not too severe. It is quite probable that some of the pupils would never have needed to come to the special classes if their parents and teachers had understood the nature of their difficulties at an early age and had provided an appropriate educational program for the children at the time of school entry.

If the only purpose of the LD classes had been to send children back to regular classes, then the LD program must be considered rather unsuccessful, for the vast majority of pupils did not return to regular classes. Yet, in a way, the long-term LD pupils, who remained in the special classes, were the ones who needed the LD classes most and who benefited most from them. For these pupils, the LD program was very successful indeed.

The LD classes did relieve regular classes by taking the most difficult children, but this function cannot and should not ever be considered a primary function of an LD program. Special classes should never be regarded as "dumping grounds." They rather represent a privilege and an opportunity for children with problems. It is wasteful and self-defeating to fill up LD classes with children who cannot benefit from them. Some youngsters who cannot be controlled in regular classes also cannot be managed in LD classes and do not belong there. More than one teacher complained that she felt like a "high-priced baby-sitter" when confronted with a youngster in her class who was grossly misplaced. Certain basic essentials have to be present if a child is to profit from a special class: The pupil has to be able to function in a group and has to be able to follow a few basic rules and directions. Inevitably, there are some children who are too disturbed or too impaired for LD classes; some groups of youngsters do not belong into public school LD classes. These include: autistic children, uncontrollable and violent psychotic children, and delinquent children with character disorders (Table 26).

In my opinion one of the greatest values of the LD program lies in its *preventive* function. Too often pupils with moderate learning disabilities are not referred to the LD classes until *after* they have developed serious emotional and behavior problems, until *after* they have acquired poor work habits and negative attitudes toward school and learning. Many of the youngsters' emotional and behavior disorders could have been avoided or minimized if the children had been given special help earlier. As it stands now, the child is usually so disturbed by the time he comes to the LD program that one or two years are required just to undo or to alleviate the harm that was done to the youngster in regular classes preceding his referral to the special classes. *It is therefore strongly recommended that the emphasis in the*

Summary and Implications of the Study 183

LD classes be shifted from remediation and rehabilitation to the prevention of learning and emotional problems. At present, the public schools actually contribute to children's learning and behavior difficulties by waiting until the youngsters' problems become serious before giving them special consideration and help.

Age and IQ Scores of LD Pupils

According to the youngsters' social histories, almost all LD pupils had experienced difficulties in school from the time they first entered kindergarten. Yet, the children were not referred to the LD program unless their learning problems were so extreme or their behavior was so disruptive that they could not be managed in regular classes. The younger the pupils were at the time of referral to the special classes, the more mentally limited and emotionally disturbed they were. It was good that these impaired children were given special attention and help early, but many youngsters with average mental ability also had learning problems. However, since these children appeared intelligent, they were usually maintained in regular classes in the hope that they would "outgrow" their difficulties. Youngsters were usually tolerated in regular classes as long as they were not *too* disruptive. Only after they had failed repeatedly and had become quite frustrated and disturbed, were these more intelligent pupils finally sent to the LD classes. It would have been far more efficient and effective, in the long run, to give these children extra help before the secondary emotional problems developed.

There is much talk these days about individual differences between children and about individualized instruction in school. Yet, the public school system decrees that all children born in a given twelve-month period must enter school at the same time. If, for instance, the admission cutoff date is December 1, then the pupils will range in age, at the beginning of kindergarten, from 5 years 8 months to 4 years 9 months, with a mean age of 5 years 3 months. School beginners vary enormously in their degree of maturity and mental ability. Even if the kindergarten curriculum is aimed somewhat below the average mental age level, a sizeable number of pupils will fall below the expected level of functioning from the very outset and will begin their school career with frustration and failure.

Table 29 shows the mental ages of kindergarten pupils of average, low average, and borderline intelligence. It can be seen that all youngsters with an IQ score of 80 or less have a mental age of less than 4 years 6 months, or below the kindergarten level. Children age 5 years

Table 29.

Mental age of kindergarten pupils with different IQ levels.

CA at beginning kindergarten	*Pupils' mental age at beginning of kindergarten*						
	IQ 75	IQ 80	IQ 85	IQ 90	IQ 95	IQ 100	IQ 105
5-8	4-3	4-6	4-10	5-1	5-4	5-8	6-0
5-6	4-2	4-5	4-8	5-0	5-3	5-6	5-10
5-3	4-0	4-2	4-6	4-9	5-0	5-3	5-6
5-0	3-10	4-0	4-3	4-6	4-9	5-0	5-3
4-9	3-7	3-10	4-0	4-3	4-6	4-9	5-0

Children functioning below kindergarten level   **Children functioning at or above kindergarten level**

3 months with an IQ score of 85 still have a mental age of only 4 years 6 months at the time of school entry, and the mental ages of pupils age 5 or younger are below the kindergarten level even when their IQ scores are 90 or 95. (It is not simply chance that the majority of LD pupils had IQ scores in the 80's and 90's [Table 1].

All youngsters with mental ages of 4 years 6 months or less are bound to have difficulty in an average kindergarten class and start school with a great disadvantage. Mental immaturity is usually also associated with emotional and social immaturity. *It is therefore suggested that all children be screened at the time of school entry for their mental, social, and emotional maturity. Such screening is especially important if the pupils are among the younger children in a given class group.* Children who function below the 4 year 6 months level are still too immature for a regular kindergarten program. A modified program for these children is needed in order to help them to develop their ability to the fullest and to prevent secondary emotional and behavior problems from developing.

It is unrealistic to expect a very young, immature child with a mental and emotional age of 4½ years or less to compete with older and more mature children who function on the 5½- or 6-year-old level. Yet, this is exactly what is done in most kindergarten classes. It is an illusion to think that these immature children will "catch up" with the other youngsters in a year's time. The child with an emotional and mental age of 4 or 4½ years needs a different kind of kindergarten program from the

Summary and Implications of the Study

child who is functioning on the 5½ or 6 year level. *Above all, the immature child needs more time in which to grow and to mature.* Immaturity is not necessarily a sign of dullness or mental slowness. A large number children of normal intelligence mature more slowly than the majority of other youngsters. They are not able to cope with an average kindergarten program at the time of school entry, but in the long run they can and do progress well, provided they were not unduly frustrated and pressured during the first years in school.

Sometimes, parents are eager to get their young children into special classes or they obtain special tutors for them in the hope of raising not only the youngsters' achievement but also their IQ scores. In general, special education does not increase the IQ levels of LD pupils. The mean IQ scores of different groups of LD pupils did not change significantly during their stay in the LD program. This was true for the children who returned to regular classes (Table 16), as well as for the long-term LD pupils (Table 20). The LD program helped children to use their mental ability to the fullest so that they functioned better and appeared brighter, but this did not imply an actual increase in intelligence.

Only in a few cases did the children's IQ scores increase considerably after the youngsters had been in the special classes for a period of time. In each of these instances, however, the admission IQ score had been invalid. Either the pupils had been so immature and withdrawn when they were referred to the LD program that they could not be adequately tested, or they had been so negativistic or discouraged when they were initially tested that they did not really apply themselves and did not put forth much effort. The low IQ scores these children had received were therefore not true measures of their ability but rather reflected their immaturity, lack of involvement, and hostility. In the small supportive LD classes, the youngsters developed more positive attitudes toward themselves and toward school; not only did their work improve, but they also did better on psychological tests.

In a few cases, the IQ scores of pupils decreased markedly during the children's stay in the LD classes. This occurred mainly among very dull youngsters who had reached a plateau in their mental development (p. 108), or among youngsters with serious problems in visual-motor *and* auditory perception *and* with memory deficits (p. 125). When this second group of children entered school, they tested in the average range. At age six, children are not expected to know a great deal of factual information, but as children get older, they are supposed to accumulate more knowledge and they have to retain much of what they learn. The LD pupils in question were unable to do this because of their multiple perceptual and memory problems. Not only did they fail to perceive correctly much of what they were taught, they also could not remember whatever they did learn. Thus, they did not grow and develop mentally at a normal rate, despite essentially normal potential. The children did not actually deteriorate intellectually, their mental development just stood still. Since the pupils' chronological ages continued to increase while their mental ages remained at the same level, their IQ scores inevitably went down.

Visual-Motor Perception of LD Pupils

At the time of entry into the LD program, 90 percent of the pupils revealed below average functioning in visual-motor perception and integration as measured on the Bender Gestalt Test (p. 16). It is characteristic of children with poor visual-motor perception that they are vulnerable and that they learn more slowly than other children since they need extra time to compensate for their difficulties. However, the mere presence of immature visual-motor perception at an early age cannot, by itself predict the youngster's long range academic progress. There is also no one-to-one relationship between a pupil's performance on the Bender Gestalt Test and his reading achievement (Bender, 1970; Koppitz, 1970). A child's ultimate success or failure in school will depend not only on his visual-motor perception or integration but also on his conceptualization, his language development, his memory and sequencing ability, and his emotional and social adjustment.

There appear to be two ways in which children with poor integration and perception can be helped: 1. They should be given extra time in which to grow and mature, and 2. They should be provided with a special training program which enables them to compensate for their difficulties. It must again be emphasized that immaturity and slow development in visual-motor perception are not synonymous with dullness or retardation. They occur among both bright and dull children. Many children of normal intelligence who suffer from minimal brain dysfunction show immaturity in integration when they enter school, but *if* they are not pressured or unduly frustrated in the primary grades and *if* they are given extra support they *can* learn to compensate for their perceptual problems *in time*.

It is recommended that *all* school beginners be given intensive training in perception, motor coordination, intersensory integration, language stimulation, memory, etc., in kindergarten and the first and second grades. Those children whose maturity level in visual-motor perception is markedly below average should be given additional consideration. They need extra time and training to compensate for their difficulties. It must be recognized, however, that a *special perceptual training program cannot speed up a child's natural rate of perceptual maturation and integration, nor can it eliminate entirely a youngster's underlying problems of neurological malfunction.* A good training program in perception and intersensory integration can help a pupil to *maximize his abilities* and can assist him in finding ways to *compensate for his weaknesses.* Bright children can do this effectively on their own if given enough time, but *children of average ability or of below-average intelligence need specific help to compensate for their integrative difficulties.*

If children are required to start with reading before their integrative ability has reached the necessary level of maturation, they cannot help failing. Failure and frustration lead to a loss of self-confidence and to a negativistic attitude. Then, a few years later, when the child's level of maturation in visual-motor perception is adequate for reading and if no other major learning problems are present and the child could theoretically begin to read, the youngster has often become so discouraged in the meantime that he does not even try to read anymore; he has lost all motivation for learning. Instead of pushing children into academic work before they are ready for it, it would be much more profitable to use the time for a good integrative and perceptual training program to lay a sound foundation on which the child can build when he is ready and able to go ahead with academic work.

Achievement of LD Pupils

The learning problems presented by the LD pupils were primarily due to some form or degree of brain dysfunction. The causes for the dysfunction varied greatly and included genetic factors as well as injury, illness, and severe early physical and emotional deprivation and neglect. Whatever the cause, the learning problems appeared to have an organic basis (Silver, 1971) and were not just the result of an "emotional block," lack of opportunity to learn, or poor motivation. In regular classes there are, of course, always some pupils who do unsatisfactory work mainly because of lack of motivation and emotional problems, but such children seldom if ever come to an LD program. The LD pupils under discussion here were a small group of youngsters with severe learning problems who typically displayed a combination of organic and emotional difficulties.

The emotional and behavior problems of the LD pupils were usually secondary in nature. Children with minimal brain dysfunction tend to experience so much frustration and failure in life that they frequently develop emotional problems as a result of these experiences. Their failure to learn is not the result of emotional problems, rather the opposite is true.

The writer is convinced that *children who can learn to read will learn to read,* sometimes even in spite of themselves. Arithmetic, on the other hand, requires a higher degree of mental integration and specific instruction. It is not something a child can just "pick up" by himself. Many of the LD pupils had a very negative attitude toward school and toward learning when they first came to the special classes. In time, their attitudes changed and they were eager to learn. Yet, despite a great deal of individual help and specific training and remediation, some children continued to have serious learning problems. An increase in motivation for learning did not automatically result in significant and lasting gains in achievement. Academic progress is, for most LD pupils, a gradual and arduous process.

Some LD pupils, age seven and older, showed an initial spurt in achievement after coming to the special classes, but this spurt was followed by a gradual leveling off in achievement (Table 17). It appeared that the youngsters were able to relax when they came to the small protective LD classes and could work up to the level of their ability, which had not been the case before. Hence, the marked increase in achievement. The extra attention and the special teaching materials and techniques provided helped the pupils to do their best, *but once a child was working up to his ability he did not advance beyond that level at any other than his own natural rate of progress. No amount of training or tutoring could speed up or basically alter his own rate of growth and achievement.* The initial spurt in achievement is often misleading and arouses undue optimism in teachers and parents. For this reason, most short-term studies of special education programs must be viewed with skepticism. The results of such studies are often quite dramatic, yet almost invariably the gains the pupils made in a few months or a year's time disappear or "wash out" in subsequent years (Silberberg and Silberberg, 1969).

The fact that learning problems do not really "go away" but, rather, are compensated for can easily be observed when an LD pupil is under stress. Many LD pupils function quite well in the small special classes

Summary and Implications of the Study

but regress when they are placed into big, less-structured classes or when they are upset or ill. Under such circumstances, children, who have not done so for a long time may again reverse letters and numbers, they may once more be unable to sequence sounds and symbols, and may have difficulty recalling facts and words. Even well-functioning LD pupils may go back to earlier patterns of hyperactivity, temper outbursts, irritability, and impulsivity when they become anxious or are under pressure. When the stress is removed, the children can usually muster the necessary energy and inner control to overcome and to compensate for their inherent poor integration and their learning difficulties. The process of compensation for areas of malfunctioning demands considerable energy and concentration. This may explain why many children with minimal brain dysfunction tire so easily from mental activity and why they find it so hard to maintain sustained attention. An LD pupil may be able to sit still and watch television by the hour, for this requires very little concentration or mental energy, but the same child may find it extremely difficult to sit and read for more than a few minutes at a time.

It seems significant that almost all the LD pupils who returned successfully from the special classes to regular classes "lost" a year or even two in the process. That is, they were placed into regular classes a year or two below their normal grade level. Such grade placements were usually quite in keeping with the youngsters' social, emotional and academic level of functioning. LD pupils are frequently slower than average in their physical and social development, even when they have normal mental potential. Many LD pupils look and act like children who are a year or two younger than they actually are. They also tend, more often than not, to select friends who are younger than they are.

Public schools are set up in such a way that all pupils are required to enter kindergarten or first grade at the same time and are then expected to progress at the same rate from one grade to the next. This lock-step grade system seems to be one of the major flaws in our public school system. No allowance is made for individual differences in the *rate* of maturation and development of children and in the *rate* of their progress in achievement. If a child grows physically more slowly than most other children, he is not penalized. Tall children do not all get As and the short ones Ds on their report cards. Yet, a child is said to fail when he lags a year or more behind in his perceptual and language development.

It appears that slowly maturing pupils need more time to master the basic academic skills in school. Since the successful LD pupils "lost" a year while in the special classes, the question arises: Could these children have succeeded as well without a special class placement if they had been kept back and had repeated a grade in regular class? The answer to this question is, in most cases, an emphatic "no." Several LD pupils had, in fact, repeated a grade before they came to the LD program. The mere repetition of a grade was not enough to help the youngsters with learning disabilities to compensate for their difficulties. A child who is held back considers himself a failure. This feeling only adds to his sense of inadequacy and his poor self-concept. Such feelings of inadequacy *could* be dealt with if the child could succeed on his second try in kindergarten or while repeating the first or second grade, or any other grade, but, usually, the child still does poorly on his second try in a given grade and is still unable to keep up with his classmates. His feeling of failure is thereby only intensified.

Repeating a grade rarely solves an LD pupil's problems. He needs a slower pace of learning and more individual help and support than he can receive in a large regular class. It is as if the school expected a child to drive a car (himself) from town A (kindergarten) to town B (first grade) at a set speed of 60 miles per hour. If the child had a well-functioning car and a straight, smooth road to travel on he could do it with ease. But LD pupils are, in effect, driving cars with poor brakes (weak inner controls) and, usually, faulty wiring systems (poor integration), or their engines are weak (low intelligence) and the road they have to travel on (home and school environment) is seldom straight or smooth. These children *cannot* drive at 60 mph without losing control of their cars, or else their engines overheat and give out. If these youngsters were given a smooth, straight road and permitted to drive at 40 mph or even 30 mph, and if they were taught *how* to drive their cars, then they too could get from town A to town B, but they need more time to accomplish this task. Asking an LD pupil to repeat a grade is equivalent to taking the driver, who ran off the road because he was being made to drive at a speed at which he could not control his car, and returning him again to town A to start all over again. He is again asked to drive to town B at the same rate of 60 mph; he still cannot do it. If the distance between town A and town B is 60 miles, the average driver will get there in one hour. The LD pupil, driving at 40 mph, could get there in one-and-a-half hours, while the 30 mph driver could make it in two hours. The LD pupil who has to repeat the run again at 60 mph may not get there even after two hours—he may end up in a ditch.

The introduction of prefirst grade and presecond grade classes or of ungraded or cluster classes in elementary schools is a step in the

Summary and Implications of the Study 191

right direction, taking into account the individual differences and different rates of progress among pupils. It is essential to realize that immature or slowly developing children cannot "make up" the extra time they require for learning. The advantage of having special classes for such youngsters is that the pupils do not have to experience failure. They can be programmed from the beginning to progress at a slower pace than that of regular classes.

Some pupils remain so vulnerable and poorly controlled that they need a protective special class at least a part of each day all the way through high school, even though their achievement level may be satisfactory. At least half of all the LD pupils could not return to regular classes at all and needed long-term special education. Most of them required vocational training. A meaningful LD program has to extend, therefore, all the way from kindergarten through high school and must include both academic and prevocational and vocational courses.

Unhappily, some LD pupils will always remain functionally illiterate, even if they are of normal intelligence (p. 124). Yet, many children who cannot learn to read *can* learn other things. LD classes have to be designed to give children an education by building on their areas of strength and competence. The youngsters' areas of weaknesses or deficits should, of course, not be ignored or neglected; special help for these areas is needed. At present, too much of special education consists almost entirely of making often vain attempts at helping children to overcome their problems while neglecting their education and the development of their abilities.

It was found that before an LD pupil age nine or older could hold his own in a regular class, he had to be able to read independently at least on the end-of-fourth–beginning-fifth grade level. It is suggested therefore that remedial reading help be concentrated on those youngsters who have progressed by age nine or ten at least to the third or fourth grade level. With intensive extra help in reading, these children may be able to achieve the independent reading level necessary for a return to regular classes.

The findings of the follow-up study convinced me that a child who is still reading at the preprimer or primer level at age ten or eleven will not become a fluent reader by age sixteen. Chances are he will never progress beyond the second or third grade reading level, if that far. Failure to learn to read does not necessarily mean that a child is dull; the valuable school years should be used to train these youngsters in areas in which they can succeed. Hopefully research into the teaching of reading will continue and some day it may be possible to teach a truly dyslexic child how to read, but until that day arrives, it is recommended that special class teachers spend more time in teaching what children *can* do and learn so that the youngsters can build up self-confidence and skills which will enable them to function successfully in society.

In public schools, and especially in LD classes, much too much emphasis is put on the printed page and on books. Much more time and effort needs to be placed on language development, direct experiences, science, social studies, art, music, work habits, human relationships, etc. Books are a status symbol in our society and every child (above all the LD pupil) needs a book, if for no other reason than to carry it around and show it off. The important thing for teachers is to know how to select the right book and how to use it. The book should always be only one of many teaching tools or devices. It is essential that teaching materials and techniques be appropriate and meaningful for the child, and that they be adapted to the pupil's level of functioning and to his particular mode of learning. Some children learn best from visually presented materials, others from aural instructions. Most educational programs do not make full use of all the children's sense modalities and of concrete experiences in the process of education. Caution is urged in adopting any *one* method for teaching *all* LD pupils or in assuming that just because one technique works with many six-year-olds that it will also be successful with many eight-year-olds. The successful special education teacher has to be flexible and able to adapt to new and difficult situations in order to meet the varied and changing needs of her pupils.

Behavior of LD Pupils

The follow-up study showed that LD pupils cannot be grouped on the basis of having *either* learning problems *or* emotional and behavior problems. The youngsters who were referred to the LD program revealed varying degrees of learning *and* behavior disorders as well as emotional difficulties. The pupil's emotional problems were usually secondary to his learning problems, while behavior disorders were either a consequence of the child's inherent impulsivity and hyperactivity, or a response to the frustrations and conflicts he experienced at home and in school, or both. It is meaningless to ask: Does the child have learning problems *or* emotional problems? The question should be: Does the youngster, have at this moment, *more* learning problems or *more* emotional difficulties? Where does he "hurt" most, where should the emphasis be placed at this time in order to help him? Which of the

Summary and Implications of the Study 193

several different needs the youngster exhibits should get top priority, which should be given attention thereafter, and so on.

In general, it was found that youngsters were more often referred to the LD program on account of their behavior than on account of their poor achievement. For each LD pupil who functioned a year or two below grade level, there were several other youngsters in regular classes whose achievement was just as poor, but who were *not* referred to the LD program. The main difference between the pupils was in their *behavior.* As long as children with learning disabilities are not aggressive or disruptive, they are tolerated in regular classes—especially if they are of normal intelligence and have some area of competence.

Girls also frequently have learning disabilities, but they are not sent to the special classes as quickly as boys are. When exposed to repeated frustration and failure in school, boys tend to act out their anger more readily and become more often overtly rebellious than girls do. Girls withdraw more often or develop somatic complaints. Consequently, boys are referred to the LD classes sooner and more frequently than girls. When a girl is sent to a special class she is usually more disturbed and more impaired than most boys of similar age and intelligence would be.

It is futile to try to teach reading or arithmetic to a thoroughly negativistic child who hates school and teachers and who is totally lacking in motivation for learning. The youngster's attitude has to be changed first, before he can even begin to profit from special education. Since the school has usually contributed to the development of the pupil's negative attitude, it is also the school's responsibility to help change that attitude. Experience with the LD pupils showed that it sometimes takes many weeks, months, or even years to bring about such a change. The LD program has to deal with the *whole* child—with his feelings and behavior as well as with his achievement. The public school's main job is of course to teach and to educate pupils, but part of that job is to work with the children so that they are *able* to learn without interfering with their natural rate and mode of learning or destroying a child's inborn desire to learn.

The LD program was actually quite successful in modifying the attitude and behavior of the younger pupils. It was more difficult to bring about lasting changes in very disturbed and acting-out older pupils. Yet, a successful return of LD pupils to regular classes depended even more on the children's behavior and attitude than on their achievement. Since it is so difficult and time-consuming to alter the attitude and behavior of LD pupils, one solution for this problem seems to lie in the *prevention* of negative and hostile attitudes toward school to begin with. There is no doubt that many behavior problems shown by LD pupils could be minimized or even avoided altogether if a modified preventive special education program could be introduced into public schools.

Unfortunately, it will not be possible to eliminate all behavior disorders of LD pupils. Some of their emotional and behavior problems obviously originate not in school but in their homes or within the youngsters themselves. In many cases, the school has to be satisfied to change the children's attitude just enough so that the youngsters' hostility will not interfere too much with their achievement. In other cases, the child's home situation may be so disturbed that it overwhelms the youngster and may make it impossible for him to profit from the special classes. Then, exclusion from the LD program becomes unavoidable. Since emotional and behavior disorders are so common among LD pupils and since their effects are so far-reaching, it is essential that the staff of a public school LD program include a clinical team consisting of a psychologist, a social worker, and, if possible, a consulting psychiatrist.

Developmental and Medical Histories of LD Pupils

It is most helpful to know an LD pupil's developmental and medical history, especially when working with the child's parents. It is important to know that the child was "difficult" or vulnerable even before he entered school and that his problems are not all the parents' or even the school's "fault." It is also essential to have a neurological and psychiatric evaluation and a medical diagnosis to rule out the possibility of epilepsy or a brain tumor and to assess the advisability of giving the youngster medication to improve his concentration and control.

The older LD pupils were frequently diagnosed as being "emotionally disturbed." Medical examinations of such youngsters usually failed to reveal any signs of neurological malfunction and their EEGs tended to show no abnormalities. Yet, the developmental and medical histories of these eleven- and twelve-year-old LD pupils reported more often than not that the children showed "soft" neurological signs and typical "organic behavior" when they were younger. In order to understand an LD pupil and his behavior, it is important to know what he was like in early childhood and while in the primary grades. "Soft" signs and immature and restless behavior tend to disappear as the youngster gets older.

No significant relationships were found between any one factor in the children's developmental and medical histories and their rate of progress or achievement during the five years of the follow-up study. Therefore, it does not appear to be meaningful or profitable to set up special classes or to group children in classes on the basis of their medical diagnoses or their developmental histories. *LD classes or groups of special education pupils should rather be formed on the basis of the youngsters' actual functioning or needs.* A child should neither be included nor excluded from a class just because he was or was not labelled as "brain-injured" or "neurologically impaired" or as "emotionally disturbed."

Social Background of LD Pupils

One of the most significant factors affecting the LD pupils' progress in the special classes was found to be their social background. Therefore, work with the children's families and with other community agencies is one of the most important aspects of any LD program. The children who made the most progress in the special classes and who returned successfully to regular classes almost all had parents who were interested, cooperative, and supportive of their youngsters and of the program. The LD pupils who failed after returning to regular classes usually lacked such parental support. Most of the children who could not profit from the LD classes and who had to be referred for hospitalization or residential treatment came from unstable and/or deprived homes and had experienced much neglect in early life.

However, it is not claimed that all of the youngsters' problems in school were caused by the pupils' social background. I am convinced that any child who has serious learning and emotional problems contributes to his own difficulties. A youngster's problems are hardly ever only the parents' fault or only the school's or the community's fault. There are obviously many children who grow up in unstable and deprived homes who do not have serious emotional and learning problems and who do not have to be referred to special classes, whereas some children from stable and adequate homes have severe learning and emotional problems. The results of the follow-up study revealed that the LD pupils' difficulties resulted most often from a *combination* of factors. Only rarely do the children's problems result almost entirely from one extreme trauma or factor in their history, e.g., a massive brain injury, a hereditary disability or a degenerative illness. In most cases, neither the extent of their difficulties nor their progress in the LD classes was determined by any one factor or event.

A child with normal mental potential can learn to compensate for minimal brain dysfunction to a remarkable degree *if* he is born into a stable, supporting, and accepting home and *if* he is given sufficient time to develop and mature at his own rate without undue pressure from parents and teachers. If the same vulnerable child were born into an emotionally unstable home with a mentally ill mother, however, or if the parents made unreasonable demands on the child, or if he experienced much deprivation and neglect in early life, then it is unlikely that he could overcome his problems on his own. He would need a great deal of extra help. A bright, well-integrated child can usually succeed in school even when he lives in an inadequate home situation. A vulnerable child with learning disabilities cannot do so.

The parents' attitude toward school and toward the LD program had a major influence on the children's attitudes and progress in the special classes. However, the children also had influence on their parents. Several parents were initially displeased when their children were sent to the LD classes; they later became "sold" on the program after they realized that their children were happy in the special classes and were making progress in their achievement.

Some families had more than one child in the special classes. In such cases the parents were usually accepting and cooperative when the first child was referred to the LD program, but they became increasingly disillusioned and angry when a second, or even a third child of theirs was found to have learning problems and was referred for special class placement. When there are several children with learning disabilities in one family it tends to point either toward a genetic "flaw" that was handed down by the parents or to a marked inadequacy on the part of the parents to bring up children. Either of these possibilities are viewed by most parents as a personal threat to them. Such parents deserve much understanding and support.

LD pupils are sometimes told by their parents that they are being sent to the LD classes because they are "bad." They are then promised that they can "get out" when they behave themselves and are "good." These youngsters often feel guilty and confused when they discover that they like the LD classes and when they experience a sense of success and security they have never known before. Some children vigorously deny their own feelings and go on protesting against the LD classes while obviously enjoying them. Other children acknowledge their liking for the small special classes. In fact, a number of LD pupils were known to hide when the school bus arrived in the afternoon so they would not have to leave the school to go home again. One little

Summary and Implications of the Study

girl proclaimed, "The thing I don't like about Christmas is that there is no school. I love school. I wish I could come every day." She did not feel that way about school before she came to the LD classes; at the beginning of the school year she had told me that she had been sent to the special classes because she was "bad."

Some LD pupils arrive in school hungry (literally) and angry. The homes of these children meet neither their physical nor their emotional needs. A preventive LD program has to take the entire child into consideration. It is both futile and wasteful to set up elaborate special education programs and to try to teach children on an empty stomach. Free lunches for those who need them are essential; so are free breakfasts in many cases. But even this is often not sufficient. If a child's home is grossly pathological or totally inadequate, the children should be, if possible, removed from such an environment. However, there will never be enough foster homes or residential schools available for all the children who could use them. The public schools are also not in a position to take children from their homes. What public schools can and should, however, do is to try to minimize the influence of the destructive homes on the children. This can be accomplished by prolonging the youngsters' school day. A preventive LD program should provide extensive after-school and weekend recreational programs for all children. The public schools should also provide dormitories where some children can live during the school week from Monday to Friday. And, finally, the public schools should plan to have a summer school as well as a summer camp.

Pathological homes and seriously disturbed parents are found among both the poor and the rich. A child with learning disabilities who has bright, ambitious, and striving, but insensitive, parents may be as much at a disadvantage as a child with neglectful and unstable parents. And many homes that may be quite adequate for the well-integrated children in the family may still be inadequate for the vulnerable youngster with minimal brain dysfunction and learning problems. An assessment of a child's home should not be made by some objective middle-class standard, but rather in terms of the particular child's needs.

CONCLUSIONS

The following conclusions were drawn from the findings of the follow-up study of LD pupils:

1. Public schools should make more *allowances for individual dif-*

ferences between pupils and for the *slower rate of maturation* and academic progress of "vulnerable" children. These are the youngsters who most often develop learning and behavior problems and who are usually referred to the LD classes.

2. Learning disabilities have no single cause and no single cure. Most pupils with learning disabilities manifest a combination of minimal brain dysfunction or some type of CNS disorder, *and* emotional and behavior problems.

3. Most children with learning disabilities tend to have difficulties in school beginning with the primary grades.

4. The emphasis in special education should be shifted from rehabilitation and the correction of learning and emotional disorders to the *prevention* of such problems, as far as this is possible, and, even if such difficulties cannot always be totally avoided, they can at least be minimized.

5. Extremely immature and vulnerable children should be *identified at the time of school entry* and should be given special consideration *before* they develop serious learning and emotional problems.

6. Pupils should be grouped in special classes according to their *functioning and needs, and not on the basis of their IQ scores or their diagnostic labels.* A medical diagnosis should be used as a means to understand a child better, but not as a criterion for his class placement.

7. An LD program should be comprehensive. It should extend from kindergarten through high school and should provide both academic classes and vocational training courses. Special help should be available for pupils in LD classes as well as for children in regular classes who require extra assistance for only part of each day.

8. The placement of a child into a special class or LD program should *never be considered final or irrevocable.* LD pupils should be reevaluated annually and should be moved from one type of class to another whenever a child is ready for such a move, or when his present class placement no longer meets his needs. The curriculum of the LD program should be flexible in order to cope with the many and changing requirements of LD pupils. No one teaching technique or one set of instructional materials can possibly benefit all children with learning disabilities.

9. LD classes should be located in regular school buildings and the LD pupils should be integrated into regular classes whenever possible. Segregation of LD pupils should be kept to a minimum. However, there will always be a few extremely vulnerable children who will need self-contained, protective classes in order to function at their best.

10. Special education teachers should be, above all, warm but firm, resourceful and flexible, and they must have patience and a good sense of humor. Each teacher should be supported and backed by a team of professionals consisting of a principal, a social worker, a psychologist, a language therapist, and a psychiatric consultant as needed. The aid of paraprofessionals and volunteers should also be solicited.

11. The LD program has to be concerned with the *whole child,* not just with his achievement. Work with *the parents* of the LD pupils is essential, as is close cooperation with other educational, health, and welfare agencies in the community.

12. The LD program should include after-school recreational activities and a summer camp program. If possible, the school should provide dormitory facilities for pupils from extremely pathological or destructive homes, so as to minimize the negative influence of the homes on the children's attitudes and on their social and emotional adjustment.

RECOMMENDATIONS FOR A COMPREHENSIVE SPECIAL EDUCATION PROGRAM

Based on the foregoing conclusions, a tentative proposal has been drawn up for a comprehensive special education program. According to this plan, all children would be screened prior to their enrollment in kindergarten. This screening would be carried out by a team consisting of an *experienced* kindergarten teacher, the school psychologist, and the school social worker, and/or school nurse. The children could be screened in small groups of six to eight youngsters. The screening should include an evaluation of the youngsters' social, emotional and mental developments, and their backgrounds. The following screening procedure is suggested:

The kindergarten teacher would observe the youngsters in a group during free play and would talk to them informally; the psychologist would administer the Vane Kindergarten Test (Vane, 1968) to the children; while the social worker and/or the nurse would interview the mothers and would obtain the social history of the children. A routine health examination and a vision and hearing test would of course also be required.

The children's social histories should include information about the youngsters' early development (e.g., prenatal and birth history, serious illnesses and accidents, onset of speech, etc.), their behavior at home (e.g., dressing, eating, toileting, etc.), their relationships to siblings and other children and adults, their ability to cope with new situations, and traumatic events (e.g., prolonged separation from parent, hospitalization of child, frequent moves, etc).

The purpose of the screening procedure is to identify youngsters who are as yet too immature or vulnerable to be able to benefit from a regular kindergarten program at the time of school entry. A child is considered ready for kindergarten if he can meet *at least three of the four criteria* listed below:

1. The pupil's social and emotional behavior, as observed by the kindergarten teacher, must be at least at the four-and-one-half-year-old level. The youngster should be able to feed and dress himself and to take care of his toilet needs.

2. The pupil's language ability, perceptual motor function, mental age and emotional adjustment as measured on the Vane Kindergarten Test should be at least at the four-and-one-half-year-old level.

3. The pupil's chronological age at the time of school entry (September) should be at least five (i.e., his birthday should be between January and August).

4. The pupil's social history should reveal no marked developmental abnormalities or delays nor any serious accidents, illnesses, or traumatic experiences that might contribute to or result in learning disabilities or emotional problems.

A child who meets three of these four criteria is considered to be a good candidate for a regular kindergarten class. For instance, a youngster has a good chance of holding his own in kindergarten even if he is less than five years old, *provided* he is functioning socially and mentally on at least the four-and-one-half-year-old level and if he has no history of serious developmental delays, emotional trauma, or medical problems. A socially immature child will also get along in kindergarten *if* he has average mental ability, a normal developmental history and is at least five years of age. So will a five-year-old pupil who is mentally a little slow but who shows good social maturity and no developmental and medical abnormalities or trauma in early life. A special class placement should never be made on the basis of any *one* factor, a single test score, or a diagnostic label.

If a child reveals weaknesses in more than one area, he will need special consideration. A child cannot cope successfully with a regular kindergarten class if he is extremely immature socially *and* slow mentally, or if he is only 4 years 9 months old and has a history of developmental delays or of severe deprivation or trauma in early life. The same applies if a pupil is mentally immature *and* suffers from brain dysfunction and epilepsy due to a head injury or if he is less than five years old and is, in addition, socially and emotionally very immature for his age.

The proposed special education plan provides that children can be

Figure 5.

Organization of regular and special classes.

Explanation of symbols:

☐ equals one year in school
→ possible movement of children from one type of class to another according to needs
R: Regular classes
I: Classes for Immature children
MP: Classes for children with Multiple Problems
T: Classes for Trainable Mentally Retarded children
RR: Resource Room
RS: Regular Slow classes
LD: Classes for children with Learning Disabilities
A: Academically oriented high school classes
G: General or nonacademically oriented high school classes
V: Vocational training program
WS: Work-Study program
SW: Sheltered Workshop

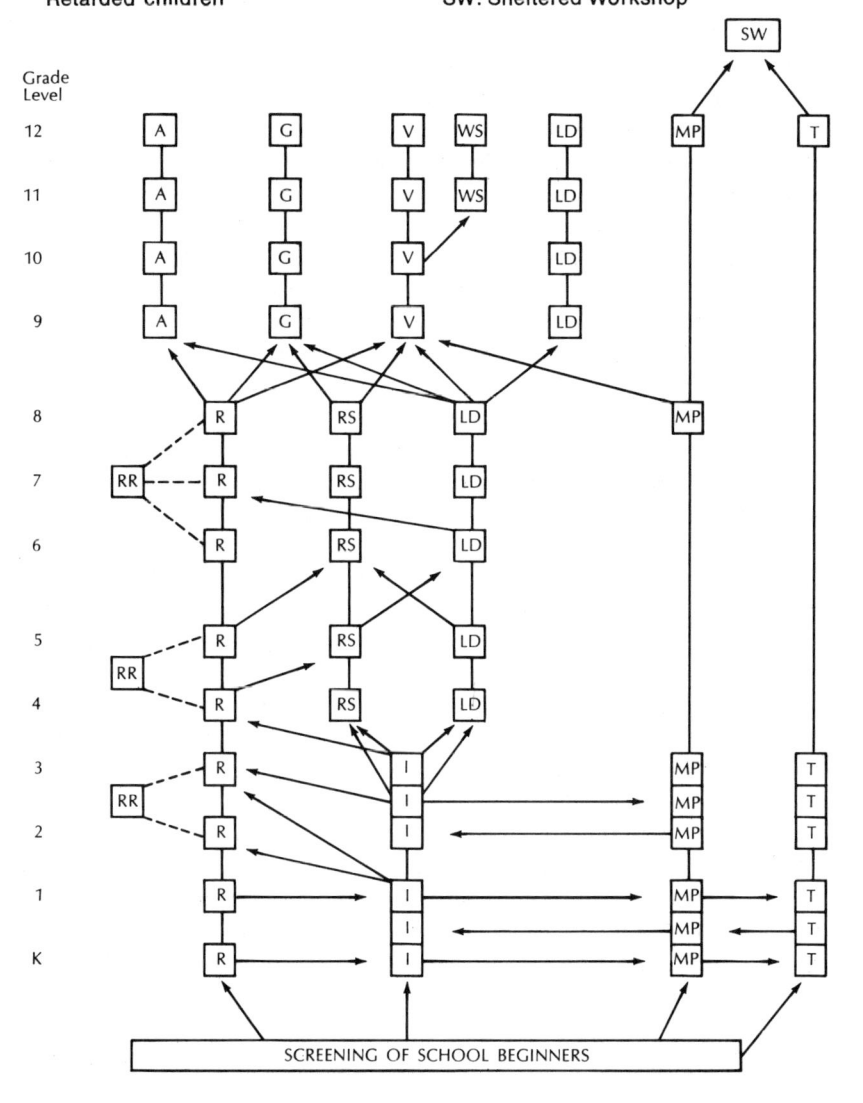

enrolled in four different types of classes at the time of school entry. The placement of each child should be guided by the results of the screening procedure. The child's age, social, emotional and mental maturity and his developmental and medical history should all be taken into account. Figure 5 shows the organization of regular and special classes in the proposed educational program. The majority of pupils would of course enter *regular kindergarten classes (R)*. Depending on the type of community the school is located in, anywhere from 5 to 15 percent of the school beginners would be placed into special *classes for immature children (I)*. Only a fraction of one percent of the pupils would have a need for the *classes for children with multiple problems (MP)* or for the *classes for severely retarded trainable children (T)*. Placement into any one of the special classes is never considered final or terminal. Each pupil in the Immature, Multiple Problems, or Trainable classes should be reevaluated annually. If it seems to be in the child's best interest, he can be transferred at any time from one type of class to another.

The suggested special education program would in effect eliminate the classes for educable mentally retarded (EMR) youngsters who are usually defined as youngsters with IQ scores between 50 and 75. Experience has shown that an IQ score is not a meaningful criterion for class placement. The more adequate, well-integrated pupils of borderline intelligence (IQs in the 70s and low 80s) can usually get along quite well in somewhat slower-moving regular classes. They should have the opportunity of being as much a part as possible of the regular school program since they will have to learn to get along on their own in the community in later life. Other children with the same level of IQ scores but with more serious neurological and emotional difficulties may need more protective and smaller classes. So will youngsters whose retardation is more severe (IQs in the 50s or 60s) and who have behavior problems. There should be no definite IQ cutoff point for placing children into specific types of classes. Special classes should be regarded as being on a continuum or gradiation, and a child should be placed where his needs are best met. Thus, a child with an IQ score of 57 might be placed in a Trainable class *or* in a class for children with Multiple Problems *or* in an Immature class depending on his behavior, integrative function, his life experiences and background, and his emotional adjustment.

The main innovation of the proposed special education plan are the *classes for immature children*. The Immature classes are designed for youngsters who mature at a slower rate than most children and who are not yet ready for regular kindergarten classes at the time of school

Summary and Implications of the Study

entry. The definition of "readiness" was outlined earlier (p. 200). Immature children whose mental ages are between 3½ and 4½ years, would not be asked to compete in regular classes with socially and emotionally more mature pupils. Instead, they would enter classes that are appropriate for their developmental level. The curriculum in the Immature classes will include much perceptual training, language stimulation, and concept formation, also training in motor coordination and social experiences, and free play and creative activities. The exact program to be followed will depend, of course, on the population of pupils and on the teacher. The essential feature of the Immature classes is that they *progress at a slower rate* than regular classes.

The Immature classes are set up in three-year units and are programmed at a slow pace. They are so designed that they will cover approximately two years (kindergarten and first grade) in three years' time. The children are allowed to advance in the classes at their own speed without undue pressure to conform to a specified rate of progress. The Immature classes should be located in regular school buildings if possible so that the pupils can participate in as many regular activities as they are able. If the school is small, the first three-year unit of Immature classes could be set up in one or two ungraded classrooms or in an open space plan in a large room. If the school is large, one or more Immature classes or class groups could be in operation at each level. Each Immature class or class group should have no more than 10 to 15 pupils with one teacher and a teacher's aide. This ratio would make individual work with the children possible and would maximize the benefits of the Immature classes. It is essential to involve the parents of the pupils in the program to get their cooperation and help and to keep them from pressuring the immature children for academic work before the youngsters are ready and able to produce it.

At the end of the school year, the immature pupils would be reevaluated and any child who has demonstrated significant maturation and mental and emotional growth could be transferred to a regular first grade class. On the other hand, if a child fails to show any progress or if he proves to be more seriously impaired or handicapped than was realized at first, he could be transferred to a class for children with Multiple Problems. Most of the pupils would continue for another year or two in the Immature classes.

The majority of youngsters who would be enrolled in the Immature classes would remain in these classes for at least three years. At the end of the three-year period, the pupils would be seven-and-one-half to eight years old. By that time, it is possible to assess fairly well their rate of learning and their mental potential. As shown in Figure 5, at this point some children will be able to transfer from the Immature classes to regular second grade classes; a few youngsters may be able to go to a regular third grade; while one or two pupils may have to be transferred to the classes for children with Multiple Problems. The remaining pupils would continue on to the second three-year unit of Immature classes. Since none of the children would have "failed" or repeated a grade, it is expected that their emotional and social adjustment would be better than it would have been if they had attended a regular kindergarten or first grade and had been retained or had been transferred to a special class *after* failing. The achievement of vulnerable pupils should also be better after three years in the Immature classes than after three years in regular classes. The youngsters would have had a chance to develop their ability to the fullest without undue frustration or failure experiences to discourage them. Thus, they should have a sound foundation on which to build further learning and their attitudes toward school should be positive.

The second three-year unit of Immature classes is again paced at a slower rate than regular classes. This unit is meant to cover, in general, only the second and third grade curriculum. However, as was pointed out before, each child is free to progress at his own rate and whenever a child is ready or able to move onto a regular class he can do so. Each child will be reevaluated at the end of each year.

At the end of the second three-year period in the Immature classes, the pupils can either go to a regular fourth or a regular fifth grade, or they can transfer to a *Regular Slow Class (RS),* which is fully integrated into the regular school program in all but the academic subjects. If, however, the youngsters are still extremely vulnerable or have specific learning disabilities and/or serious emotional problems, they can move to a small, more protective class for children with *Learning Disabilities (LD).* These classes would be mostly self-contained. LD pupils would be integrated into regular classes only on an individual basis for isolated subjects, when they were ready for it. Some children may always need a self-contained class.

Youngsters who transfer from the Immature classes to Regular classes *(R)* in elementary school and who still require some extra help can get it from the *Resource Rooms (RR).* The Resource Rooms are set up to provide daily one-half-hour to one-hour individual or small group supplementary instruction for second and third graders and for fourth and fifth graders (Figure 5).

At the sixth grade level—that is, at the beginning of middle school—

Summary and Implications of the Study

most youngsters have three possibilities for class placements. Depending on his needs, a regular class pupil can continue in a regular middle school class or he can enroll in a Regular Slow class or if needed he can transfer to the small, protective LD class. The child in the Regular Slow class will most likely continue in such a class if he is well placed, but if he is able to do so, he may transfer to a regular middle school class, or, if need be, to an LD class. The youngster in the LD class, who is by now twelve years old, may have matured sufficiently in the intervening years to hold his own in a regular sixth grade either with or without the aid of a Resource Room. Or the child may have stabilized and can move along now with other somewhat slower pupils in a Regular Slow class, or he may need to continue in the supportive LD class in the middle school.

At the beginning of high school, in the ninth grade, the pupils can select or be assigned to four different types of programs (Figure 5). The options are open to all who qualify. They can attend an Academic program *(A)*, a General program *(G)*, a self-contained academically oriented LD class, or a Vocational program *(V)*. This choice should be made on the basis of the youngsters' abilities and interests. It is expected that many regular and LD pupils will select a general or vocational program, as will most of the pupils in the Regular Slow classes. LD pupils whose achievement and adjustment is good may transfer to the academic program or they may pursue an academic course in the LD class. There is precedent for LD pupils graduating from an LD class and going onto college. The vocational program should include one or two years of prevocational training and the study of basic skills followed by one or two years of Work-Study *(WS)*. Work-Study would include part-time vocational training at the high school and part-time work under supervision in the community.

The proposed special education plan would appreciably reduce the amount of frustration and failure children with learning disabilities would experience, especially during the crucial first three years in school. During these early years, children's attitudes toward school and toward learning are formed. These attitudes are extremely important since they influence the pupils' adjustment to school and work in the years to follow.

The suggested special class plan would make it possible for children to move through school, beginning with kindergarten, at a faster or slower pace without having to repeat a grade. Thus, most youngsters would graduate after thirteen years in elementary and secondary school (including kindergarten), but some pupils would need fourteen or fifteen years to do so. The children with multiple problems and the trainable retarded children would stay in school until they are 20 years old. A few youngsters with multiple problems might be able to take vocational training courses, but most of the pupils in these two groups would move on to a Sheltered Workshop *(SW)* or to an institution if necessary.

Some people object to any and all special classes in public schools and claim that such classes stigmatize the pupils and deprive them of normal educational opportunities and stimulation. It is indeed deplorable if children are "dumped" into ill-defined or poorly run "special" classes and are left there without any further evaluation or consideration, but just because some unfortunate experiences have occurred with some special classes is not sufficient reason to deprive children with learning and emotional problems of the special help they need. It is also well to remember that children do not develop problems *because* they are in special classes, but rather that children are *in* special classes *because they have problems*. Of course, a special class placement has some drawbacks; this cannot be denied. However, these are minor compared to the advantages a well-run special class can offer youngsters with minimal brain dysfunction, developmental lags, or with specific learning difficulties. These youngsters would be at a much greater disadvantage if they did not have special classes to go into.

The writer is convinced that a failure to provide special classes early enough for more children contributes to the ever-increasing number of youngsters with learning and behavior problems. It is sincerely believed that the slower-paced classes for immature children and the LD classes proposed here would greatly help to prevent or to minimize the development of serious emotional problems and learning disabilities in vulnerable, immature school children. By placing the special Immature and LD classes into regular schools and by integrating the pupils as much as possible into regular classes and activities, the children will feel less like "failures" and "rejects." No special class program can prevent or eliminate *all* learning problems since most of them have an organic basis, but a good special education program can help pupils to function up to the limits of their ability and can make school a happier and more meaningful experience for them.

No one school will have enough children with serious multiple problems or with severe retardation to allow for good class grouping for these children within a single school. It is therefore suggested that the Trainable classes and the classes for Multiple Problems be placed into central locations so that pupils from several schools or school districts

Summary and Implications of the Study

can be enrolled in them. A joint or cooperative larger program for these severely handicapped children will allow for better educational services than an isolated class in a regular school could offer. Such a central facility would most likely involve segregation from the regular school, but the advantages of such placement would, in this case, outweigh the disadvantages.

The same applies for the vocational school. Few high schools are large enough to be able to afford a comprehensive vocational training program with the latest equipment and workshops. A large cooperative or regional vocational school in a separate location can offer better services to more youngsters from several different schools than several small vocational training programs could provide if they were attached to individual high schools.

References

Ackerman, P., Peters, J. E., and Dykman, R. A.: Children with specific learning disabilities: WISC Profiles. *Journal of Learning Disabilities,* 4:33-49, 1971.

Ames, L. B.: A low intelligence quotient often not recognized as the chief cause of many learning difficulties. *Journal of Learning Disabilities,* 1:735-739, 1968.

———: Children with perceptual problems may also lag developmentally. *Journal of Learning Disabilities,* 2:30-33, 1969.

Bender, L.: A Visual Motor Gestalt Test and its clinical use. *The American Orthopsychiatric Association Research Monograph, No. 3, 1938.*

———: Use of the Visual Motor Gestalt Test in the diagnosis of learning disabilities. *Journal of Special Education,* 4:29-39, 1970.

Birch, H., and Gussow, J. D.: *Disadvantaged Children: Health, Nutrition, and School Failure.* New York, Grune & Stratton, 1970.

Black, F. W.: An investigation of intelligence as a causal factor in reading problems. *Journal of Learning Disabilities,* 4:22-25, 1971.

Bloom, B.: *Stability and Change in Human Characteristics.* New York, John Wiley & Sons, 1964.

Bortner, M., and Birch, H. G.: Patterns of intellectual ability in emotionally disturbed and brain-damaged children. *Journal of Special Education,* 3:351-369, 1969.

Brenner, M. W., Gillman, S., Zangwill, O. L., and Farrell, M.: Visuo-motor disability in school children. *British Medical Journal,* 4:259-262, 1967.

References

Christoplos, F., and Renz, P.: A critical examination of special education programs. *Journal of Special Education,* 3:371-379, 1969.

Cruickshank, W., and Johnson, G. O.: *Education of Exceptional Children and Youth.* Englewood Cliffs, Prentice-Hall, 1958.

Dubnoff, B.: "Perceptual training as a bridge to conceptual ability." In: Hellmuth, J.: *Educational Therapy.* Seattle, Special Child Publications, 1966.

Early, G. H.: *Perceptual Training in the Curriculum.* Columbus, O., Charles E. Merrill, 1969.

Ebersole, M. L., Kephart, N. G., and Ebersole, J. B.: *Steps to Achievement for the Slow Learner.* Columbus, Charles E. Merrill Publishing Co., 1968.

Fenichel, C.: "Psycho-educational approaches for seriously disturbed children in the classroom." In: Hellmuth, J.: *Educational Therapy.* Seattle, Special Child Publications, 1966.

Hallahan, D. P.: Cognitive styles: preschool implications for the disadvantaged. *Journal of Learning Disabilities,* 3:6-9, 1970.

Haring, N. G., and Phillips, E. L.: *Educating Emotionally Disturbed Children.* New York, McGraw-Hill, 1962.

Harvey, J.: To fix or to cope: a dilemma for special education. *Journal of Special Education,* 3:389-392, 1969.

Hellmuth, J.: *Educational Therapy.* Seattle, Special Child Publications, 1966.

———: *Learning Disorders.* Seattle, Special Child Publications, 1966.

Jastak, J., and Bijou, S.: *Wide Range Achievement Test,* Wilmington, C. L. Story, 1946.

Jastak, J. F., Bijou, S. W., and Jastak, S. R.: *Wide Range Achievement Test,* rev. ed. Wilmington, Guidance Associates, 1965.

Johnson, D., and Myklebust, H. R.: *Learning Disabilities.* New York, Grune & Stratton, 1967.

Kirk, S. A.: *Education of Exceptional Children.* Boston, Houghton-Mifflin, 1962.

Koppitz, E. M.: *The Bender Gestalt Test for Young Children.* New York, Grune & Stratton, 1964.

———: *Psychological Evaluation of Children's Human Figure Drawings.* New York, Grune & Stratton, 1968.

———: Brain damage, reading disability and the Bender Gestalt Test. *Journal of Learning Disabilities,* 3:429-433, 1970.

Kotting, C. and Brozovich, R.: *A descriptive follow-up study of a public school program for the emotionally disturbed.* U.S. Department of Health, Education and Welfare, Office of Education, Bureau of Research, 1969.

Lazure, D. and Roberts, C. A.: *One million children: the commission on emotional and learning disorders in children report.* Toronto, Leonard Crainford, 1969.

Mackie, R. P.: Spotlighting advances in special education. *Exceptional Children,* 32:77-81, 1965.

Mallison, R.: *Education as Therapy.* Seattle, Special Child Publications, 1968.

Miller, J. G., and Schoenfelder, D. S.: A rational look at special class placement. *Journal of Special Education,* 3:397-401, 1969.

National Education Association: *Programs for Handicapped Children.* pp. 115-117. Washington, NEA Research Division, 1967.

Rawson, M. B.: *Developmental Language Disability: Adult Accomplishments of Dyslexic boys.* Baltimore, Johns Hopkins, 1968.

Richards, C. J., and Clark, A. D.: Learning disabilities: a national survey of existing public school programs. *Journal of Special Education,* 1:223-226, 1968.

Ritvo, E. R., and Ornitz, E. M.: A new look at childhood autism points to CNS disease. In: *Roche Report: Frontiers of Hospital Psychiatry,* 7:6-7, 1970.

Silver, L. B.: A proposed view on the etiology of the neurological learning disability syndrome. *Journal of Learning Disabilities,* 4:6-16, 1971.

Silberberg, N. E., and Silberberg, M. C.: Hyperplexia: special word recognition skills in young children. *Exceptional Children,* 34:41-42, 1967.

——— and ———: Case histories in hyperplexia. *Journal of School Psychology,* 7:3-7, 1968-69.

——— and ———: Myths in remedial reading. *Journal of Learning Disabilities,* 2:209-217, 1969.

Strauss, A. A., and Lehtinen, L. E.: *Psychopathology and Education of the Brain-injured Child.* New York, Grune & Stratton, 1947.

Swift, M., and Spivack, G.: The assessment of achievement-related classroom behavior. *Journal of Special Education,* 2:137-147, 1968.

Terman, L. M., and Merrill, M.: *Stanford-Binet Intelligence Scales.* Boston, Houghton-Mifflin, 1960.

Thomas, A., Chess, S., and Birch, H. G.: The origin of personality. *Scientific American,* 223:102-109, 1970.

Towne, R. C., and Joiner, L. M.: Some negative implications of special placement for children with learning disabilities. *Journal of Special Education,* 2:217-222, 1968.

Vane, J. R.: *The Vane Kindergarten Test.* Brandon, Clinical Psychology Publishing Co., 1968.

Wechsler, D.: *Wechsler Intelligence Scale for Children.* New York, The Psychological Corporation, 1955.

Wepman, J. M.: *Auditory Discrimination Test.* Chicago, Language Research Associates, 1958.

Index

Achievement of LD pupils. *See* LD pupils, achievement of
Ackerman, P., 122, 208
Acting-out. *See* Behavior, acting-out
Adjustment. *See* LD program, adjustment to
Administrator, 3, 5-7, 13, 40, 52, 93, 168, 175, 180, 181
Admission. *See* LD program, admission to
Age of LD pupils. *See* LD pupils, age of
Aggressive behavior. *See* Behavior, aggressive
Ames, L., 42, 64, 208
Anxiety, 21, 22, 27, 28, 32, 48, 49, 53, 54, 56, 69, 80, 81, 88, 89, 102, 108, 109, 111, 134, 146, 153-155, 158, 164, 189
Aphasic, 118
Arithmetic, 19, 20, 32, 46, 60, 62, 82, 93, 96, 97, 108, 113, 119, 122, 138, 151, 155, 188, 193
Association of sounds and symbols, 125, 162, 172

Attitude. *See* LD pupils, attitudes of *and* Parents, attitudes of
Auditory discrimination, 172
Auditory perception. *See* Perception, auditory
Autism, 21, 47, 53, 139
Autistic children, 15, 22, 47, 49, 53, 55, 139ff, 182

Behavior. *See also* LD pupils, behavior of
  acting-out, 21, 23, 27, 38, 49, 53, 65, 67, 76, 81, 84, 86-88, 92, 138, 145, 146, 149, 163, 164, 174, 193
  aggressive, 21, 22, 27, 38, 48, 49, 54, 56, 68, 77, 80, 88, 90, 92, 138, 140, 148, 149, 160-163, 193
  bizarre, 21, 47, 145, 155, 174
  deterioration of, 27, 47, 88, 146, 147, 149, 152, 175
  temper outbursts, 10, 21, 28, 68, 77, 134, 147, 148, 153, 155, 160, 189

211

unpredictable, 29, 86, 128, 172, 185, 188
withdrawn, 21, 22, 27, 29, 32, 48, 54, 71, 72, 81, 82, 88, 89, 113, 114, 125, 126, 151, 155, 170, 185
Behavior problems, 12, 15, 20, 22, 27, 28, 47, 49, 65, 74-76, 80, 82, 91, 98, 99, 101, 111, 112, 116, 126ff, 158, 170, 172, 174, 175, 181, 182, 188, 194, 198, 202
Bender, L., 16, 186, 208
Bender Gestalt Test, 8, 16, 18, 29, 32, 44-46, 59, 60, 62, 64, 102, 108, 138, 142, 186
Bijou, S. W., 8, 19, 209
Birch, H. G., 22, 25, 51, 158, 208, 210
Birth trauma, 23, 49, 50, 117
Black, F. W., 122, 208
Bloom, B., 62, 208
Bortner, M., 51, 208
Brain dysfunction. *See* Minimal brain dysfunction
Brain injury, 1, 81, 125, 148, 152, 195
Brain-injured. *See* Diagnosis of brain injury
Brenner, M. W., 46, 208
Brozovich, R., 2, 4, 36, 46, 51, 209

Central Nervous System (CNS), 12, 139, 198
Cerebral palsy (CP), 24, 102
Character disorder, 163, 164, 182
Characteristics of LD pupils. *See* LD pupils, characteristics of
Chess, S., 25, 158, 210
Childhood autism. *See* Autism
Christoplos, F., 2, 209
Clark, A. D., 2, 210
Class groupings, 4, 6, 51, 84, 175, 178, 192, 195, 198, 206
Class placement, 101, 112
special, 2, 19, 37, 47, 56, 69, 75, 80, 85, 133, 135, 146, 160, 166, 168, 174, 196, 198

kindergarten, 5, 15, 27, 42, 54, 68, 77, 81, 82, 91, 101, 110, 111, 125, 127, 134, 151, 160, 161, 169, 170, 178, 181, 183, 184, 186, 189-191, 198-200, 202-205
first grade, 15, 27, 42, 54, 75, 82, 111, 112, 125, 134, 161, 170, 172, 186, 189, 190, 203, 204
second grade, 27, 68, 82, 111, 112, 134, 172, 187, 190, 204
third grade, 33, 76, 111, 172, 191, 204
fourth grade, 71, 80, 191, 204
fifth grade, 76, 89, 91, 191, 204
sixth grade, 76, 82, 93, 204, 205
seventh grade, 76, 90
eighth grade, 72, 173
College, 72, 87, 109, 157, 205
Compensation for neurological problems, 34, 80, 115, 121, 187-190, 196
Comprehension, 11, 86, 102, 111-114, 122, 131
Compulsivity, 21, 85, 129, 153, 154
Concepts, 11, 98, 111-113
Control, weak inner, 10, 11, 27, 29, 32, 54, 78, 117, 127, 133, 146
Convulsions, 23, 147
Coordination. *See* Motor coordination
Counseling, 136, 161, 162, 178
Cruickshank, W., 1, 209

Delinquent, 21, 22, 48, 49, 56, 92, 138, 163ff, 182
Depressed, 21, 99, 123, 149
Developmental history, 5, 22-24, 28, 49, 50, 51, 54, 194, 195
Developmental lag, 1, 11, 23, 49, 169, 172, 186, 189, 200, 206
Diagnosis
of brain injury, 22, 24, 50, 102, 117, 126, 128, 160, 162
of emotional disturbance, 4, 23, 194
of minimal brain dysfunction, 22, 24, 28, 49, 54, 74

Index

Diagnostic label, 4, 51, 100, 117, 142, 198, 200
Disorganization
of behavior, 90, 132, 146, 148
of thinking, 80, 128
Distractible, 10, 11, 21, 54, 68, 74, 77, 82, 102, 128, 132, 151
Dormitories, 136, 164, 197, 199
Drawings. See Human Figure Drawings
Dubnoff, B., 51, 206
Dykman, R. A., 122, 208
Dyslexic, 2, 117, 119, 173, 192

Early, G. H., 1, 209
Ebersole, J.B., 1, 209
Ebersole, M. L., 1, 209
Educable children. See Mentally retarded, educable, and EMR classes
EEG (electroencephalogram), 22-24, 28, 49, 117, 126, 128, 149, 162, 194
Elementary school, 2, 15, 37, 65, 71, 74, 90, 102, 138, 153, 175, 178, 190, 204, 205
EMR (educable mentally retarded) classes, 36, 99, 100-102, 202
Epilepsy, 194, 200
epileptic equivalent, 149
grand mal, 24, 148
petit mal, 24, 86, 87
Evaluation of LD pupils. See LD pupils, evaluation of
Exclusion. See Psychiatric exclusion
Expression
oral, 85, 119
written, 77, 119

Farrell, M., 46, 208
Fenichel, C., 51, 209
Foster home, 21, 25, 26, 51, 68, 71, 92, 93, 139, 145, 147, 149, 150
Frustration tolerance, low, 10, 21, 22, 26, 27, 29, 47, 53, 74, 78, 88, 93, 125, 146, 153, 163

Genetic, 1, 117, 119, 187, 196
Gillman, S., 46, 208
Grade placement. See Class placement
Grouping of pupils. See Class groupings
Gussow, J. D., 22, 25, 208

Hallahan, D. P., 117, 209
Haring, N. G., 1, 209
Harvey, J., 2, 209
Hellmuth, J., 1, 209
High school, 5, 37, 86, 87, 90, 91, 101, 110, 124, 173, 178, 179, 181, 191, 198, 205, 206
Home tutoring, 35, 147, 154, 164
Hospital. See Mental hospital
Human Figure Drawing, 29, 32, 69, 72, 78, 82, 129, 142, 155, 170
Hyperactive, 11, 21-23, 53, 54, 68, 69, 71, 77, 118, 128, 131, 132, 147, 149, 161, 163, 189, 192
Hypersensitive, 21, 27, 68, 71, 77, 88-90, 125, 127, 133, 147, 149, 150, 155, 174, 175
Hypertalkative, 87, 118, 153
Hypoactive, 10

Immaturity, 16, 23, 49, 50, 68, 74 77, 81, 98, 102, 127, 142, 158, 169, 175, 184, 200
emotional, 76, 133, 163, 184
perceptual, 19, 29, 60, 133
physical, 23, 76, 133, 184
Impulsive, 10, 21, 29, 71, 78, 80, 82, 92, 127, 129, 140, 153, 154, 189, 192, 194
Incoordination, 127, 132
Individual differences, 74, 183, 189, 191, 197
Individualized instructions, 135, 173, 183
Integrative ability, 10, 12, 16, 19, 27, 29, 46, 54, 55, 60, 76, 81, 88, 127, 128, 138, 142, 186, 187, 189
Intelligence. See Mental ability
Intersensory integration, 15, 120, 186

IQ scores of LD pupils. *See* LD
    pupils, IQ scores of
Jastak, J. F., 8, 19, 209
Jastak, S. R., 8, 19, 209
Johnson, D., 1, 209
Johnson, G. O., 1, 209
Joiner, L. M., 2, 210

Kephart, N. G., 1, 209
Kirk, S. A., 1, 209
Koppitz, E. M., 8, 16, 29, 32, 46, 69,
    108, 129, 186, 209
Kotting, C., 2, 4, 36, 46, 51, 209

Language
    ability, 77, 81, 148, 200
    development, 23, 53-55, 129,
        133, 140, 151, 186, 189, 192
    problem, 161, 175
Laziness, 116, 118, 161, 162
Lazure, D., 2, 75, 209
Learning disability
    cause of, 1, 32, 116, 187, 198
    cure for, 36, 198
    definition of, 1
LD class. *See* Special class
LD program
    adjustment to, 55, 67ff, 154,
        166, 177
    admission to, 4-6, 12, 20, 21,
        27, 37, 42, 59, 61, 100, 141
    description of, 4
    purpose of, 34, 180
    return to, 35-37, 66, 89, 92,
        146-150, 155, 159, 161, 162,
        174-176ff
    withdrawal from, 8, 36, 37, 40,
        56, 166ff, 177
LD pupils
    achievement of, 16, 19, 27, 40,
        53, 55, 59, 61, 64, 69, 77, 78,
        88, 89, 95, 99, 100, 117, 123,
        133-135, 167, 187, 188, 193
    age of, 3, 5, 8, 14, 41, 59, 60, 88,
        97, 98, 117, 127, 183ff
    attitudes of, toward school, 67,
        134, 151, 152, 155, 159-161,
        163, 166, 169, 170, 174, 185,
        188, 193
    behavior of, 20-22, 47, 56, 67,
        74, 76, 85, 126ff, 141, 192-194
    characteristics of, 2, 9, 10ff,
        26, 27, 52, 53, 67, 97, 101
    evaluation of, 7, 8, 12, 95, 99,
        100, 119, 125, 133
    failure of, 64, 66, 87, 92-94,
        119, 174
    fathers of, 25, 26, 28, 32, 33, 36,
        134, 147, 148, 151, 152, 155,
        157
    IQ scores of, 8, 15, 27, 42, 43,
        54, 55, 60-62, 81, 88, 95, 99,
        111, 117, 119, 121, 125, 127,
        131, 138, 183ff, 198
    long-term, 35, 36, 42-45, 54, 55,
        95ff, 182, 185
    mothers of, 7, 23, 26, 28, 32, 33,
        91, 134, 145, 147-150ff, 158,
        163, 164, 196, 199
    referral of, 5, 12, 13, 15, 19, 20,
        22, 27, 38, 42, 54, 68, 71, 74,
        78, 81, 82, 86, 102, 111, 138,
        185, 193
    selection of, 3, 4, 37, 39, 40, 44,
        178, 180, 181
    sex of, 13, 14, 41
Lehtinen, L. E., 1, 210

Mackie, R. P., 2, 210
Mallison, R., 1, 210
Maturation, 12, 47, 61, 74, 76, 78, 80,
    82, 100, 169, 181, 187
    rate of, 64, 74, 76, 78, 81, 102,
        133, 185, 187, 189, 196, 198,
        202
Medical histories of LD pupils, 11,
    22-24, 28, 49, 50, 54, 117,
    148, 194
Medication, 48, 69, 71, 129, 147-149,
    159, 194
Memory, 16, 19, 33, 36, 53-55, 97,
    99, 110, 111, 115ff, 131, 148,
    185, 186
    deficit, 115, 116, 118, 119, 122,
        125, 126, 185, 186
Mental ability of LD pupils, 42-44,
    62, 88, 98, 127, 138, 181

Index

above average, 18, 77, 81, 85, 112, 129
average, normal, 1, 8, 15, 29, 53, 74, 77, 85, 101, 116
borderline, 15, 99
low average, dull normal, 15, 18, 27, 54, 81, 95, 163
retarded. *See* Mentally retarded children
Mental hospital, 8, 35, 39, 42, 137, 141, 142, 146, 149, 150, 155, 159, 195
  return from, 146, 148-151, 154, 155, 161, 177
  return to, 146, 149, 150, 177
Mentally retarded children, 4, 38, 99, 100, 108-110, 117, 126, 162, 202
  Educable, 4, 38, 99, 100, 202
  Trainable, 4, 142, 202, 206
Merrill, M., 15, 210
Middle school, 15, 71, 81, 82, 86, 90, 91, 102, 132, 135, 138, 153, 172, 173, 175, 204, 205
Miller, J. G., 2, 210
Minimal brain dysfunction, 18, 27, 47, 71, 76, 77, 88, 92, 98, 117, 119, 145, 149, 153, 158, 186-189, 197, 206
Mother-child relationship, 139, 157
Motivation for learning, 36, 56, 64, 75, 116, 118, 119, 158, 173, 187, 188, 193
Motor coordination, 77, 78, 82, 88, 102, 131, 133, 146, 153, 203
Myklebust, H. R., 1, 209

National Education Association (NEA), 2, 210
Neglect, physical and/or emotional, 25, 51, 54, 68, 92, 110, 117, 139, 145, 147, 150, 157, 158, 163, 164, 187, 195, 196
Neurological examination, 22, 23, 28, 117, 126, 128, 149, 194

Neurological malfunction or impairment, 1, 4, 28, 54, 68, 74, 76, 127, 128, 129, 151, 153, 155, 161, 187, 194, 195, 202
Number concepts, 111, 113
Nursery school, 102, 127

Observation
  class, 38, 100, 102, 109
  of LD pupils, 99, 154
One-to-one situation, 55, 56, 77, 135, 140, 142
Organic signs, 23, 194
Ornitz, E. M., 139, 210

Parent
  attitude toward LD pupil, 28, 32, 33, 37, 56, 68, 71, 81, 84-86, 91, 92, 110, 111, 113, 116, 125, 126, 128, 139, 150, 157-160, 162, 166, 167, 169, 170, 172-174, 195
  attitude of, toward LD program, 5, 21, 28, 35, 37, 40, 56, 69, 85, 91, 93, 100-102, 109, 127, 142, 147, 161, 166-168, 172, 173, 177, 196
  work with, 7, 23, 26, 33, 51, 52, 72, 90, 110, 114, 141, 155, 157, 168, 182, 194, 199
Parents of LD pupils. *See* LD pupils, parents of
Peers
  attitudes of, toward LD pupils, 11, 28, 32, 66, 68, 71, 82, 84-88, 112, 123, 128, 153-155, 162, 173
  LD pupils' attitudes toward, 11, 33, 55, 56, 67, 74, 77, 85, 87, 90-93, 102, 134, 135, 147, 148, 153, 158, 161, 162, 164, 169, 174
Perception
  auditory, 10, 15, 16, 19, 45, 53-55, 115, 116, 119, 120, 122, 124, 125, 131, 160, 162, 163, 185
  visual, 77, 119, 125, 131

visual–motor, 10, 11, 15, 16, 18, 19, 27, 29, 33, 53-55, 60, 61, 82, 85, 88, 92, 102, 115, 116, 133, 138, 147, 148, 151, 153, 155, 160, 163, 185-187
Perceptual malfunctioning, 38, 44, 74, 90, 100, 115, 117, 118, 124-126, 175, 185, 186
Perceptual training, 33, 63, 75, 109, 114, 169, 186, 187, 202
Perfectionism, 78, 85
Perseveration, 29, 142
Peters, J. E., 122, 208
Petit mal. *See* Epilepsy, petit mal
Phillips, E. L., 1, 209
Preadolescent, 14, 71, 138, 163, 164
Predicting progress. *See* Progress of LD pupils, predicting
Prevention of emotional problems, 75, 76, 81, 136, 180, 181, 183, 194, 198, 206
Prevention of learning problems, 180, 183, 198, 206
Primary grades, 15, 42, 53, 80, 81, 179, 186, 194, 198
Private schools, 2, 4, 6, 36, 40, 56, 84, 86, 87, 141, 154, 162, 168
Progress of LD pupils, 9, 13, 16, 45, 52, 56, 58ff, 82, 86, 93, 100, 116, 118, 124, 135, 151, 166, 195, 196
  actual, 2, 58ff, 96, 97, 108, 113, 114, 118, 119, 128, 152
  initial spurt of, 63, 64, 100, 188
  long-range, 39, 100
  predicting, 34, 38, 46, 48, 50, 52, 53, 169, 186
  rate of, 62, 63, 75, 91, 97, 100, 108, 109, 114, 133, 188, 189, 191, 195, 198, 203
Psychiatric
  evaluation, 22, 28, 68, 113, 137, 149, 194
  exclusion, 8, 35, 39-42, 47, 48, 80, 137ff, 142, 159
Psychiatrist, 5, 6, 24, 28, 40, 72, 110, 147, 160, 194
Psychological testing, 16, 55, 56, 99, 100, 140, 142, 185

Psychologist, 5-8, 12, 28, 33, 40, 72, 99, 110, 120, 125, 140, 142, 160, 194, 199
Psychotherapy, 69, 71, 72, 136, 141, 146, 149, 155, 159, 160, 162
Psychotic, 56, 137, 145, 154, 182

Rawson, M. B., 2, 4, 210
Reading
  achievement, 20, 45, 46, 60, 62, 63, 82, 96, 97, 111-113, 118, 119, 127, 131, 151, 152, 188
  problems, 29, 77, 86, 89, 122, 124, 125, 162, 172, 173, 187, 191
  remedial, 114, 172, 191
Reasoning, 29, 98, 101, 110, 111, 114, 115, 121, 131, 163
Recall, 16, 29, 54, 110, 121
Referral to LD program. *See* LD program, referral to
Regression, 47, 78, 89, 90, 93, 147, 150, 152, 174, 189
Regular class
  adjustment to, 22, 60, 65ff, 169, 172, 174, 177
  return to, 2, 7, 13, 34, 36, 38, 40-42, 44, 54, 58ff, 110, 159, 168, 172-174, 181, 182, 185, 189, 191, 195, 198
  modified program, 7, 87, 90, 91, 93, 168, 173, 178
Renz, P., 2, 209
Repeating grade, 75, 76, 163, 190, 204, 205
Residential treatment center, 7, 8, 35, 37, 43, 51, 56, 80, 93, 137, 138, 142, 149, 152, 153, 159, 163, 177, 195
Restless, 10, 21-23, 27, 29, 47-49, 53, 68, 71, 77, 82, 87, 88, 90, 118, 148, 163, 175, 194
Resource room, 2, 178, 204, 205
Retarded. *See* Mentally retarded
Return to regular class. *See* Regular class, return to
Reversal of letters, 28, 29, 122, 189
Richards, C. J., 2, 210

Index

Rigid, 71, 85, 128, 132, 133, 153
Ritvo, E. R., 139, 210
Roberts, C. A., 2, 75, 209
Routine, 66, 128, 129, 139, 142

Schizoid, 21, 22, 47, 87, 89, 150, 151, 175
Schizophrenic, 146, 149, 151
Schoenfelder, D. S., 2, 210
School dropout, 164, 176
School placement. *See* Class placement
Screening committee, 5, 7, 87-91
Screening pupils, 5, 6, 184, 199
Secondary problems, 38, 98, 126, 181, 183, 184, 188, 192
Self-concept, 32, 33, 56, 75, 78, 114, 135, 190
Self-confidence, 32, 64, 69, 80, 134, 187, 192
Sequencing, 10, 16, 29, 33, 53, 54, 85, 92, 116, 120-122, 162, 172, 186, 189
Sex. *See* LD pupils, sex of
Silberberg, N. E., and Silberberg, M. C., 111, 167, 188, 210
Silver, L. B., 187, 210
SLD (Slow class for children with learning disabilities), 101, 109, 112, 114
Slow development. *See* Developmental lag
Slow learner, 81, 82, 101, 110
Slow-track class, 76, 81, 82, 86, 90, 93, 135
Social
    adjustment, 11, 12, 29, 32, 33, 86, 88, 89, 127, 134, 186, 199
    background, 25, 27, 32, 40, 51, 55, 56, 195
    isolates, 28, 32, 84, 88, 112, 126, 134, 158
    judgment, 86, 131
    worker, 5-7, 33, 72, 110, 125, 147, 157, 160, 194, 199
Soft neurological signs, 23, 194
Somatic complaints, 21, 22, 47, 113, 114, 153, 193

Special classes (LD classes), 2, 204
    self-contained, 2, 198, 204, 205
    goal of, 2, 34
    enrollment in, 4, 5, 37
Specific learning disabilities, 38, 81, 97, 99, 100, 109, 115ff, 169, 204, 206
Speech problem, 23, 118, 125
Spelling, 20, 60, 62, 77, 96, 97, 119
Spivack, G., 116, 210
Staff of LD program, 5, 6, 194, 199
    recommendations of, 36, 40, 86, 88, 90, 109, 110, 141, 153, 159, 161, 162, 164, 168, 170, 173, 177
    role and tasks of, 75, 93, 114, 126, 150, 152, 154, 157, 168
Stanford-Binet Intelligence Scale, 15, 42, 77, 102, 129
State hospital. *See* Mental hospital
Strauss, A. A., 1, 210
Structure, 71, 77, 89, 128, 131, 132, 135, 147, 148, 153, 175
Swift, M., 46, 210
Symbiotic disorders, 139, 150ff

Teacher
    attitude of, toward LD program, 13, 64, 180
    expectations of, 111, 116, 182, 188
    function of, 33, 78, 122, 125, 134, 157, 160, 199
    personality of, 7, 80, 135, 148, 199
    recommendations of, 5, 7, 27, 40, 68, 88
    reports of, 3, 20, 65, 67, 77, 82, 86, 87, 131, 135, 142, 174
    methods and techniques of, 1, 3, 6, 7, 36, 118, 122, 125, 188, 192, 198
Temper. *See* Behavior, temper outbursts
Terman, L. M., 15, 210
Therapy. *See* Psychotherapy
Thomas, A., 25, 158, 210

Time spent in LD program, 3, 7, 34, 36, 40, 59, 60, 65, 66, 133, 137
Towne, R. G., 2, 210
Trainable children. *See* Mentally retarded children, trainable
Treatment center. *See* Residential treatment center
Tutoring, 28, 102, 109, 125, 128, 172, 185, 188

Unstable home, 25-27, 51, 55, 56, 88, 139, 146, 175, 195, 196

Vane, J. R., 199, 210
Vane Kindergarten Test, 199, 200
Visual memory, 112, 114, 151
Visual-motor perception. *See* Perception, visual-motor

Vocational training, 7, 53, 91, 100, 112, 114, 124, 135, 148, 157, 162, 178, 179, 191, 198, 205, 207

Wechsler, D., 15, 210
Wechsler Intelligence Scale for Children (WISC), 15, 29, 32, 42, 77, 95, 119, 121, 122, 125, 131, 133, 152, 172
Wepman, J. M., 44, 210
Wepman Test of Auditory Discrimination, 44, 45, 120
Wide Range Achievement Test, 8, 19, 29, 32, 45, 77, 95, 108, 151
Work habits, 71, 75, 78, 82, 131, 169, 182, 192
Work-study program, 100, 124, 148, 178, 205

Zangwill, O. L., 46, 208

DATE DUE

MAY 14	MAY 16		
JUN 13	OCT 6		
JUN 27	AUG 3 1988		
OCT 13	AUG 23 1988		
3/15	NOV 14 1986		
OCT 9	MAR 0 1 2001		
NOV 15			
NOV 29	DEC 1 7 2001		
DEC 8	APR 0 7 2002		
DEC 17	NOV 0 6 2003		
APR 14			
APR 26			
DEC 12			
MAR 17			
APR 25			
JAN 29			
OCT 11			
DEC 15			
GAYLORD			PRINTED IN U.S.